OPALESCENT GLASS
FROM A—Z

Revised edition of William Heacock's
Encyclopedia of Victorian Pattern
Glass, Books 2 and 9

William Heacock, Author
Revised by JoAnn Elm

 Antique Publications
a Division of

The Glass Press, Inc.
dba Antique Publications
P.O. Box 553• Marietta, OH 45750
www.antiquepublications.com

PB ISBN:1–57080–075–8
HB ISBN:1–57080–076–6

It is probably safe to assume that the majority of people buying this book will have never met the original author, Bill Heacock, and may not even know his name. So as Yogi Berra once said (or maybe it was Julie Andrews), "Let's start at the very beginning."

Back in 1974, a young man in his mid–twenties came to my father's print shop in Marietta, OH., seeking help in printing a book on toothpick holders. The young man was Bill Heacock, and he was gifted in the area of glass research. He felt that the world needed another researcher to follow in the footsteps of Kamm, Lee, and Metz and he wanted to write, illustrate and publish a series of books on pattern glass.

Bill decided to name the series *Encyclopedia of Victorian Colored Pattern Glass.* The first volume was *Toothpick Holders from A to Z.* Over the next twelve years he added seven volumes to his series, the last one being Book 9—*Cranberry Opalescent Glass from A to Z.*

William R. Heacock
1947-1988

(It is worth mentioning at this point that Book 8, entitled *Amethyst, Amber, and Other Stained Glass from A to Z,* was never completed because of Bill's ill health.) He died in 1988, one of the early victims of AIDS.

Almost all of the original editions of the *Encyclopedia* series are out of print. Books 2, *Opalescent Glass from A to Z,* and 9, *Cranberry Opalescent Glass from A to Z* were two of the most popular and sold out very quickly. As the years have passed, many, many readers have written to us asking that these books be revised and once again made available to the public. After months of considering this, I finally decided to accede to their request and the book you have in your hands is the result.

As you read and study this publication, you will notice it's almost as if there are two voices being heard. There is a difference in style, pronouns and time period references and sometimes even tense differences. This results from our decision to leave in as much of Mr. Heacock's original materials as we could. However, in the years since he first wrote these books we have learned a great deal more about glass and know that some of his conclusions were incorrect. Our editor, JoAnn Elmore, has revised the text and added her own comments and observations which we interspersed into the original text. For the most part, we have used two different type faces in an effort to help you keep track of who is speaking. Although the pattern section is also a combination of Heacock and Elmore's research, we did not use the different "voices" there in order to keep the format from becoming confusing.

Also, since we are combining two books into one, some pages from the original editions have been rearranged and others eliminated as unnecessary. New photographs were taken and different illustrations added to the text, but much of the art is from the first editions. We hope that you find this combined volume to be interesting and useful while you pursue your passion of glass collecting.

It is with great pleasure and a sense of pride that I reintroduce this portion of Bill's original research on opalescent glass to an entirely new generation of glass collectors.

David Richardson
February, 2000

INTRODUCTION

How it came about that I am revising a book by William Heacock is a mystery to me. I am the kid whose mind went blank when a pen was put in my hand in English class; I am not glib of tongue or pen. As the years passed, I managed to overcome this problem somewhat and wrote to Dave Richardson lamenting the fact that there was such a dearth of good, current information on opalescent glass. I finished my letter with the following sentence: "Please let me know if there is a possibility you may consider revising William Heacock's Victorian Colored Pattern Glass Book 2, Opalescent Glass from A to Z. I would like to see it live again." Dave responded with: "As a matter of fact I have been thinking about doing something with the entire outdated Heacock series—would you like to work on the project?" I thought about it for 30 seconds, then said that I would like to try, but I had never written anything before. Dave replied, "Don't worry about that, everything will work out in the end." Now they want me to write an introduction!

After I agreed to do this revision, I had a lot of second thoughts. I did not even know where to begin or where I wanted to go. After much "stewing" I decided I would take the things I liked about the books and build on that. I liked the way Bill put everything he knew about each pattern in one place. I believe the collector wants to be able to find all pertinent information quickly.

So much of Book 9 was a repetition of Book 2, vague and speculative. This made the rewrite very difficult, as I believe the reader wants a book that is factual and to the point. I have removed the "what ifs" and the "maybes"; I also removed Heacock's and Gamble's differing ideas and only wrote the facts, as they are known.

Each pattern listed in this volume has been thoroughly researched using as much information as I could lay my hands on. Many times I found two or three different answers to each question. I then had to decide which "fact" I thought most accurate. If any readers disagree with my decisions, I can be contacted through Antique Publications at P.O. Box 553 Marietta, OH 45750. Include a self addressed stamped envelope, if you wish to have a reply.

This has been a wonderful learning experience. I am pleased that I have been instrumental in keeping the works of William Heacock alive for the next generation. Bill worked diligently to bring this information to us. I worked hard to update and revise these books. I hope you like the result.

I would like to thank the following: my friend Ronnie Robinson, who first introduced me to the antique and collecting world twenty years ago; my friend Libby Yalom, author of Shoes of Glass and Shoes of Glass 2, who further educated me in the delights of having a definitive collection and the wonders of the writing and publishing world; my new friend Betty Chism, who introduced me to the exciting moment when you get the most incredible buy at an auction, and who was kind enough to share her knowledge and extensive pattern glass library with me; Fred and Arna Simpson, who are continually there to answer a question; Joan Chester, who has been willing and able to broaden my knowledge of cruets; and Frank Fenton of the Fenton Art Glass Co. who always makes time to share his vast knowledge with an interested collector. Finally, to my husband Charlie, who has invariably been there for me for forty plus years.

JoAnn

EXCERPTS FROM WILLIAM HEACOCK'S BOOK 2 AND BOOK 9 ACKNOWLEDGEMENTS

Please bear in mind that Heacock published Book 2 in 1975 and Book 9 in 1987. Although some of these people are deceased, we are reinstating Heacock's text to give credit where it is still due. Much of the research and parts of the text of this new book remain the work of Bill Heacock, and those he acknowledges here.

How do you really thank someone? I owe so many people for their completely unselfish help in this project. Book 2 is indeed a group effort. No less than forty collectors and dealers from all over th country will be seeing their pieces pictured within the covers of this book. Two particular individuals, whose collections comprise more than 40% of this book, asked not to be mentioned...I cherish their friendship and can never truly thank them enough.

A tremendous share of credit must go to Mr. Joe B. Bell, whose devotion to this project has been unequalled. He unselfishly packaged and mailed more than 20 boxes of glassware from his collection...Joe shared every bit of information with me, no matter how trivial it may have seemed to him. His name really should accompany mine on the byline.

One hot day in June, 1975, I made a trip through Ohio, picking up glassware on my way to Marietta for yet another of the seemingly endless photography sessions. The day literally swept by, and will remain in my memory as long as I live. The first stop was at Bob & Jean Brocke's, collectors of blue opalescent. I walked out of their home with a considerable chunk our of their collection; but they never once showed any hesitancy. Further on, I stopped at the home of Tom and Betty Laney...I walked out with three full boxes—mostly extreme rarities—and they never once pleaded for the safe–handling of their glass. Another two hours down the road to the Wendell Graves residence, the family insisted

that I stay for dinner. I spent three precious hours with this delightful family, and a box full of glass was removed trustingly from their home. To all of you, I extend the sincerest of thank you's. I want my readers to witness what lovely, fine and unselfish people you are.

From Indiana, Jack and Julie Mavis were the very first people to offer their collection for this project. Most of the items shown on the cover [of Heacock's Book 2] and practically all of the syrups and sugar shakers were borrowed from them. They are very good friends of mine, and it is a continual delight to be in their company.

From Michigan, I want to thank Mr. and Mrs. La Verne Sweet, the Robert Hefners, Ms. Dayna Alexander, the Goldsberry's, and the staff at one of Michigan's finest antique shops, "The Sign of the Peacock." From nearby Ohio, considerable credit goes to my dearest friends, Ted and Hugh Heischmann, Judge Wilbur Armstrong and his adorable wife, Martha. Mr. and Mrs. Jay Bollinger, Mr. and Mrs. Al Berry, Loren Yeakley, Penny Sulley, and a big thank you to the well–known Cambridge glass experts, Lyle, Mary, and Lynn Welker.

Others who cannot go unmentioned are Ruby Fink, Jack Burk, Mr. and Mrs. Ed Sawicki, Mr. and Mrs. Gary Ellis, Robert and Pat Costa, Jennie Shultz, Jim Broom, don Farrell Sr., Elmer Sharpe, and my dear dear friends from down Georgia, Ed and Kathy Wait.

A word of praise for the fantastic work done by the photographer, Dale Brown. His insistence on perfection was sometimes nerve–wracking, but it is obvious that he knew what he was doing from the outstanding results you hold in your hands. I thank him for these high standards which made my book something of real beauty.

An equally high word of praise for the friendly management and staff of Richardson Printing Corporation, who always made me feel at home as I roamed among them admiring the work they were doing on this book.

A final thank–you to the staff at the Oglebay Institute of Wheeling, W.Va., and its director, John A. Artzberger. They granted me permission to reprint some of the pages from the Hobbs Glass Co. catalog. I highly recommend this fine museum to any lover of American glass.

Bill Heacock dedicated Book 2, *Opalescent Glass from A to Z* as follows:

For the Gambles
With Everlasting Gratitude

❦

Bill dedicated Book 9, *Cranberry Opalescent Glass from A to Z* as follows:

To David Richardson
For 10 years of friendship and support,
and without whom my work could not continue.

ACKNOWLEDGEMENTS FROM BOOK 9

First and foremost, I must thank my co–author, William Gamble, who first presented the idea for this book to me and pursued its publication. He gathered the glass from his own personal collection, and solicited other collectors across the Midwest to send their glass to him. He presented a manuscript with his own observations as a collector and dealer, which included valuable, "field research". Combining Mr. Gamble's facts with my own research from trade journals, an important contribution to glass history could be prepared.

Joe and Audrey Humphrey unselfishly offered to pack and remove hundreds of pieces from their home. Audrey is known around Ohio as "The Cranberry Kid", and her love for the glass extends form the very old to the very recent Fenton production.

Many other collectors and dealers were involved in this book through the loaning of glass, some of whom packed a dozen or more examples to mail to us for photography. Taking such risks deserves special mention: Robert and Jean Brocke, Jim Broom, Jack Burke, Virginia Ellison, Dorothy Frazee, Steve Gehring, Ray and Jennie Goldsberry, John and Eve Gordon, Leonard and Marie Gyles, Chuck Hardy, Norman and Noreen Koch, Lawrence Loxterman, Joan McGee, Tom Neale, Mr. and Mrs. Les Norman, Ward Rohm, Glen and Juanita Wilkins.

Our sincere thanks to Steve Jennings for reprint permission from an L.G. Wright Glass Co. catalog, and to Frank M. Fenton for reprints of Fenton Art Glass Co. catalogs. The cranberry glass sold since 1939 by both of these firms (all of it made by Fenton) has kept the Victorian traditions alive for new generations of glass lovers.

For early trade journal ads, we thank the helpful staff of the Rakow Library at the Corning Museum of Glass, Corning, N.Y.

EXCERPT FROM WILLIAM HEACOCK'S BOOK 9 INTRODUCTION

The oft–told tale of the cranberry color being accidentally discovered when a worker dropped a gold coin into a boiling batch of crystal could not be further from the truth. This color is an overlay, requiring a layer of crystal coated with a layer of cranberry, and then blown into shape. It requires strict temperature control and cannot be made successfully in pressed form. It must be a blown pattern to have the true pink coloration for which it is known.

Cranberry opalescent was originally called "ruby opalescent" or "pink opalescent" in the early trade journals and catalogs. The use of the term "cranberry glass," much like the glass terms "custard" and "Carnival", was introduced by the antiques collectors—not the glass industry. The first commercial production of the color in America appears to have gained momentum in 1884. The English–bred glass workers at the Mt. Washington Glass Works and the Phoenix Glass Co. were competing at this time for the art glass market. The Hobbs, Brockunier concern at Wheeling joined in immediately.

The trade journals for the mid–1880s are clearly filled with references to colors like "Peach Blow," "Coral" and "Amberina", but these colors were not excluded to single factories. Neither was the color "ruby" (cranberry). The workers apparently moved from factory to factory, carrying with them valuable formulas and glassmaking secrets, which made it possible for other manufacturers to compete with popular, marketable production colors. We collectors tend to think of the final product as a work of glassmaking craftsmanship, which it is, but we lose sight of the fact that it was also originally a commercially manufactured product conceived by businessmen to make a profit. A number of patents and lawsuits are recorded during this period, as manufacturers sought to protect their ideas, usually with little success. Other companies which made "ruby" color during the 1880s include New England Glass Works, La Belle, and Northwood's own factory which opened in 1888.

Thus we note the problem in attributing many of the patterns shown in this book. With very few ads and catalogs available which illustrate this glass, naming manufacturers can sometimes be a matter of comparing colors and moulds to existing attributable items. In a few cases, naming the maker is virtually impossible. It becomes a matter of eliminating the obvious and focusing on the most likely possibilities, particularly on the staple designs know as *Coinspot*, *Swirl*, and *Stripe*. Just about every factory making blown opalescent was using these patterns. These three are particularly difficult to research.

Unfortunately, moulds were sometimes relocated, factories changed owners and names, designs and shapes were copied, workers and designers moved from location to location. If an item is called "Northwood", collectors must note that he had four different factories, and worked at four others. Also, his moulds were used by other firms. Percy Beaumont designed for Hobbs, West Virginia and his own two factories. An item called "Beaumont" could have been made earlier in the same or a different shape by Hobbs or West Virginia Glass. (Excerpted from Heacock's *Book 9*, Main Pattern Motifs.)

DO YOURSELF AND YOUR HEIRS A FAVOR!

If you do not keep a record of your collection, start doing so TODAY. This little chore only takes a few minutes of your time, and you will thank yourself a hundred times over in the years to come. So will your children, should something suddenly happen to you.

I have always kept a notebook (and now also a computer) for this purpose since I first began collecting in 1980. Why I did this I do not know, since by nature I am not really that exacting. First, give each piece an inventory number. I use a Sharpie pen for this and write the number on the bottom of the piece. Then, write the number and information about the piece in the notebook. (For example: #400. Cranberry Eye Dot cruet, made by Fenton for L.G. Wright, circa 1950–1960, see Heacock's Book 9, page 100, fig. 291. Purchased 2/85, Atlantic City Show, paid $000.00.)

I always write down where the piece can be found in a reference book if such information exists. Some collectors go so far as to keep a record of who they purchased the item from, including address and phone number. Other collectors prefer to keep this information on index cards in a card file or on a computer. It does not matter how you do it, it just matters that you DO IT.

It is amazing what wonderful memories are brought back when you search to see when you bought piece #2 or #50 or #1000. It is also helpful if you tell your heirs about your friends who are collectors, and the organizations to which you belong. The majority of these people will be more than willing to help your heirs in the event they need to dispose of your cherished collection. I have even listed several auctioneers in case my children decide they would prefer to follow that route. This type of record keeping is often all an insurance company needs, should you decide that your collection has grown to a size and value that warrants coverage.

Do not say, "It's too late, I should have started years ago." It is never too late. If you decide to keep a record, and then run a total, you may be in a state of shock—and your heirs will smile all the way to the bank.

TABLE OF CONTENTS

HOW TO USE THIS BOOK

I have tried to make this book as "user" friendly as Bill Heacock tried to make the originals. All the information Bill knew about a specific pattern he put in one place. However, he did not write his books in novel form, which could cause the reader to have to skip from page to page to find information on a specific piece. I have re–organized the text to avoid that situation, and updated the index for easier reference, as well.

The dates used for "years of production"(Y.O.P.), represent only the date that a catalog or other such material has been confirmed. This means a pattern could have been made years before that date or for years after that date. It is to be remembered that all pieces were not made in all colors listed and vice versa. I have listed as many reproductions as have come to my attention, but there are probably many more. I have also done away with all the abbreviations and spelled out the words instead, as I find the abbreviations confusing.

NOTE FROM THE EDITOR: This book is a revised compilation of William Heacock's *Encyclopedia of Victorian Colored Pattern Glass, Book 2, Opalescent Glass from A to Z* and *Book 9, Cranberry Opalescent*. We have combined the introductory text sections of both Book 2 and Book 9 in the first part of this edition.

Following that organization, we have simplified two separate pattern sections for Opalescent and Cranberry Opalescent glass into one large pattern section. The color photographs are separated, however; Book 2's color section precedes Book 9's color. New color plates follow those photographs.

As mentioned in the Publisher's Foreword, JoAnn Elmore's "voice" is denoted by italicized text in the first section of this book. We opted not to continue that in the pattern section for clarity's sake, even though JoAnn made numerous revisions and editions to that part of the book.

ORIGINAL MANUFACTURER'S NAMES

This book is written on the premise of returning to the original manufacturer's name for a pattern. Following is an excerpt from Bill Heacock's 1986 book, Encyclopedia of Victorian Colored Pattern Glass Book 7, Ruby-Stained Glass From A to Z:

"Glass enthusiasts may notice as they flip through this volume that their favorite pattern may be alphabetized under a name which is totally foreign to them. This is probably because the new computer research makes it easier for us to single out and identify original manufacturer's names for certain lines from trade journal descriptions. Let me try to explain the reasons for this practice.

Perhaps some will criticize me for being so rigid in reinstating original names over far more popular collector names. Even Kamm, who made such an effort to reintroduce original names, did not attempt to change the name of the popular Sprig pattern which she thought was Bryce, Higbee's Royal line. The Royal name seems to have been used by as many different factories as Columbia, and Victoria. But mankind has lasted for centuries with thousands of Marys, Williams, Georges and Annes. What made them distinct was their surname, their parentage. Think of this book as an exercise. We

have to start calling all those Columbia, Victoria, Royal, Puritan, and Peerless patterns by their surname, the name of their parents—the factory of origin.

My work as a glass historian has become increasingly important to me. Since this is virtually a lost history in glass with which we are dealing, I feel I must make my readers more aware of the "roots" of their glass. Reinstating original names is part of this. The long-time collectors and dealers may balk. It is hard to accept change. But these reference books I am writing will be used by thousands of future collectors, dealers, and as the decades progress, museums. Naming the manufacturer of a line of glass is important. Almost as important is knowing what the parent's named the child."

In view of the foregoing I have done my best to use the original manufacturer's names as I became aware of them. I have cross–referenced the names in the index, so there should be no problem in finding a piece no matter which name you know it by.

I believe the name that was hardest for me to change must be "S Repeat". Dugan Glass Co.'s original name for the pattern, "National", does nothing to describe the design, but then very few of the original names did.

A PICTURE IS WORTH A THOUSAND WORDS

Yes, "a picture is worth a thousand words," and a color picture showing a detailed pattern is worth a thousand more. Illustrated in this book are representative examples of many different patterns. This was done mainly to show the reader how the pattern changes when applied to the different shapes. Depending on the size of the piece, a pattern can have parts omitted, shortened or elongated, all of which change the pattern's appearance.

As the value of colored pattern glass increases, each purchase becomes more and more of an investment. With a certain amount of dedication and effort, there are a few "sleepers" and a number of "bargains" to be found, giving a larger return on your investment in the long run. But as more and more people become knowledgeable, as the numbers of collectors increase and as opalescent glass gets harder and harder to find, we will have to resign ourselves to pay the asking price.

Thus this book represents one of the best investments you can make. Is this the original stopper to this cruet? Or, is it a reproduction? Is this the correct base to this butter dish? Has this been ground down or polished? A quick check through the pages of this book will answer some of these questions, and hopefully prevent some costly mistakes.

All too often, quality antiques are appearing on the market repaired, polished and with mismatched parts. It is hoped that this book, with hundreds of different examples illustrated, will help you to make better and safer investments.

ALL THAT IS WRITTEN IS NOT NECESSARILY TRUTH

The market for books on antique glass is somewhat limited and most never make it into a second printing, let alone a second edition. But there are several which have become "standards" and continue to be reprinted over and over again. However, when later research proves many of their earlier reports to be incorrect, it is sad to see the useless, out–of–date data sold to an unsuspecting public. I am not saying that I do not want to see the fine works of glass pioneers sold any more; I am saying that they should be updated. Literally thousands of facts have surfaced since publication of these priceless early works.

Glass documentation is still in its early stages. Were it not for my plans to continually update each printing, then even my books would be relics of limited use in about 20 years. As the years pass new discoveries will be made, early catalogs will surface, and information presented by me could be proved wrong. I look forward to this day, because I have such a serious interest in glass research. Knowing the truth is far more important to me than any discredit new discoveries may bring to my own works.

Unfortunately, the untimely death of William Heacock prevented him from carrying out his master plan for his series of Victorian Colored Pattern Glass books. In this book, a revised compilation of his Book 2 and Book 9, we have tried to carry out his promise of updating his books. These volumes were combined to give the reader a more complete view of the subject and to avoid so much repetition. Antique Publications is also planning to publish a revised and combined book on three of Heacock's other Encyclopedia books: Book 3, Syrups, Sugar Shakers & Cruets; Book 4, Custard Glass; and Book 6, Oil Cruets.

The difference between a reproduction and a "reintroduction" (a term which Heacock coined) is simple. A *reproduction* is a copy of an exact shape and color made much earlier by a now–existent factory. A *reintroduction* means taking an old design idea and placing it back on the gift ware market in new shapes or in new colors, never before made.

This book includes reprints from the catalogs of the Fenton Art Glass Co., Williamstown, W.Va. and the L.G. Wright Glass Co., New Martinsville, W.Va. Fenton made almost all the cranberry opalescent offered by L.G. Wright, a glass jobber firm which manufactured no actual glass (they did maintain a decorating force, however). Fenton built much of their business manufacturing reintroductions of old design ideas. The majority of Fenton glass made after 1972 was trademarked. Anyone who collects Victorian opalescent and wishes to avoid buying Fenton reintroductions must study and learn to recognize Fenton shape moulds. In Fenton's catalog and publication, *Glass Messenger*, Fenton explains that the L.G. Wright Glass Co. built their business on reproductions and reintroductions. Wright produced many old Victorian patterns in colors and shapes never before made. If an item was never made in a certain color by the original manufacturer, then that item in the new color is technically not a reproduction. In order for a piece to be a reproduction, it must be exactly the same in shape and in color as that made by the original manufacturer; any variation makes the piece a reintroduction.

The Wright firm began business slowly in the late 1930s and expanded during World War II, after the purchase of many original moulds from the Northwood—Dugan—Diamond factory in Indiana, PA. During the war, the glass market in America faced no challenges from cheaper European competitors. Mr. Wright had much of his glass made by Fenton, which he in turn sold directly to his customers as his own glass. As the business grew, new moulds were made, many of them reproducing the popular patterns of the Victorian era, *Westward Ho*, *Three Face*, *Moon and Star* and many others. The reproductions were almost identical to the originals, causing considerable confusion.

Most of the opalescent glass offered by Wright was made from the old spot moulds used by Northwood and Dugan in Indiana, PA. *Opal Stars and Stripes* seems to be the single exception. Some of the shape moulds found there were also used. But, in most cases, the Wright pieces were blown into their own shape moulds, making these pieces easy to determine as "reintroductions." There are a good number of reproductions and differentiating these items from the originals is a matter of experience. Only a person who has done a lot of studying can tell the difference. The most difficult pieces to identify as Wright repro's are the melon–rib barber bottle (a few rare old examples do exist) and some of their earliest water pitchers (from the 1940s) which now have almost 60 years of age wear on the base.

The opalescent glass made from the late 1930s through the 1990s has become very collectible in its own right. This glass is very expensive to make and in some cases a new piece can retail for almost as much as an astute collector can purchase an old example. All cranberry or any opalescent glass, be it Victorian or reproduction or reintroduction, has value. It is up to the individual collector to determine the purity of his or her collection. Heacock and I think age is only one factor to a collection's value. Quality is another and Fenton's quality is unquestionable—they are masters of the art of reintroduction.

On the other hand, there is some cranberry opalescent of limited quality made for A.A. Importing Co., which is heavy and poorly made. Only inexperienced or over–exuberant collectors have been stung by these cheap reproductions.

BLOWN OPALESCENT AFTER 1905 —ARE THEY REPRODUCTIONS?

The peak production years of blown opalescent tableware and novelties were from about 1884–1904, about a twenty year period. However, a limited amount appeared from time to time on the market. No cranberry opalescent was made by Fenton Art Glass Co. until the 1930s. From 1910–1920 this firm made three opalescent water sets in flint, green and blue opalescent with pressed tumblers in the *Coindot* (Coinspot), *Spiral* (Swirl) and *Buttons And Braids* patterns. These were copies of sets made earlier by Frank L. Fenton's former employer, Jefferson Glass Co., a firm which did make cranberry before 1910.

In the 1920s, a few lemonade sets were made by Fenton in blown opalescent, but none in cranberry. These were usually with the popular ice–lip of the period, or with lids. The tumblers were iced–tea size, taller than those of the Victorian period.

In 1939, the Fenton Art Glass Co. brought out a major line of opalescent *Spiral* (Swirl), *Dot Optic* (Coinspot), *Rib Optic* (Stripe) and *Wide Rib Optic* (Wide Stripe) in vases, bowls and other shapes, in colors of blue, topaz, flint and cranberry opalescent. These were abandoned after a single year in the line, so most are extremely rare today and command prices—especially in cranberry—comparable to prices of much earlier glass.

At about this time, L.G. Wright, a road salesman for the New Martinsville Glass Co., learned of a warehouse of old moulds from the glass factory at Indiana, PA., and among them were moulds from the Northwood, Dugan and Diamond Glass companies which had operated there. He purchased these moulds and took one, the *Hobnail* barber bottle (fig. 954) to Fenton at Williamstown, and had a number of these bottles made in the cranberry opalescent which Fenton was producing at the time. Frank Fenton got the idea for his own *Hobnail* line of ware from this bottle, and the rest is history. Fenton Art Glass Co. has produced *Hobnail* in one form or another ever since, and its name has become associated with the design.

Thus, an original Northwood mould (itself a reproduction of a Hobbs, Brockunier mould) continued to influence the production of glass well into the 20th century. When Fenton produced their successful *Hobnail*, other firms were producing competing lines. Fenton's moulds were entirely new shapes distinctive to the company, and this was the only firm to produce a line in cranberry opalescent since 1940. The *Hobnail* which Duncan & Miller called "cranberry pink" was more of a salmon color, and Frank M. Fenton recalls his uncle's amusement at the competition calling this color "cranberry". Duncan's ads after 1940 call this color "peach", which is more descriptive.

There was another cranberry *Hobnail* on the market just prior to this time from Czechoslovakia. Other opalescent designs, particularly *Swirl* and *Stripe*, have also been spotted with acid stamped marks "made in Czechoslovakia". When World War II broke out in Europe, a hungry market for this color and design must have opened up. The Czech *Hobnail*, and the Fenton and D & M *Hobnail* are relatively easy to find on today's collectors' market, indicating extensive and lengthy production.

Since the late 1930s, the Fenton Art Glass Co. has been doing contract work for L.G. Wright Glass Co. at New Martinsville, and has produced all of this firm's cranberry opalescent and cased colors. First relying heavily on the old Indiana, PA., moulds, the Wright concern had additional hundreds of moulds made to expand its line of gift and novelty glass over the years. Many of the items found in cranberry opalescent are in shapes never originally made, and are easy to distinguish from the old. But when an original Northwood/Dugan/Diamond mould is used, it becomes more difficult for beginning collectors to avoid paying an "antique" price for a reproduction. The distinctive "melon rib" shape found on many Wright cranberry pieces was apparently taken from an old Beaumont Glass Co. bitters bottle and expanded to include other shapes (pitchers, lamps, open sugars, etc.). The L.G. Wright pressed glass was made at a variety of factories, including Fenton, Westmoreland, Viking and Imperial.

Fortunately, depending upon your perspective, the high collectability of cranberry opalescent, and Fenton glass in general, has led to a revived interest in collecting the copies made since 1938. The new, limited edition cranberry opalescent being made by Fenton today is very expensive to produce, and an awareness of this fact has led many collectors to seek out, whereas they formerly avoided, the L.G. Wright items.

The Steuben Glass Works at Corning, N.Y. produced a line of cranberry opalescent in the 1930s under the auspices of Frederick Carder, another Englishman from the Stourbridge area. Much glass was made here in the style of the early English Victorian period. The opalescent glass is very lightweight, usually has a polished pontil, and is styled in the contemporary shapes of the period. Revi AANG lists colors of cranberry, green and orchid opalescent. The cranberry was called "Oriental Poppy." When finished with a lustre surface inside and out, it was called Clouded Glass. The *Swirl* and *Stripe* motifs were primarily used. Revi indicates it was never signed.

This book concentrates primarily on American production, but examples from England and the Continent are included. Cranberry opalescent was made in England from about 1880 to as late as the 1930s.

I have gone on record in the past with some fairly harsh statements about reproductions and the harm they do to collectors' investments. But since I entered the 20th Century with my research, and have expanded my "boundaries" in glass history, and have seen one famous factory after another close its doors forever, I have begun to appreciate all glass for what it is. If it is a reproduction/reintroduction, then it should be represented and sold as one. The reproduction was made with the same care, and considerable more expense, than the original was made one hundred years ago. It is this high cost of fuel and labor, as well as the competition from cheaply made, government subsidized, foreign glass, that is hurting our struggling American glass industry. When something becomes scarce, it becomes more precious to the beholder. Some day all glass may come from foreign shores, and you will then perhaps understand how special handmade American glass is, no matter how old.

Listed below are some flaws to watch for when buying glass. If the flaw was caused by faulty workmanship in the manufacturing of a piece, this imperfection should not have bearing on its value:

Annealing cracks: These are often referred to as "heat checks" to limit their value destructiveness. These little lines usually appear at the top of the applied handle on cruets, syrups, creamers, and water pitchers where they are applied to the body of the piece. Often they have darkened with age, a good sign that the lines truly developed "in the making." These annealing cracks occur due to the contraction of the glass as it cooled. Do not confuse these tiny cracks with a cracked handle. A cracked handle is considered major damage and has great bearing on the item's value.

Roughness under the tops of salt and sugar shakers: Many sugar shakers and salt shakers are mould blown (not pressed) and were taken off the pontil rod at the top. This often left rough edges, even chips, which the makers saw no need to polish since they would be covered by the screw–top.

Roughness on the top of blown tumblers: Blown tumblers were taken off the pontil rod from the top and then the rough edges were smoothed down. Frequently, small chips went unnoticed and the tumbler made it to store shelves anyway. These edges are extremely brittle and highly susceptible to flaking, so if you are holding out for a perfect piece, you will either have a long hard look or will have to buy one that is professionally polished. The same applies to the berry dishes.

Rough mould lines: Even pressed glass has its problems, although on a much smaller scale. When the finished piece is removed from the mould, occasionally pieces of glass will stick to the mould and pull glass from the body of the finished piece. This will happen on patterns of intricate design that have many separate raised surfaces, or on footed platters.

Straw marks or shear lines: These long, hair-like or scratch–like crevices occur when the surface of the glass comes into contact with the plunger of the press.

Polished bottoms on pressed tumblers: Pressed tumblers frequently came out of the mould with a lopsided base, which caused the tumbler to lean slightly. They were put to the grinder's wheel to level them off. In some cases, these pressed tumblers were taken off the mould at the base and polished to smooth the rough edges. Check the sides of the base. If these have a polished look, then you can suspect professional mending. The above also applies to table setting pieces with pedestal bases.

Pontil scars on the rims of opalescent pieces: The opalescence on many of the novelties was achieved by treating a formed piece of glass with chemicals and then re–firing the piece. When the finished product was taken off the rod, sometimes a little scar would remain behind. When the tool was removed, the glass usually melted back into shape, but not always. Occasionally, a sharp little protrusion of glass will appear to have "dripped" down the glass; also, a deep hole can occur where the glass stuck to the tool, instead of to the finished piece of glass. This should not be considered damage.

Air bubbles, grit and sand deposits: These also appear in glass and are not considered to be flaws that detract from the value of the piece. A burst air bubble may detract somewhat from the value.

THE REEDED AND TWISTED HANDLES

Most opalescent has a plain, clear glass applied handle. Reeded handles found on most reproductions have caused some collectors to avoid any pieces found with this handle. The term "avoid or beware of reeded handles" was designed for beginning collectors who are looking for simple answers. But investing in glass is not that simple. It requires a considerable amount of study and even the "experts" are learning new rules every day.

The early art glass made in America, produced by such fine manufacturers as Hobbs, Brockunier & Co., Mount Washington, New England, Phoenix, Duncan and others, was made in the style used by many young glass-workers introduced to this country from England. For many years, some of these pieces were considered to be English. But we now have more knowledge at our disposal and we know many pitchers and oil cruets with reeded handles are indeed American–made, from the 1880s. Most pieces from this period have polished pontils at the base. Examples of early glass with reeded handles are shown in this book, see figs. 878, 880, 881 (English) and 898.

The "twisted" handle is a variation of the reeded handle. See figs. 745, 825 and 833, these pitchers were made by Northwood.

Butler Brothers was the largest wholesale outlet of glassware from as early as the 1880s to as late as the 1940s. It is interesting to scan these ads and witness the prices that our glass collectibles originally sold for 100 years ago. However, Butler Brothers bought the glass outright from the factories, and did not name the manufacturers in their ads.

After much studying, we realized that many of the glass groupings and pieces contained as many as a dozen different patterns. The ads stated that they were packed in barrels for immediate shipment. Butler Brothers did not pack the barrels; the manufacturer shipped the glass to them already packed in the barrels. This could mean only one thing: all pieces shown in the ad were made by the same manufacturer. If you could identify the manufacturer of one piece in the grouping, you then could know the maker of all the items. This discovery has been a great help in the attribution of glass patterns.

THE TRIALS AND TRIBULATIONS OF NAMING UNLISTED PATTERNS

The following text is from Heacock's Book 2, published in 1975:

This book contains dozens of patterns and novelties which have never before been listed. Following the precedent set by other glass authors, I have named those unlisted items for easy reference for collectors. This practice is not as simple as it sounds.

The extreme similarity in names of patterns has caused considerable confusion for many years. There must be literally scores of patterns which include the words "Loop", "Fine–cut," "Honeycomb", "Thumbprint", "Sunburst", "Fan", "Block", and the much over–used "Diamond." Get one word wrong or out of context and you have another pattern.

Due to the rising popularity of mail order sales in antiques, it becomes absolutely essential that any newly uncovered patterns have names assigned to them that will create as little confusion as possible. Unfortunately this does not always occur. Certain researchers have even gone as far as naming patterns identically to others already named. How many *Maple Leaf* patterns will we have to bear? And there seems to be one too many *Regal* patterns. It has gotten to the point that the name of the pattern has to be preceded with the name of the company or with the words "opalescent" or "late."

I have often thought how useless it is to name a pattern according to its design. Some of the loveliest pattern names have nothing whatsoever to do with their design. A quick check reveals that in almost every case these turn out to be the original manufacturer's name. If this practice of calling patterns *Louis XV, Doric, Excelsior, Czarina* and *Famous* was good enough for the brilliant craftsmen who made this glass, then it is good enough for this author.

Yet, when picking a name for an unlisted pattern, you can't just draw it out of a hat. The name you choose must come from the look and the feel of the piece it is assigned to. The name *Leaf Medallion* (Kamm) appropriately described the look of the now–known Northwood line, but the original name *Regent* describes its very presence, its very "aura." How unfortunate that we may never know the original manufacturer's names for the many lovely patterns undermined by sterile pattern names.

Thus, I have studied long and hard before finally deciding on names for several of the pieces illustrated in this book. I owe a sincere debt of gratitude to Mr. Joe B. Bell of Memphis, TN., who offered considerable help and advice in providing names for several of the patterns in this book.

The Victorian oil cruet was an important part of the seasoning set. Because of its importance, the cruet was used extensively—thus it suffered a multitude of abuses. The pouring spouts were frequently chipped, the handle could become cracked and the stopper could easily be dropped and broken or lost.

Original stoppers cannot be easily determined, especially in the blown glass cruets. Pressed pattern cruets often have a matching pattern stopper or a pressed stopper of uniform dimension. The blown cruet most frequently includes a cut glass stopper. It is difficult to say if the cut stopper in any cruet is original. If the stopper fits the neck of the cruet well, if the top of the stopper is not too large or too small, if the shank (neck) of the stopper is not too close or too far away from the top of the cruet—all of these factors determine whether the stopper can be considered original. It takes experience in seeing and handling Victorian cruets over a long period of time to determine this. One might say it takes an "eye" to judge the originality of a cruet's stopper.

Original catalogs have helped determine the originality of cruet stoppers, but even these could have been changed over the production life of a particular pattern. We know that Hobbs, Brockunier & Co. used special cut stoppers (often in color) in their blown pattern cruets. It appears that Northwood used pressed glass stoppers in some of his blown cruets.

Most old blown opalescent cruets, with few exceptions, have plain, applied clear handles. The *Opaline Brocade (Spanish Lace)* cruet is one notable exception. This cruet always seems to have a reeded handle. Examples with colored handles in amber or blue are probably English or Bohemian.

Victorian blown cruets will have basically two styles of pouring spouts: either a pulled out lip or a tri-corner spout. There are no known Victorian cruets with a ruffled spout. The *Stars and Stripes* (fig. 886) and the *Curtain Drapery* (fig. 887) are not cruets made during the Victorian period. These cruets were made by the Fenton Art Glass Co. of Williamstown W.Va., for the L.G. Wright Glass Co. of New Martinsville, W.Va., (who owned the moulds) from the 1950s through the 1970s. Even so, they are very collectable and command a healthy price.

There is nothing wrong with having "collectible" glass in an opalescent collection. Just don't be duped into paying Victorian prices for pieces produced in the second half of the twentieth century. Age has little to do with the value of glass. In most cases, collectibility is the determining factor in an item's value.

The Victorian syrup remains one of the most highly collectible items of the seasoning set. The metal tops, made of brass (often silver plated), tin, and a pot metal of a pewter-type substance, often decayed or became loose from the glass vessel. Often, the lids were thrown away. Replaced metal tops are commonplace. While the original tops are preferred, collectors of syrup jugs do not object to the replaced tops.

The tops appear in two different shapes—a dome lid and a "duck bill" lid. In replacing a syrup lid, it is most desirable to use the style which was original to the syrup. Replaced syrup lids do not affect the price of the jug.

The three basic jug shapes are bulbous, oval and cylindrical. The *Opaline Brocade (Spanish Lace)* syrup is the only known jug which originally came with a reeded handle. All other Victorian opalescent syrups have a plain (not reeded) handle.

There have been many reproductions of the opalescent syrups. All of the repros (with one exception) have reeded or crimped handles. The re-make of the *Ring Neck Stripe* syrup uses a plain handle. The difference between the new and old is found in the number of rings on the neck of the jug. The old syrup has one ring on the neck, while the reproduction has two rings.

The sugar shaker has few reproductions with which to deal. The one which causes most concern is the *Nine Panel* mould (fig. 789). In judging the age of a sugar shaker, remove the metal top. On an old example, the top edge is slightly rounded and often has a rough, lightly chipped rim where the piece was removed from the blow pipe. Since this rim was covered by the screw top, there was no reason for the manufacturer to polish the rim. However, on the L. G. Wright reintroductions (made by Fenton Art Glass Co.), these rims are usually ground flat with a grainy, frosted appearance.

Chips under the metal lid do not hurt the value of the sugar shaker. Replaced or reproduction lids are not objectionable to most collectors. However, in order to receive the best price for an old sugar shaker, it should be correctly lidded.

There are many reproductions of Victorian salt and pepper shakers on the market today, and it is very difficult to tell the old from the new. One of the best ways is to study the shapes and colors of the old. Many of the new shakers are a different size or shape and are made in colors not found in the originals. Removing the tops of the salt and pepper shakers, as with the sugar shakers, will sometimes give you a clue as to its age.

SHAPE MOULDS USED IN OPALESCENT PRODUCTION

Some shape moulds have pattern names of their own; most are listed below. These moulds can be found in colors and with decorations other than an opalescent motif. All of these moulds are blown–glass, not pressed moulds.

Apple Blossom. Northwood at Indiana, PA. Main line in decorated milk glass.

Ball–Shaped Syrup. Opaline Brocade (Spanish Lace), Daisy and Fern, Swastika, Coinspot, Coinspot and Swirl.

Buckeye Swirl. Used on table pieces in Reverse Swirl and Big Windows, both by Buckeye Glass Co., but also possibly made at American Glass Co. These moulds were also used for non-opalescent speckled glass and opaque glass.

Bulbous Base. A Hobbs shape mould used on a Frances Ware decorated line, and also with an inside optic pattern. Mould may have also been used by Northwood after 1902.

Fancy Fans. Used on the Polka Dot pattern and milk glass at Northwood's Ellwood City factory.

Hobbs' Swirl. No. 326 mould, used on the Frances Ware Swirl line.

Jewel (Threaded Swirl). Northwood at Martins Ferry, OH. Primarily made in the plain Rubina color. Could also have been made at Ellwood City and Indiana, PA.

Melon With Sprig (Paneled Sprig). Northwood at Ellwood City and Indiana, PA. Also made at the Dugan Glass Co., Indiana, PA.

Multi-Ribbed Rose Bowl. Yellow opalescent; Seaweed example known.

Nine Panel Syrup And Sugar Shaker. Swirl, Stripe, Coinspot, Daisy and Fern, Twist Blown, Opaline Brocade (Spanish Lace).

Northwood Swirl. Used on Royal Ivy, Parian Swirl, Daisy and Fern, Coinspot, and Swirl by Northwood at Martins Ferry OH., Ellwood City, and Indiana, PA.

Oval Indiana. Cruet mould. Opaline Brocade (Spanish Lace), Daisy and Fern, and Coinspot.

Ribbed Pillar. Mould which Northwood made at Ellwood City and Indiana, PA.

Ribbon Tie. Mould was used mainly for Opaline Brocade (Spanish Lace) tankard and salt

Ring Neck. Water pitcher, sugar shaker, syrup, cruet, toothpick. Used on Stripe, Coinspot and in Rubina and cased Vasa Murrhina and Aurora.

Utopia Optic. Shape moulds used on Opaline Brocade (Spanish Lace). Northwood at Indiana, PA.

West Virginia Optic. Used on Daisy and Fern, Polka Dot and Fern by West Virginia Glass Co. in 1893-1894.

Wide–Waist Sugar Shaker. The same patterns as the Nine Panel: Swirl, Stripe, Coinspot, Daisy and Fern, Twist Blown, Opaline Brocade (Spanish Lace).

HOW IS MOULD BLOWN CRANBERRY OPALESCENT GLASS MADE?

Cranberry opalescent is a color which cannot be pressed successfully. The color requires exacting temperature control which is not compatible with pressing techniques.

A "gather" of molten cranberry glass is attached to the end of a blow pipe. This glass is then coated with an outer layer of clear glass which has bone ash in the formula. This unformed ball of glass is then blown into the "spot" mould. This spot mould has the basic design of the pattern in relief, that portion of the final piece which is white (opalescent). The formed object is then removed from the mould, still attached to the blow pipe, and then reheated in the glory hole of the furnace; this reheating turns the raised portions of the glass white. At this point, the hot glass is immediately re–blown into a "shape" mould. The mould is opened, the formed object removed, and the piece is again reheated in the glory hole at the top in order to crimp or "finish" the rim. With careful examination of a piece of cranberry opalescent, especially an item with a polished top (like a tumbler), you can see the two layers of glass, the cranberry interior and the crystal opalescent exterior. See page 206.

ENGLISH OPALESCENT GLASS

The English opalescent pressed glass era predates ours by a good ten years. There is little doubt that Northwood's English heritage and his extended visit to England during the National Glass Co. trauma directly influenced much of the pressed opalescent production, which enjoyed its hey–day after the turn of the century.

The major manufacturers of pressed opalescent glass in England were: George Davidson and Co., Gateshead–on–Tyne; Henry Greener and Co., Sunderland; Bartles, Tate and Co., Manchester; Molineau, Webb and Co., Ancoats, Manchester; Sowerby and Co., Gateshead–on–Tyne. Davidson was the primary manufacturer of opalescent glassware in England. In fact, the Davidson name is as well–known in England as the Northwood name is in the States.

The major manufacturers of mould blown opalescent glass in England were: George Bacchus and Sons, Birmingham; Thomas Webb and Sons, Stourbridge; Stevens and Williams, Stourbridge; Richardsons of Wordsley, Stourbridge area.

The English were quite helpful in that many of their patterns of glass were marked with a registration number, often referred to as an Rd. #. If you write to the London Public Record Office asking about specific numbers they will be able to tell you who made the item and when. Following is a list of known English patterns and their Rd. #.

RD #	Pattern Name/Description & Year	Manufacturer	Notes/Shapes
262018	Ascot (1895)	Greener	Cracker jar/complete set
130643	Brideshead	Davidson	Complete set
217749	Camelot (new name) (1893)	Greener	Wine shape known
150277	Carriage (1890)	Greener	Novelty item
160244	Contessa (1890)	Greener	Complete set
42947	Daisy Block Rowboat (1886)	Sowerby	Novelty boat
193365	Dover Diamond (new name) (1892)	???	Two shapes known
39807	Driftwood and Shell	Burtles, Tate	Novelties
23527 & 39414	Grace Darling Rowboat (1885)	Edw. Bolton	Novelty boat
176566	Lady Chippendale (1891)	Davidson	Complete set
237038	Linking Rings (1894–1895)	Davidson	Complete set
285342 or 285312	Lords And Ladies (1896)	Davidson	Complete set
217752	Prince William (1893)	Davidson	Complete set
320124	Queen's Crown (1898–1899)	???	Complete set
96945	Richelieu	Davidson	Complete set
154027	Somerset (1895)	Davidson	Complete set
138051	Sunderland (new name)	Greener	Twisted, rope–hdl. basket and tumbler
20086	Swan novelty (1885)	Burtles, Tate	Two sizes
303519	Victoria And Albert (1897–1898)	Davidson	Complete set & cracker jar
212684	War of Roses (1893)	Davidson	Novelties only
413701	William And Mary (1903)	Davidson	Complete set

•No RD number reported on the following: *Princess Diana* by Davidson (complete set), *Quilted Pillow Sham* (limited set), *Lady Caroline* from 1891 (novelty items), *Crown Jewels, Coronation* (by Greener), *Daisy and Greek Key* (by Davidson), *Piccadilly* (by Sowerby).

OPALESCENT DOTS AND THEIR NAMES

For years, there has been quite a controversy over what each "dot" pattern should be named. Howard Seufer, a former engineer with the Fenton Art Glass Co., gave a seminar in August of 1996 which included an effort to come up with an "official" list of dot names. Seufer's list was passed on to me with the suggestion that I utilize his first attempt, refine it, and use it as a topic for one of our club meetings. I, in due course, came up with my "official" list of dot names and sent if off to Frank M. Fenton for his comments and corrections.

Following is the final list from the three of us:

Names For "Dot" Patterns—Late 1800s Through Early 1900s:

Baby Coinspot—Small opaque staggered dots with clear* net.

Big Windows—Large, opaque net with clear* dots.

Coinspot—Clear* background with opaque dots.

Inverted Thumbprint—Large round dots that are the same color as the base color.

Polka Dot—Large, opaque net with clear* dots lined up in columns, not staggered.

Windows—Opaque net with small clear* dots.

Following is a comparison of the Fenton/ L.G. Wright pattern names, versus the Victorian:

Fenton/L. G. Wright Name:	Victorian Name:
Coin Dot	Big Windows
Dot Optic	Coinspot
Eye Dot	Polka Dot
Fine Dot	
Honeycomb	Windows
Opal Dot	Coinspot
Polka Dot	Baby Coinspot
Thumbprint	Inverted Thumbprint

Names For "Dot" Patterns—Mid 1900s through Late 1900s:

Coin Dot—Large, opaque net with clear* dots. (Fenton)

Dot Optic—Clear* background with opaque dots. (Fenton)

Eye Dot—Large, opaque net with clear* dots lined up in columns, not staggered. (L.G. Wright)

Fine Dot—Small, clear* staggered dots with clear* net. (Fenton)

Honeycomb—Small, opaque net with clear* staggered dots. (L.G. Wright)

Opal Dot—Clear* background with opaque dots. (L.G. Wright)

Polka Dot—Small opaque staggered dots with clear* net. (Fenton)

Thumbprint—Large round dots that are the same color as the base color. (L.G. Wright and Fenton)

* "Clear" indicates any glass that is not opaque, regardless of its color, such as cranberry, blue, white, green etc.

THUMBNAIL SKETCH OF MOST OF THE OPALESCENT GLASS MANUFACTURERS

Adams and Co. Pittsburgh, PA. Began in 1851 as Adams, Macklin and Co. In 1860 the name was changed to Adams and Co. They produced numerous crystal patterns, the usual colors of the era and some opalescent glass. In 1891, they became Factory A of the United States Glass Co.

Aetna Glass and Manufacturing Co. Bellaire, OH. Began in 1880. During their years of operation they produced bar glass, tableware, opalescent glass, gas lamp shades and lamps. Aetna closed its doors in 1891.

A. J. Beatty and Sons, Steubenville and Tiffin, OH. Began in 1851. During their years of operation, they produced cut crystal, opalescent glass, pressed and blown ware. In 1891 they became part of the United States Glass Co. Their factory in Tiffin became Factory R and the factory in Steubenville became Factory S.

Beaumont Glass Co. Martins Ferry, OH. Began in 1895 by Percy Beaumont. In the beginning, they only decorated other manufacturer's glass but by 1899 they were producing their own. They produced both pressed and blown ware, much of which was opalescent. Some of the opalescent patterns were copies (or reissues from the original moulds) of lines, possibly designed earlier by Beaumont while at Hobbs Co.

Lines particularly thought to be Beaumont's are Seaweed, Stars and Stripes, Windows and Swirl. Beaumont also produced a copy of one of his West Virginia designs, Fern. His No. 27 bitter bottle is a shape which has been copied by L.G. Wright Glass Co. for their line of reproductions. (See figs. 951 and 952) In 1902, Beaumont built a new factory at Grafton, W.Va., then sold the company in 1906.

Belmont Glass Co. Bellaire, OH. Began in 1866. By 1881, Bellaire was known as "The Glass City" with fifteen glass houses in operation. They mainly produced tablewares, lamps, goblets and bar goods; some were opalescent. Blown tumblers were their speciality. Belmont also made their own moulds and manufactured moulds for other companies such as: Central Glass Co., McKee Glass Co., Riverside Glass Co., Gillinder and Fostoria Glass Co. Belmont closed in 1890.

Buckeye Glass Co. Martins Ferry, OH. Began in 1878 by Henry Helling. They produced all types of glass from pressed glass to mould blown opalescent glassware. Among their noted employees were John F. Miller, and for a short time, Harry Northwood. Their best known patterns are: Big Windows, Coinspot, Daisy and Fern, Lattice, Reverse Swirl, Ribbed Opal Lattice and Stripe. Buckeye was brought to a close as a result of a fire in 1896.

Consolidated Lamp and Glass Co. Coraopolis, PA. Consolidated began in 1893 and moved their factory to Fostoria, Ohio in 1895. Consolidated Lamp and Glass Co. is probably best known for the outstanding array of colors they produced. Many of the wonderful colors and designs are credited to Nicholas Kopp who was with the company until 1902. With the usual ups and downs faced by the glass industry, Consolidated managed to stay in business until its closing in 1964.

Coudersport Tile & Ornamental Glass Co. Coudersport, PA. Began in 1900. This short–lived company went through several reorganizations and ended its days as the Bastow Glass Co, when fire destroyed the factory in 1904. Their glass was very much like the products made at Northwood and Jefferson, including blown opalescent, pressed glass in opalescent, opal, custard, and decorated lemonade sets.

Perhaps Harry Bastow's major contribution to glass history, and to the art of blown opalescent glass production was his association with the Fenton brothers. Bastow helped the Fenton brothers establish their factory in Williamstown, W.Va.; Fenton Art Glass Co. continues the production of blown opalescent glass today.

Dalzell, Gilmore and Leighton Co. Findlay, OH. This company began as Dalzell Brothers & Gilmore in Brilliant, OH., at the abandoned Brilliant Glass Works factory until their new factory was finished in Wellsburg, W.Va. Cheap fuel convinced the firm to move to Findlay, OH., in 1888 at which time they also changed their name.

Dalzell, Gilmore and Leighton Co. joined the National Glass Co. in 1899. Dalzell's greatest claim to fame was their Onyx and Floradine line. Unfortunately, the line was a financial disaster because it was costly to make, chipped easily and quite often had annealing cracks. Many pieces you manage to find today will have some flaking on them, or have a crack. Fuel problems made it necessary for them to close in 1901. For more information on this company, read: *Findlay Glass Company* by James Measell and Don E. Smith.

Dugan Glass Co. Indiana, PA. Began in 1904, when Thomas Dugan and others purchased the old Northwood factory from the disbanding National combine. In their early years, they produced a great deal of opalescent glass but by 1910 they became deeply involved with the production of doped ware or, as we know it today, Carnival glass.

Perhaps the most unique pattern made by Dugan was Swastika, a tankard water pitcher in blue opalescent, produced in their Diamonds and Clubs mould. They remained in business until 1913 when Thomas Dugan resigned from the firm. The new owners renamed the company Diamond Glass Ware Co. Diamond remained in business until 1931 when the plant was destroyed by fire. For a complete history of this company read *Dugan—Diamond, The Story of Indiana, Pennsylvania Glass* by William Heacock, James Measell and Berry Wiggins.

Fenton Art Glass Co. Williamstown W.Va. Began in 1905 as a glass decorating firm. By 1907, they found producing their own glass ware much more to their liking. Thus began a long life for the company—Fenton is the only early glass company still in operation. They have made every kind of glass imaginable, from the most simple pressed glass to very intricate mould blown art glass. Their color range is endless. It is said that Fenton first developed the formula for doped ware (Carnival glass). Hopefully, they will remain in business for many more years, and continue developing new colors and patterns. For a complete history, read: *Fenton, The First Twenty-Five Years, Fenton, The Second Twenty-Five Years* and *Fenton, The Third Twenty-Five Years,* by William Heacock.

Hobbs, Brockunier & Co. Wheeling, W.Va. Began in 1863. They changed their name to Hobbs Glass Co. in 1888 after much reorganization. The Hobbs Glass Co. became part of the United States Glass Co. in 1891, and was known as Factory H. Factory H closed in 1893. This factory produced splendid cut and engraved pieces, chandeliers, apothecary ware, pressed tableware, opalescent, lamps and art glass. They are probably best known for their Francis Ware, Cranberry and Peach Blow (Coral). Factory H was reopened by Harry Northwood in 1902 under his own name. For a more complete history of the glass company, read: *Hobbs, Brockunier & Co., Glass Identification and Value Guide* by Neila & Tom Bredehoft.

Jefferson Glass Co. Steubenville, OH., and Follansbee, W.Va. Began in 1900 in an abandoned factory, Jefferson moved to their new facility in Follansbee in 1906. The majority of their opalescent glassware was produced between 1901 and 1907. In 1912, the firm established another factory in Canada, transferring many of their moulds to the new location. Consequently, some of their patterns can be found north of the border.

Jefferson produced blown and pressed colored glass ware, opalescent glass in all the colors of the time, and an extensive line of custard glass. By the Twenties they had dropped the glassware line and centered their interests around the lighting industry. The Depression took its toll on this company and they went bankrupt in 1933.

La Belle Glass Co., Bridgeport, OH, began in 1872. La Belle first concentrated on the production of pressed tableware, and then branched out to other fields which included some production of opalescent and art glass. Only two patterns shown in this book can positively be attributed to them, Hobnail, Four–Footed and Hobnail. The factory burned down in September of 1887, and was immediately rebuilt. However, the financial drain of this new construction caused the firm to enter bankruptcy; it was sold in late 1888. **Journal quote**: *Pottery and Glassware Reporter,* January 27, 1887. "The La Belle Co.'s new line of opalescent tableware, the 'Dew-drop,' is simply superb, and those wanting something rich and novel for the spring trade should lose no time in ordering it. This firm has made a marked success in the production of fine colored glass and their latest effort is worthy of the previous successes."

McKee and Brothers. Pittsburgh and Jeanette, PA. Began in 1850 with the name of J & F McKee. A third brother joined the firm in 1865, and the name changed to McKee and Brothers. In 1889, the factory moved to Jeanette, PA. In 1899, they joined the National Glass Co., and in 1903 McKee reorganized and became known as McKee Glass Co.

They remained the McKee Glass Co. until 1951, when they became the McKee Division of the Thatcher Glass Co. In 1961, Jeannette Glass Corporation bought the McKee Division. During the early years McKee was probably best known for their production of opaque wares and pressed patterns. Many of their old moulds were purchased by the Fenton Art Glass Co. in Williamstown, W.Va. All of the new pieces will be marked with an "F" in a circle. (right)

Model Flint Glass Co. Findlay, OH. Began in 1888 in Findlay, OH. In 1893, they moved to Albany, IN., where they had their own gas wells and felt they were in a better position to fulfill their commitments. Their major lines were colored glassware, some opalescent, bar ware and lamps. Model Flint became part of the National Glass Co. in 1899, and closed in 1903. For more information about this company, read: *Findlay Glass, The Glass Tableware Manufacturers, 1886-1902,* by James Measell and Don E. Smith and *Albany Glass, Model Flint Glass Co. of Albany, Indiana* by Ron Teal, Sr.

National Glass Co. Began in 1899 with the hope of bringing profits and controls back into the glass industry. National faced many insurmountable problems and was forced into receivership in 1908. The combine was composed of 19 factories:

Beatty-Brady Glass Works, Dunkirk, IN
Canton Glass Co., Marion, IN
Central Glass Co., Summitville, IN
Crystal Glass Co., Bridgeport, OH
Cumberland Glass Co., Cumberland, MD
Dalzell, Gilmore and Leighton Co., Wellsburg, W.Va.
Fairmount Glass Works, Fairmount, WV
Greensburg Glass Co., Greensburg, PA
Indiana Tumbler and Goblet Co., Greentown, IN
Keystone Glass Works, Rochester, PA
McKee and Brothers, Pittsburgh, PA and Jeanette, PA
Model Flint Glass Co., Albany, IN
The Northwood Glass Works, Indiana, PA
Ohio Flint Glass Works, Lancaster, OH
Riverside Glass Works, Wellsburg, WV
Robinson Glass Co., Zanesville, OH
Rochester Tumbler Co., Rochester, PA
Royal Glass Co., Marietta, OH
West Virginia Glass Co., Martins Ferry, OH

Nickel Plate Glass Co. Fostoria, OH. Began in 1888, it was named Nickel Plate because it was built next to the Nickel Plate railroad tracks. They made a blown line of tableware, and bar goods in crystal and opalescent colors. Some of their patterns were so extensive that they contained 40 different pieces. Nickel Plate joined the United States Glass Co. in 1891 and became known as Factory N; they stayed in operation only until 1894. For more information about the Nickel Plate Glass Co., read: *Fostoria Ohio Glass 2* by Melvin L. Murray.

Northwood Glass Co. Harry Northwood was deeply involved with many different glass companies. It is extremely difficult to tell which pattern was made at which factory at what time, as some moulds were transferred from factory to factory. Listed here are the known factories and the approximate dates of Harry Northwood's association with them. The reader can draw his own conclusions.

•Hobbs, Brockunier & Co., Wheeling, W.Va., 1882.
•La Belle Glass Co., Bridgeport, OH., 1884; returned to La Belle in1886.
•Phoenix Glass Co., Phillipsburg, PA., (now Monaca) 1885.
•Buckeye Glass Works, Martins Ferry, OH., 1887. Northwood stayed for two weeks and returned to La Belle for more money.
•The Northwood Glass Co., Martins Ferry, OH.,1888.
•The Northwood Glass Co. built a new factory in Ellwood City, PA., 1893.
•The Northwood Co., Indiana, PA., 1896.
•The Northwood Co. of Indiana, PA., joined the National Glass Co. in September of 1899 and Harry Northwood headed the London office of that company.

Harry Northwood purchased the old Hobbs, Brockunier plant in Wheeling W.Va., in 1902 and established the H. Northwood & Co. where he remained until his death on February 4, 1919, at the age of 58. The factory remained in business until 1925. This book is full of the beautiful glass Mr. Northwood created. For a complete history of Harry Northwood and his glass, read: *Harry Northwood, The Early Years 1881-1900* and *Harry Northwood, The Wheeling Years 1901-1925* by William Heacock, James Measell and Barry Wiggins.

Phoenix Glass Co. Began in 1880 in Phillipsburg, PA. The town's name was changed to Monaca in 1892. Phoenix commenced business as a manufacturer of chimneys and gas shades. When they employed Joseph Webb, nephew of Thomas Webb, the focus changed to art glass. After the turn of the century they returned to the manufacturing of lighting ware. For a brief period in the 1930s they produced glass from moulds acquired at Co-operative Flint and Consolidated Lamp and Glass, and today they are part of the Anchor Hocking conglomerate.

Following is an 1884 newspaper quote describing their wares during the art glass period: "The diversity of colors in itself is not so remarkable as the fine shading of one color into another and the different shades in the one and the same article, which shows a different color as one changes its position in relation to the light. Some of the articles have a body of one color and are plated or cased inside with a different color and the effect is very fine. Also on pieces cased outside the colored part is cut away by machinery in any desired pattern and leaves the crystal to be seen beneath, forming a crystal design on colored ground.

"Among the colors are carnelian, topazine, amberine, azurine, all shades of opalescent, such as flint, spotted blue, crystal, canary, pink, etc., rose, blue, green, all shades of red, ruby, amber, blue and gold and numerous others."

Richards and Hartley Glass Co. Tarentum, PA. Began in 1869 at Pittsburgh and moved to nearby Tarentum in 1884. They joined the United States Glass Co. in 1891, and became known as Factory E. In 1894, Factory E was sold to the Tarentum Glass Co,. but this sale did not include the Richards and Hartley moulds.

Riverside Glass Co. Wellsburg, W.Va. Began in 1880, their major production seems to have been in crystal, ruby-stained and a beautiful emerald green glass, with some production of opalescent glass. The factory burned in 1887, but was rebuilt. In 1899, they joined the National Glass Co.; unfortunately, many of their moulds were transferred to other National factories. With the dissolution of the National Glass Co., Riverside became independent again in 1904. They struggled along for four years and closed in 1908.

United States Glass Co. Began in 1891 with the merger of the eighteen independent glass companies listed below:

A—*Adams & Co., Pittsburgh, PA.
B—* Bryce Brothers, Pittsburgh, PA.
C—Challinor, Taylor & Co., Tarentum, PA.
D—George Duncan & Sons, Pittsburgh, PA.
E—Richards & Hartley, Tarentum, PA.
F—*Ripley & Co., Pittsburgh, PA.
G—Gillinder & Sons, Greensburg, PA.
H—Hobbs Glass Co., Wheeling, W.Va.
J—Columbia Glass Co., Findlay, OH.
K—*King Glass Co., Pittsburgh, PA.
L—O'Hara Glass Co., Pittsburgh, PA.
M—Bellaire Glass Co., Findlay, OH.
N—Nickel Plate Glass Co., Fostoria, OH.
O—Central Glass Co., Wheeling, W.Va.
P—*Doyle & Co., Pittsburgh, PA.
R—*A. J. Beatty & Sons, Tiffin, OH.
S—A. J. Beatty & Sons, Steubenville, OH.
T—Novelty Glass Co., Fostoria, OH.
Factories built by U. S. Glass:
U—Gas City, Indiana
GP—Glassport, PA

Only the factories marked with a * were still operating after 1900. The majority of their production at that time was from the original moulds of the member companies. The United States Glass Co. continued in business for many years, developing their own styles and colors. In their later years they produced marble glass, Carnival, iridescent and stretch glass. The Interpace Corporation purchased the company in 1969 and produced crystal "by Tiffin". For more information about this interesting company, read: *Victorian Colored Pattern Glass Book V, U. S. Glass From A to Z* by William Heacock and Fred Bickenheuser.

West Virginia Glass Co. Martins Ferry, OH. Began in 1894, and closed in 1899 when they joined the National Glass Co. During West Virginia Glass Co.'s short life, it produced pressed and blown glassware in cranberry, opalescent, opaque and crystal. It also produced bar ware. This short–lived glass company seems to have had more than its share of reorganizations. Following are its transitions: Elson Glass Co. (1882-1893); West Virginia Glass Co. (1893-1896); West Virginia Glass Mfg. Co. (1897–late 1899); and finally, West Virginia Glass Works (1899-1903) operated by National Glass Co.

L. G. Wright Glass Co. New Martinsville, W.Va. Began in 1937 or 1938 as a distributor of the glass Wright had made from moulds he owned. L. G. Wright never made any of its own glass. They did, however, decorate some of their glass and assembled many of their unique lamps from parts made specifically for them. The mainstay of the Wright line was reproduction glass made in the image of old pattern glass. Fenton Art Glass Co. of Williamstown, W.Va., made the majority of Wright's mould blown glassware. Wright had companies such as Westmoreland, Imperial, Fostoria, Paden City, Viking and New Martinsville make the balance of their glass. Unfortunately, they have closed their doors; their moulds went on the auctioning block on May 27, 1999. For a complete history, read: *The L. G. Wright Glass Company* by James Measell and W. C. "Red" Roetteis.

GLIMPSES FROM THE GLASS HOUSES

(Excerpted from Heacock's Book 2, published in 1975.)

The following notes appeared in various trade journals regarding the companies which produced opalescent glass. I thought it might interest my readers to scan these for bits of information, just as this author did for clues that might prove important.

January, 1897

"Northwood at Indiana, PA., specialities are table articles of all kinds, lemonade sets, fancy novelties, and lamps of all sizes and descriptions. These goods are in ruby, blue, crystal opalescent, and various combinations of colors and shades are of the finest lead glass."

January, 1902

"The Beaumont Glass Co. has a pattern which they call No. 106, in plain, rose pink and gold and crystal and gold. They have this in decorated, etched and gold band as well. There are new water sets in crystal, blue, green and ruby, all handsomely decorated. Other things in the exhibit are opalescent novelties in great variety, vases in the No. 106 pattern, and numerous miscellaneous articles."

March, 1902 (in reference to National Glass Co.)

"The company has prepared plans for the erection of another furnace at the factory in Indiana, PA. This is the plant where most of the fine colored ware is made, and its product enjoys a prestige equalled by no other in the country."

January, 1904 (at a 1904 Glass Exhibit)

"The name of Northwood is synonymous with high–grade colored glass to everyone in the trade. When Mr. Harry Northwood sold out his Indiana, PA., plant to the National Glass Co. about two years ago, he went abroad, and the leisure afforded to a man of such artistic tastes, retentive memory and original ideas meant added capital of the richest kind for the new plant, which he opened in Wheeling, W.Va., in May, 1902.

He bought the old Barnes & Co. site, where glass-making was in vogue in 1830. The new buildings and additions are modern; equipped with the best appliances for his special lines.

Everything in the Northwood display is practically new. There are 125 lemonade sets alone, arranged in a most effective way. The chief feature of the room is several complete lines of tableware, radically different in design and finish from anything in the house. One of these, the Mikado, in frosted glass with transparent colored enamel flowers artistically trimmed in gold, is novel, almost too novel, but it grows in favor the more it is inspected. The Encore and Regent are regal looking patterns, in several solid colors, rich in heavy gold trimmings."

January, 1904

"Among the most lasting impressions gained by (a buyer's) first round will be the exhibit managed by Mr. George Mortimer, of the Jefferson Glass Co. of Steubenville, Ohio. Not only are the lines exceptionally full, but the arrangement is so good that all its beauty is retained in spite of the inevitable confusion of so much sight–seeing along somewhat similar lines. The number of new patterns in colored lemonade sets, wine sets, toilet ware, etc. is certainly not smaller than elsewhere, and there are numerous effects in decoration that are both distinctive and in the rarest good taste. The toilet line, *Iris* and *Vogue*, have merit that appeals to one instinctively, while the entire display justifies the praise given it by men of discriminating judgement."

April, 1902

"Harry Northwood has made another proposition to the Wheeling Board of Trade relative to securing inducements toward starting up part of the old Hobbs glass plant. The option given by President D.C. Ripley of the United States Glass Co. on the plant expired April 1, and a conference was arranged to get it renewed. Mr. Northwood proposes to make novelties."

September, 1902

"Harry Northwood is very busy preparing his factory at Wheeling, W.Va., for active work. Everything is being overhauled and put in proper shape and it's expected that operations will begin early next month. Tableware and novelties in crystal, colored and opalescent glass, plain and decorated, will be the product, and in the manufacture of these specialties, Mr. Northwood has few peers, if any at all."

(Month unknown) 1898

"The Northwood Co., Indiana, PA., represented in New York by Frank M. Miller, is coming prominently to the fore as producers of opalescent and decorated lemonade sets. In these wares, which have long been regarded as a prerogative of the importer, the Northwood Co. is now prepared to make prices which will compare favorably with any asked for foreign goods. The popularity of the Klondyke and Alaska patterns in tableware, which have had such a phenomenal run, would seem by the orders daily received to be unabated. They certainly were original and new, and for next season Harry Northwood promises something that dealers will like even better."

(Month unknown) 1896

"The Buckeye Glass Works, Martins Ferry, recently destroyed by fire, was one of the oldest west of the Alleghenies. It was first established in 1849 and run as a bottle factory for three years with one small furnace. Michael Sweeny, known as the 'glass king', was the chief owner and manager for many years. It was known as the

Excelsior Glass Works until 1879, when it was changed to the Buckeye. Mr. Seamon has been president since 1884. The cause of the fire is a mystery."

(Month unknown) 1896

"Fires have been drawn in the factory of the Northwood Glass Co., Ellwood, PA., and no prospects of an early resumption are apparent. Mr. Harry Northwood, who has purchased the large factory in Indiana, PA., has put fire in the furnace and is prepared to book orders and ship at an early date, all the lines of fine colored and opalescent water sets, novelties and fine lemonade sets formerly made by him at the Ellwood works. New lines of artistic lamps will be put on the market as soon as possible, and early orders for these goods are solicited."

(Month unknown) 1896

"The Northwood Co. is working full hand, and one of the most expert set of off hand workmen to be found in this country are gathered at the works. A fine line of opal tableware, lemonade sets, lamps and colored novelties are being made, and Harry is just letting himself out on fine shapes, color combinations and handsomely decorated glassware."

May, 1902

"At this writing—May 5—all but $1,000 of the required $10,000 public subscription has to be raised to secure the plant Harry Northwood proposes to operate in the old Hobbs factory. He intends to make ruby (cranberry) and opalescent ware. The U.S. Glass Co., which owns the Hobbs property, extended the options from April 1 to May 3, and a further continuance until May 8 has been secured. It is known that a small syndicate stands ready to make up the balance of the money, if necessary, so that the scheme is practically assured.

Mr. Northwood, who worked in the Hobbs factory in its palmy days, says other towns have made better monetary inducements, but he prefers Wheeling because of its being a better labor market than the smaller communities. This fact actuated his display of patience in waiting throughout the delay. Wheeling never had to cash bonus any industrial proposition before, which accounts for the long time in getting the comparatively small amount."

October, 1902

"John F. Miller, manager of the National's plant at Albany, IN., and formerly with the Buckeye at Martins Ferry and the Riverside at Wellsburg, was in Wheeling a few days ago and reports the glass business is brisk and all factories in his company working to the limit."

January, 1905

"The name of Harry Northwood is the best evidence that in parlor #6 will be found one of the most frequented exhibits of the house. Mr. Northwood inherits the artistic sense through several generations of glass makers. He not only creates beautiful designs and shapes, but he has a large plant well equipped to quickly produce what the dealer requires. In colored lemonade sets, wine sets, vases, one fire gold decorations and tableware, novelties, ten cent goods, etc., the display is unexcelled. Many buyers think of the output of the concern as chiefly colored ware, but the display of crystal, opal and enamel goods is proof of the variety of pieces made."

October, 1904

"The Jefferson Glass Company continue to bring out goods which attract the instant favor of the trade because of their elegance and quick selling qualities. Mr. Magee, the chief designer and mould maker here, is somewhat responsible for this not unpleasant condition of affairs. His experience at the Heisey works and with other celebrated glass makers has given him ideas and a standard of taste of much practical value. When Mr. C. Grant Fish or his associates, Messrs. Findt and Mortimer, have a new conception in mind they find Mr. Magee able to produce a mould expressing their best ideas."

September, 1904

"A little more than four years ago, Messrs, Fish, Findt, Mortimer and their associates took the present plant of the Jefferson Glass Co. and determined to make a specialty of colored lemonade sets, fine table ware, both color and crystal, opalescent glassware, vases and novelties of especial merit. They had a good plant, but it was not until about a year ago that they caught exactly what the trade most desired. Since then, they have met that want fully, and have become leaders in designing some peculiarly attractive goods."

September, 1906

"H. Northwood & Co. are fairly swamped with orders for their new lines. The strikingly beautiful and altogether original 'Verre D'Or' ware in royal blue, amethyst and green, with a massive gold treatment, has taken like wild fire. On first sight, it looks like a proposition for the jeweler, so heavily encrusted and richly embossed are the gold decorations."

OPALESCENT GLASS PATTERNS

ABALONE
(See fig. 406)

Maker: Jefferson Glass Co., Steubenville, OH.
Named by: Joe B. Bell
Y.O.P.: Circa 1904
Other name: None
Colors made: Blue, white, green, possibly canary.
Pieces made: Two handled bowl.
Reintroduction or Repros: None known at this time.

ACORN BURRS
(See fig. 153)

Maker: H. Northwood Co., Wheeling, W.Va.
Named by: Presznick l
Y.O.P. Circa 1911
Other name: Acorn Burrs and Bark
Colors: Blue and white opalescent; Carnival colors of amethyst, green, marigold, ice blue, ice green, purple, white and aqua opalescent.
Pieces made: Water set, table set, berry set, punch bowl and base, punch cup and swung vase.
Reintroduction or Repros: None known at this time.
Note: Highly collectible in Carnival, but extremely rare in opalescent.

ADMIRAL (FLORA)
(See fig. 209, 219)

Maker: Beaumont Glass Co., Martins Ferry, OH.
Named by: Original manufacturer's name.
Y.O.P. From 1898
Other name: Flora, Kamm 7 and pattern #99.
Colors made: Blue, white and canary opalescent, crystal and emerald green.
Pieces made: Table set, water set, berry set, cruet, toothpick, syrup, assorted novelty bowls, salt shaker, jelly compote and celery vase.
Reintroduction or Repros: None known at this time.
Notes: This is an extremely attractive pattern which is very hard to piece together as a set. In opalescent, this pattern is scarce. Heacock initially called this pattern *Flora*. In his series, *The Glass Collector, Collecting Glass,* he began advising the reader of the original manufacturer's name. Heacock believed original factory names should be used when known. Thus, the name change for this edition.

ADONIS HOBNAIL (GONTERMAN HOB)
(See fig. 166)

Maker: Aetna Glass & Mfg. Co., Bellaire, OH.
Named by: Original manufacturer's name.
Y.O.P. Circa 1888
Other name: Gonterman Hob, Heacock
Colors made: Amber top with an opalescent or frosted base, rare with a blue base.
Pieces made: The cruet seems to be the only piece made.
Reintroduction or Repros: None known at this time.
Notes: This pattern is very hard to find. It was made with the same annealing process used on the *Adonis Swirl* pattern. Heacock attributed this pattern to Hobbs, Brockunier & Co. In *Hobbs, Brockunier & Co., Glass Identification and Value Guide,* the Bredehoft's state "Gonterman Swirl was not made by them (Hobbs, Brockunier & Co.)." Thus, the attribution change for this edition.

Heacock originally called this pattern *Gonterman Hob*. In his series *The Glass Collector, Collecting Glass,* he began advising the reader of the original manufacturer's names. Heacock believed original names should be used when known. Thus, the name change for this edition. See notes for *Adonis Swirl*.

ADONIS PINEAPPLE

Maker: Aetna Glass and Manufacturing Co., Bellaire OH.
Named by: Original manufacturer's name
Y.O.P. Circa 1888
Other name: Gonterman Pineapple
Colors made: Top portion in blue or amber with the bottom opalescent or frosted.
Pieces made: Claret bottle
Reintroductions/Repros: None known at this time.

Adonis Pineapple claret bottle with original stopper.

ADONIS SWIRL
(GONTERMAN SWIRL)

(See figs. 173-178, 195, 562, 563)

Maker: Aetna Glass & Mfg. Co., Bellaire, OH.

Named by: Original manufacturer's name.

Y.O.P. Circa 1888

Other name: Ribbed Swirl and Gonterman Swirl, Heacock

Colors made: Blue or amber top, frosted or opalescent base.

Pieces made: Table set, water set, berry set, cruet, celery vase, syrup, lamp shade, cologne bottle*, covered butter, finger bowl, and toothpick holder (sometimes in a frame). Other possibilities are the salt shaker and sugar shaker.

Reintroduction or Repros: None known at this time.

Notes: Quite often signed "Pat'd Aug 4, 1876." The patent date refers to the annealing process whereby two separately formed pieces of glass are attached to form a single item.

  *The top half of this cologne bottle is amber and the base is opalescent white.

  Heacock originally called this pattern *Gonterman Swirl.* In his series *The Glass Collector, Collecting Glass,* he began advising the reader of the original manufacturer's names. Heacock believed original names should be used when known. Thus, the name change for this edition. See notes for *Adonis Hobnail.*

ALA–BOCK

(See fig. 1273)

Maker: Model Flint Glass Co., Albany, IN.

Named by: Ron Teal, Sr.

Y.O.P. Circa 1900–1902

Other name: None

Colors made: Blue and canary opalescent.

Pieces made: Rose bowl and water set.

ALASKA

(See figs.1–18, 202 & 217)

Maker: The Northwood Co. with continued production by Dugan Glass Co., Indiana, PA.

Named by: Original manufacturer's name

Y.O.P. Circa 1897

Other name: Lion Leg, Kamm

Colors: Crystal, emerald green, white, blue and canary opalescent. Sometimes found with tiny enameled forget-me-nots and big "elephant ear" leaves—with or without gold decoration.

Pieces made: Table set, water set, berry set, cruet, banana boat, celery tray (or jewel tray), salt and pepper (see notes) and bride's basket.

Reintroduction or Repros: None known at this time.

Notes: The tumblers and salt shakers are interchangeable with the *Klondyke* pattern, unless decorated as with figure 1. The interchangeable tumbler and salt were obviously a production shortcut. The original cruet stopper is a crystal pressed, faceted stopper.

See catalog reprint in the *Dolphin Compote* section.

Ad from *China, Glass and Pottery Review* (February, 1898).

Alaska table set from G. Sommers and Co. wholesale catalog (April 6, 1898).

ALHAMBRA

(See figs. 1271, 1272)
Maker: Model Flint Glass Co., Albany, IN.
Named by: Heacock
Y.O.P. Circa 1894
Other name: None
Colors made: White, blue, and canary opalescent.
Pieces made: Rose bowl, tumbler. A pitcher is probable.
Reintroduction or Repros: None known at this time.

Blue opalescent *Alhambra* tumbler

ANIMALS, ENGLISH

Note: The small vaseline alligator was blown into a mould and cut off at the end of the tail. It has been seen with its tail attached to a small, shell–like, mould–blown vase with applied rigaree. This rare example was photographed at a museum in England and is about 4" long.

The tiny 3" pig was photographed at the same museum and shown with the original Thomas Webb & Sons, Ltd. box. This pig was free blown, made for the Franco-British Exhibition at the turn of the twentieth century.

Yellow opalescent pig

Yellow opalescent alligator

AQUATIC

(See fig. 1222)
Maker: Unknown. Best guess would be a French origin for this interesting piece.
Named by: Elmore
Y.O.P. Uncertain. Possibly the 1950s or 1960s.
Colors: White opalescent
Pieces made: Vase and under plate
Reintroductions/Repros: None

ARABIAN NIGHTS

(See figs. 260, 809, 810)
Maker: Possibly Beaumont Glass Co., Martins Ferry, OH.
Named by: Heacock
Y.O.P. Circa 1900
Other name: None
Colors made: White, blue, and cranberry opalescent. Rare in canary.
Pieces made: Pitcher, tumbler.
Reintroduction or Repros: None known at this time.
Notes: The attribution is highly questionable. The shape mould on the water pitcher matches that on *Daisy in Criss Cross*, which was made by Beaumont. This pattern, unlisted until 1975, is seldom seen for sale. *Arabian Nights* is a fascinating and highly embellished pattern which apparently was made only in a water set. Production must have been limited.

See the picture on the following page.

This *Arabian Nights* pitcher is similar in shape to the mould used on the *Daisy in Criss Cross* pitcher.

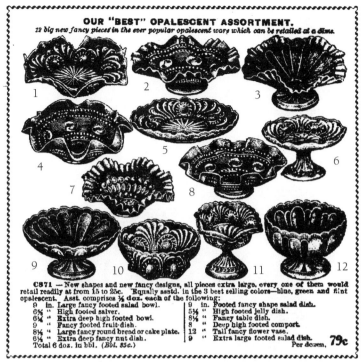

Grouping of Jefferson Glass Co. pieces, circa 1905. 1. *Tokyo* 2. *Astro* 3. *Popsicle Sticks* 4. *Astro* 5. *Tokyo* 6. *Barbells* 7. *Astro* 8. *Tokyo* 9. *Popsicle Sticks* 10, 11. *Tokyo* 12. *Popsicle Sticks*.

ARGONAUT SHELL (SEE NAUTILUS)

ASCOT

(See fig. 545)
Maker: Henry Greener & Co., Sunderland, England.
Named by: Heacock
Y.O.P. Circa 1895 sometimes marked with the Rd #262018
Other name: None
Colors made: Blue and yellow opalescent
Pieces made: Table set
Reintroduction or Repros: None known at this time.

ASTRO

(See fig. 512)
Maker: Jefferson Glass Co., Steubenville, OH.
Named by: Hartung, *Opalescent*
Y.O.P. Circa 1904
Other name: None
Colors made: White, blue, green and canary.
Pieces made: Bowl
Reintroduction or Repros: None known at this time.
Notes: This pattern was previously attributed incorrectly to Northwood. The 1905 Butler Brothers catalog shown above reveals this to be a Jefferson product.

AURORA BOREALIS

(See figs. 467, 538)
Maker: Jefferson Glass Co., Steubenville, OH.
Named by: Heacock
Y.O.P. 1903
Other name: None
Colors made: White, blue, and green opalescent.
Pieces made: Vases
Reintroduction or Repros: None known at this time.

AUTUMN LEAVES

(See fig. 486)
Maker: H. Northwood Co., Wheeling, W.Va.
Named by: Heacock
Y.O.P. Circa 1905
Other name: None
Colors made: White, green and blue opalescent.
Pieces made: Bowls
Reintroduction or Repros: None known at this time.
Notes: Presznick calls this *Maple Leaf, Variant* but it does not have that pattern's characteristics—thus the name change.

BABY COINSPOT

(See fig. 306)

Maker: Belmont Glass Co. Martins Ferry, OH., and Nickel Plate Glass Co., Fostoria, OH.

Named by: Taylor

Y.O.P. Circa 1887

Other name: None

Colors made: White opalescent.

Pieces made: Syrup and pitcher, plus others.

Reintroduction or Repros: Yes—See fig. 620, which is Fenton Art Glass Co.'s *Polka Dot*. See also text for *Polka Dot* (Fenton).

Nickel's *Baby Coinspot* pitcher with unique opalescent reeded handle.

BARBELLS

(See fig. 511)

Maker: Jefferson Glass Co., Steubenville, OH and H. Northwood Co., Wheeling, W.Va.

Named by: Heacock

Y.O.P. Circa 1905

Other name: None

Colors made: White, blue, green, and canary opalescent; also purple slag.

Pieces made: Bowls

Reintroduction or Repros: None known at this time.

Notes: Attribution based on a grouping in the 1905 Butler Brothers catalog. See catalog reprint in the *Astro* pattern section.

BASKET, FENTON

(See fig. 460)

Maker: Fenton Art Glass Co., Williamstown, W.Va.

Named by: Original manufacturer's name.*

Y.O.P. Circa 1911

Other name: Basketweave, Basketweave Base Open—Edged, Fenton Basket and Pattern 1092.

Colors made: White, blue, green and canary opalescent; crystal, royal blue, and ruby; Carnival colors of marigold, amethyst, green, blue and ruby; stretch colors of Celeste blue, Florentine green, Florentine Ruby and Florentine Pearl.

Pieces made: Bowls of varying sizes, vase, plate, candle holder and novelties.

Reintroduction or Repros: Fenton may reintroduce a pattern or color at any time, as they have here. If the piece was made after 1972, it should be marked with the Fenton logo.

Note: *A catalog reprint shown in *Fenton, The First Twenty-Five Years* shows that Fenton called this pattern *Basket*. The word "Fenton" has been added to avoid confusion with other patterns named *Basket*.

BEAD AND PANEL (CHRISTMAS PEARLS)

(See fig. 182)

Maker: Jefferson Glass Co., Steubenville, OH.

Named by: Peterson, Glass Salt Shakers

Y.O.P. Circa 1902

Other name: Christmas Bead and Christmas Pearls (Heacock)

Colors made: Blue, white and green opalescent

Pieces made: Cruet and salt shakers

Reintroduction or Repros: None known at this time.

Note: It is not understood why Heacock felt it was necessary to change the name of this pattern to *Christmas Pearls*. In three other reference books I have on file, this pattern was listed as *Bead and Panel*. Heacock's name change seems unnecessary and contrary to his belief that the first name published, other than the original manufacturer's name, should be used. Therefore, I have listed this pattern as *Bead and Panel*.

BEADED CABLE

(See fig. 461)

Maker: H. Northwood Co., Wheeling, W.Va.

Named by: Presznick 1

Y.O.P. Circa 1903–1908

Other name: None

Colors made: Opalescent colors of white, blue, green and canary, custard (sometimes decorated with nutmeg), purple slag; Carnival colors of marigold, purple, blue, green, ice green, aqua opalescent, peach opalescent and aqua opalescent.

Pieces made: Rose bowl, bowl, and card receiver.

Reintroduction or Repros: None known at this time.

Note: For many years Heacock believed *Beaded Cable* to be one of the patterns made by both Jefferson Glass Co. and Northwood. In *Collecting Glass, Volume III,* he stated: "Beaded Cable is NOT one of the patterns which was made by both Jefferson and Northwood."

BEADED DRAPES
(See fig. 502)
Maker: Jefferson Glass Co., Steubenville, OH.
Named by: Presznick 2
Y.O.P. Circa 1904
Other name: None
Colors made: White, blue, green and canary opalescent, sometimes with cranberry border.
Pieces made: Bowls
Reintroduction or Repros: None known at this time.

BEADED FAN
(See fig. 509)

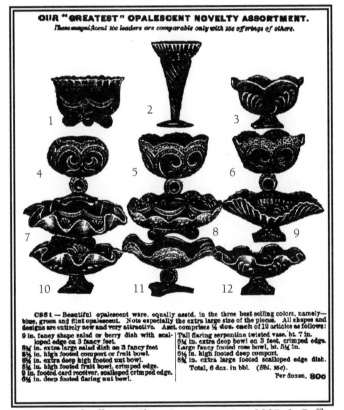

OUR "GREATEST" OPALESCENT NOVELTY ASSORTMENT.
These magnificent 10c leaders are comparable only with 35c offerings of others.

C881 — Beautiful opalescent ware, equally asstd. in the three best selling colors, namely—blue, green and flint opalescent. Note especially the extra large size of the pieces. All shapes and designs are entirely new and very attractive. Asst. comprises ¼ doz. each of 12 articles as follows:
9 in. fancy shape salad or berry dish with scalloped edge on 3 fancy feet.
8¼ in. extra large salad dish on 3 fancy feet.
6½ in. extra deep high footed nut bowl.
5¼ in. high footed fruit bowl, crimped edge.
9 in. footed card receiver, scalloped crimped edge.
6½ in. deep footed flaring nut bowl.
Tall flaring serpentine twisted vase, ht. 7 in.
6½ in. extra deep bowl on 3 feet, crimped edge.
Large fancy footed rose bowl, ht. 5½ in.
6¼ in. high footed deep compart.
8¼ in. extra large footed scalloped edge dish.
Total, 6 doz. in bbl. (Bbl. 95c).
Per dozen, **80c**

Grouping of Jefferson Glass Co. pieces, circa 1905. 1. *Ruffles and Rings* 2. *Dahlia Twist* 3. *Beaded Fan* 4, 5, 6. *Beaded Fleur–de–Lis* 7, 8. *Ruffles and Rings* 9. *Beaded Fan* 10. ? 11. *Beaded Fleur–de–Lis* 12. *Beaded Fan.*

Maker: Jefferson Glass Co., Steubenville, OH.
Named by: Presznick 2
Y.O.P. Circa 1905
Other name: Shell and Dots, and Pattern #211.
Colors made: White, blue, and green opalescent.
Pieces made: Novelties
Reintroduction or Repros: None known at this time.
Notes: The earlier Presznick name for the pattern is

retained for two reasons. First, her name for the pattern was from an earlier publication, and Heacock believed in the right of priority. Second, he was trying to clear up the confusion over Northwood's *New York* pattern, which both Kamm and Hartung called Jefferson's #211. The patterns are not the same at all.

BEADED FANTASY
(See fig. 1247)
Maker: Uncertain. In *Collecting Glass, Volume 2,* Heacock stated that the color of figure 1247 was identical to the "cranberry pink" opalescent made by Duncan & Miller Glass Co., Washington, PA., beginning in 1940. It is unlike any color made by Fenton at that time.
Named by: Elmore
Y.O.P. Circa 1940s
Other name: None
Colors made: Pink, yellow and blue opalescent.
Pieces made: Perfume
Reintroductions/Repros: None known at this time
Note: This perfume was originally attributed to Fenton in *Fenton Glass, The Second Twenty-Five Years.* Frank M. Fenton stated some years later that they did not make this perfume, even though the perfume was found in Fenton's storage. Mr. Fenton believes the bottle was probably sent to them by the perfume packager for a production quote, but was never made. Despite the DeVilbiss look, this bottle was made for a company in Chartley, Mass. and marketed under the trade name "HomSpray".*
*A perfume with a paper label stating this information has been documented.

BEADED FLEUR–DE–LIS
(See fig. 396)
Maker: Jefferson Glass Co., Steubenville, OH.
Named by: Presznick 2
Y.O.P. Circa 1905
Other name: None
Colors made: White, green, and blue opalescent.
Pieces made: Novelties
Notes: Attribution is based on the 1905 Butler Brothers catalog, which shows this pattern with a grouping of known Jefferson patterns. See catalog reprint in *Beaded Fan.*
Reintroduction or Repros: None known at this time.

BEADED OVALS IN SAND
(SEE ERIE)

BEADED STAR AND MEDALLION
(See fig. 398)
Maker: Reportedly, Imperial Glass Co., Bellaire, OH.
Named by: Presznick 2
Y.O.P. Circa 1910
Other name: None
Colors made: White, green opalescent, and marigold carnival.

Pieces made: Novelties and lamp shades.

Reintroduction or Repros: None known at this time.

Notes: The Imperial Glass Co. was started by Mr. Edward Muhleman. Muhleman was president of La Belle Glass Co., and then National Glass Co. before founding Imperial. Perhaps this lamp globe was made earlier in opalescent glass, and later in Carnival glass, at the Imperial firm.

BEADED STARS AND MOON

Maker: Fenton Art Glass Co., Williamstown, W.Va.

Named by: Heacock

Y.O.P. Circa 1908

Other name: None

Colors made: Crystal and opalescent; white, blue and green.

Pieces made: Bowls, plate, and bonbon.

Reintroductions/Repros: None known at this time. Fenton may reintroduce a pattern or color at any time. If made after 1972, it should be marked with the Fenton logo.

Blue opalescent *Beaded Stars and Moon* bowl.

BEADED STARS AND SWAG

(See fig. 418)

Maker: Fenton Art Glass Co., Williamstown, W.Va.

Named by: Heacock

Y.O.P. Circa early 1908

Other name: None

Colors made: Crystal and opalescent, white, blue and green.

Pieces made: Bowls, plate and bonbon

Reintroduction or Repros: None known at this time, but Fenton may reintroduce a color or pattern at any time.

BEADS AND BARK

(See figs. 469, 470, 536)

Maker: H. Northwood Co., Wheeling, W.Va.

Named by: Hartung, *Northwood.*

Y.O.P. Circa 1903

Other name: None

Colors made: White, blue, green, canary opalescent and purple slag.

Pieces made: Novelties and vase

Reintroduction or Repros: None known at this time.

BEADS AND CURLY--CUES

(See fig. 500)

Maker: H. Northwood Co., Wheeling, W.Va.

Named by: Heacock

Y.O.P. Circa 1906

Other name: None

Colors made: White, blue, and green opalescent.

Pieces made: Novelties

Reintroduction or Repros: None known at this time.

BEATTY HONEYCOMB

(See figs. 194, 554, 576, 577, 581–583)

Maker: Beatty & Sons, Tiffin, OH.

Named by: Lee, *Victorian Glass*

Y.O.P. Circa 1888

Other names: Beatty Waffle, Checkered Bar and Crossbar Opal.

Colors made: Blue and white opalescent.

Pieces made: Table set, water set, berry set, cruet, toothpick, celery, salt shakers, mustard, mug, sugar shaker, individual creamer and sugar.

Reintroduction or Repros: Yes—by Fenton Art Glass Co., Williamstown, W.Va. (See text for *Beatty Waffle* and figs. 585, 591 and 612). In 1976, the Westmoreland Glass Co. of Grapeville, PA., produced a covered sugar No. 339; pieces are marked with an embossed *WG*.

Notes: This pattern seems to have had a limited production.

BEATTY RIB

(See figs. 129, 213, 555, 579, 580)

Maker: Beatty & Sons, Tiffin, OH.

Named by: Lee, *Early American Pressed Glass*

Y.O.P. Circa 1889

Other name: Beatty Ribbed

Colors made: Blue and white opalescent; scarce in canary.

Pieces made: Table set, water set, berry set (round or rectangular), celery, mug, assorted nappies, mustard, salt shakers, salt dip, cracker jar, sugar shaker, toothpick, finger bowl, match holder and covered butter.

Reintroduction or Repros: Yes, but not in opalescent. The Fenton Art Glass Co., Williamstown, W.Va., produced a sugar bowl in milk glass, circa 1958.

Notes: This pattern apparently purples in the sun easily, and the blue will sometimes have a deep reddish caste.

BEATTY SWIRL

(See figs. 50, 63, 64, 186, 380, 1212)

Maker: Beatty and Sons, Tiffin, OH.

Named by: Kamm 8

Y.O.P. Circa 1889

Other name: Beatty Swirl Opal

Colors made: Blue and white opalescent; very rare in canary opalescent.

Pieces made: Table set, water set, berry set, celery, mug, water tray and syrup.

Reintroduction or Repros: None known at this time.

BEATTY WAFFLE

(See figs. 585, 591, 612)

Maker: Fenton Art Glass Co., Williamstown, W.Va.

Named by: Fenton

Y.O.P. Circa 1960

Other name: Victorian name Beatty Honeycomb

Colors made: White milk glass, blue and dark green opalescent; other colors are probable.

Pieces made: Sugar bowl, vase and basket.

Reintroduction or Repros: Fenton may reintroduce a pattern or color at any time. If the piece was made after 1972, it should be marked with the Fenton logo.

BERRY PATCH

(See fig. 448)

Maker: Jefferson Glass Co., Steubenville, OH.

Named by: Joe B. Bell

Y.O.P. Circa 1905

Other name: Pattern No. 261

Colors made: White, blue, and green opalescent.

Pieces made: Novelties

Reintroduction or Repros: None known at this time.

Notes: This little novelty seemed to escape everyone's attention. It is shown in the blurred reprints in *Kamm 7*, page 156. The ad reprint shows a cake plate. Figure 448 illustrates what the catalog called a "jelly".

BIG WINDOWS AND BIG WINDOWS REVERSE SWIRL

(See figs. 796, 864, 865, 902, 925)

Maker: Buckeye Glass Co., Martins Ferry, OH.

Named by: Uncertain

Other name: Pattern No. 527

Colors made: White, blue and cranberry opalescent.

Pieces made: Butter dish, creamer, covered sugar, spooner, sugar shaker, syrup, pitcher, tumbler, barber bottle and oil lamps.

Reintroduction or Repros: Yes, by Fenton Art Glass Co., Williamstown, W.Va. Fenton calls their pattern *Coin Dot*. See text for *Coin Dot*.

Note: The water pitcher was made in the same mould as used on *Lattice*. The rest of the set was made in the swirled mould used to make *Reverse Swirl*. *Big Windows Swirl* pieces will all be round, not oval.

Big Windows master berry and syrup pitcher in cranberry opalescent, made by Buckeye Glass Co. The same moulds were used on their *Reverse Swirl* line.

BLACKBERRY, FENTON

(See fig. 475)

Maker: Fenton Art Glass Co., Williamstown, W.Va.

Named by: Presznick 1, #20

Y.O.P. Circa 1907

Other name: None

Colors made: Blue, white, green opalescent; custard and Carnival colors of marigold, green, amethyst, blue, ice blue, ice green and red.

Pieces made: Bowl, plate, vase and cuspidor.

Reintroduction or Repros: None known at this time, but Fenton may reintroduce a pattern or color at any time. If made after 1972, it should be marked with the Fenton logo.

Notes: Frequently found with goofus decoration.

BLACKBERRY SPRAY

(See fig. 1128)

Maker: Fenton Art Glass Co., Williamstown, W.Va.

Named by: Fenton

Y.O.P. Circa 1915

Other name: None

Colors made: White, blue, amethyst (violet) opalescent, custard; Carnival colors of marigold, green, red, blue, amethyst and aqua.

Pieces made: Vases, bonbon, and nappy.

Reintroductions/Repros: Fenton may reintroduce a pattern or color at any time. If made after 1972, the piece should be marked with the Fenton logo.

BLOCKED THUMBPRINT AND BEADS

(See fig. 457)

Maker: Dugan Glass Co., Indiana, PA.

Named by: Heacock

Y.O.P. Circa 1906

Other name: None

Colors made: White, blue, and green opalescent.

Pieces made: Bowls

Reintroduction or Repros: None known at this time.

Notes: This pattern is similar to *Leaf Rosette & Beads*, except that the flowers are missing. See catalog reprint in *Winterlily* pattern section.

BLOCK, JEFFERSON

(See fig. 196)
Maker: Jefferson Glass Co., Steubenville, OH.
Named by: Heacock
Y.O.P. Circa 1905
Other name: Northwood's Block—Hartung, *Opalescent*.
Colors made: White, blue, green and canary opalescent, sometimes with a cranberry border on the top rim.
Pieces made: Bowls and celery vase.
Reintroduction or Repros: None known at this time.
Notes: The celery vase was sometimes flattened out into a bowl. No table set pieces were made to accompany this pattern.

BLOCK OPTIC

(See fig. 1143)
Maker: Fenton Art Glass Co., Williamstown W.Va.
Named by: Fenton
Y.O.P. Circa 1939, or possibly as early as 1933.
Other name: None
Colors made: White opalescent
Pieces made: Vase, ginger jar on satin glass base, and hats.
Reintroductions/Repros: Fenton may reintroduce a pattern or color at any time. If made after 1972, it should be marked with the Fenton logo.
See catalog reprint in the *Wide Rib* section.

BLOOMS AND BLOSSOMS (SEE MIKADO)

BLOSSOMS AND PALMS

(See fig. 412)
Maker: H. Northwood Co., Wheeling, W.Va.
Named by: Heacock
Y.O.P. Circa 1905–1908
Other name: None
Colors made: Green, white and blue opalescent.
Reintroduction or Repros: None known at this time.
Notes: Care should be taken not to confuse this pattern with the very similar Northwood pattern, *Shell and Wild Rose*. They are most definitely two different patterns.

BLOSSOMS AND WEB

(See fig. 483)
Maker: Uncertain—see notes
Named by: Hartung, *Opalescent*
Y.O.P. Circa 1905
Other name: None
Colors made: Primarily white opalescent, frequently with goofus decoration; very, very hard to find in colored opalescent.
Pieces made: Bowls

Reintroduction or Repros: None known at this time.
Notes: Heacock believed this pattern was made by Northwood. This pattern is not shown in either *Harry Northwood, The Early Years 1881–1900*, or *Harry Northwood, The Wheeling Years 1901–1925*, so the attribution is doubtful.

BLOWN TWIST (SEE TWIST, BLOWN)

BOGGY BAYOU (SEE REVERSE SWIRL)

BRIDESHEAD

Maker: Davidson and Co.
Named by: Chris Molinar, winner of a pattern naming contest in Heacock's *The Glass Collector*, Spring 1982.
Y.O.P. Circa 1889–90
Other name: None
Colors made: The color was advertised as "Blue Pearline" in an English trade journal. Also yellow opalescent.
Pieces made: Butter dish, creamer, vase, fairy lamp and jelly compote, pitcher, tumbler and covered biscuit jar with underplate. More pieces are likely.
Reintroductions/Repros: None known at this time
Note: *Brideshead* is marked with the English Rd. No. 130643, which means it was registered in 1889.

Brideshead butter dish, creamer and jelly compote.

BUBBLE LATTICE
(SEE LATTICE)

BUCKEYE (CONCAVE COLUMNS)

(See figs. 459, 533)

Maker: National Glass Co. and Dugan Glass Co., Indiana, PA.

Named by: Heacock

Y.O.P. Circa 1902 and 1908

Other name: Concave Columns and Coinspot, Pressed. Carnival collectors know this pattern as Formal.

Colors made: White, blue, and canary opalescent. Also Carnival colors.

Pieces made: Vases, compotes, tumblers, and novelties.

Reintroduction or Repros: None known at this time.

Note: The name has been changed because a catalog reprint shown in *Dugan/Diamond, The Story of Indiana, Pennsylvania, Glass* shows that Dugan named this pattern *Buckeye*.

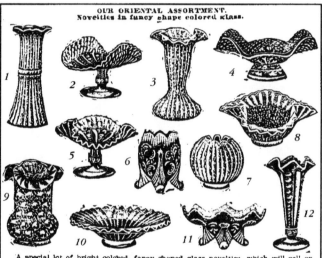

OUR ORIENTAL ASSORTMENT.
Novelties in fancy shape colored glass.

A special lot of bright colored, fancy shaped glass novelties, which will sell on sight. The shapes are entirely new, and the pieces are useful as well as ornamental. Most of the pieces could be sold at a quarter each, but will be wonders if offered at 15 cents or 2 for a quarter. Each assortment contains 6 dozen pieces, consisting of ½ dozen each of the following 12 numbers:

8-inch Flower Vase—Coraline glass; fancy shape; assorted flint blue and yellow opalescent.
Celery Stand—6 inches tall; fluted top; assorted green, blue and rose coraline glass.
Card Tray—Fancy footed stand; 7 inches wide;; high crimped sides; assorted flint blue and yellow opalescent.
Footed Jelly Dish—Fancy shape bowl, measuring 6½ inches; assorted colored opalescent glass.
Card Receiver—7-inch flared and crimped dish; very useful; in assorted opalescent colors.
Coraline Vase—Large base and small stem; 7 inches tall; imitating expensive foreign glass; assorted colors.
Fruit Stand—Large size, fancy shape dish, in assorted colors; showy and useful.
Coraline Rose Bowl—Very rich and showy, making a beautiful article; assorted blue, green and rose.
High Footed Receiver—Richly embossed, with pointed edges; flint blue and yellow opalescent.
Fruit Bowl—Fancy coraline glass, in three colors, measuring 7 inches wide; a very handsome dish.
Buckeye Vase—Heavy opalescent vase, in assorted flint blue and yellow colors; always a quarter article.
Rose Bowl—Solid opalescent colors; richly embossed; with four feet.
Total, 6 dozen assorted pieces. Per dozen, 95 cents.
Barrel, 35 cents.

G. Sommers and Co. catalog reprint dated March 4, 1901. 1, 3, 7 and 8. "Coralene" glass (wares decorated with minute glass beads or powered glass [frit] which is fired-on.) 2.,5, and 12. *Buckeye* 4. *Nautilus* card receiver 6 and 11. *Inverted Fan and Feather* 9 and 10. Unidentified.

BULL'S EYE, OPALESCENT

(See figs. 285, 572)

Maker: Attributed to Hobbs, Brockunier & Co., Wheeling, W.Va., by Oglebay Institute*. Other possibilities are La Belle Glass Co., Bridgeport, OH., and Phoenix Glass Co., Monaca, PA.

Named by: Heacock

Y.O.P. Circa 1890

Other name: None

Colors made: Cranberry and white opalescent.

Pieces made: Water bottle, bride's bowl, oil lamp, hall lamp (cylindrical) and lamp shades.

Reintroduction or Repros: None known at this time.

Notes: This pattern is much like *Coinspot,* but has heavily raised "bumps" of opalescence, about the size of a quarter. The spots on *Coinspot* are usually flat and bleed in with the glass.

Bull's Eye, Opalescent or *Bullseye* are not shown in *Hobbs, Brockunier & Co. Glass Identification and Value Guide,* by Neila & Tom Bredehoft. Therefore, the attribution is doubtful.

BUSHEL BASKET

(See fig. 420)

Maker: H. Northwood Co., Wheeling, W.Va.

Named by: Presznick 2

Y.O.P. Circa 1905

Other name: Basket

Colors made: Opalescent colors of blue and white; custard, sometimes with nutmeg decoration. Carnival colors of marigold, blue, red, purple, white, ice blue, ice green, aqua opalescent, lime green opalescent and other hues described as "clambroth", canary and "smoke".

Pieces made: Baskets; occasionally octagonal.

Reintroduction or Repros: None with the feet.

Note: Usually marked with an "N" in a circle.

BUTTON PANELS

(See fig. 476)

Maker: The Northwood Co., National Glass Co., and Dugan Glass Co., Indiana, PA.

Named by: Hartung, *Opalescent.*

Y.O.P. Circa 1899-1906

Other name: None

Colors made: White, blue and canary opalescent, rare in green opalescent; also made in emerald green and possibly crystal.

Pieces made: Rose bowl

Reintroduction or Repros: None known at this time.

Notes: Many dealers and collectors have been buying and advertising this as the *Alaska* pattern. It is strikingly similar, but close inspection reveals a couple of minute differences.

The rigaree on the side of the pattern lacks the little bee found at the base of most *Alaska* pieces. Also, *Alaska* is usually square or rectangularly based, whereas *Button*

Panel is round. Finally, this pattern has an interior design of faint cross-hatching, not found in *Alaska*.

Button Panel has been attributed to the Coudersport Tile & Ornamental Glass Co., of Coudersport, PA., circa 1903. Mr. Floyd W. Bliss, in an article published in the November, 1972, issue of *Spinning Wheel*, states that a former decorator from the factory claims that Coudersport made this pattern, and called it *Shadow*.

However, Hartung states that *Button Panel* was advertised by Northwood, with no dates or actual location offered. Shards have been unearthed at Indiana, PA., with later production by Dugan Glass. A catalog showing *Button Panel* has now been found showing the Northwood/Dugan attribution to be correct

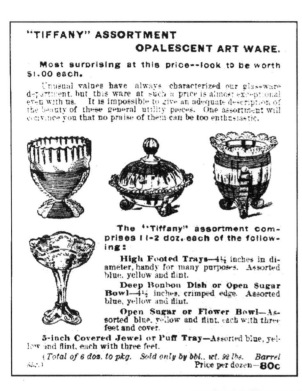

BUTTONS AND BRAIDS
(See figs. 181, 274–276, 807, 808, 1199, 1200)

Maker: Jefferson Glass Co., Steubenville, OH., and Fenton Art Glass Co., Williamstown, W.Va.
Named by: Hartung, *Opalescent*.
Y.O.P. Circa 1903 Jefferson–1910 Fenton
Other name: Jefferson pattern #182, Fenton pattern #351.
Colors made: White, blue, green, and cranberry opalescent. No early production in cranberry by Fenton.
Pieces made: Pitcher, tumbler, vases and bowls.
Reintroduction or Repros: By Fenton Art Glass Co., Williamstown, W.Va. They produced a vase in cranberry opalescent in 1995 as their first piece for the Showcase Dealer offering.
Notes: According to Frank M. Fenton, the Fenton pattern has five "backward C's" on the scroll design, whereas the Jefferson version has seven. Hopefully, you can see this in detail on figures 1199 and 1200. The Fenton tumblers are usually pressed; the Jefferson tumblers are usually mould-blown. The blown tumblers were delicate and brittle and highly susceptible to flaking at the upper rim. The blown tumblers have opalescence in the pattern detail while the pressed variety carries opalescence at the top edge of the tumbler. Both tumblers are old.
See catalog reprint in *Coinspot* and *Old Man Winter*.

Butler Brothers catalog, Spring, 1899. 1. *Button Panels* 2. and 3. *Klondyke* 4. *Intaglio*.
Also see catalog reprint in the *Dolphin Compote* section.

Assortment of Fenton opalescent mould–blown pitchers and pressed tumblers: *Curtain Optic, Buttons and Braids and Dot Optic.*

CABBAGE LEAF

(See fig. 401)

Maker: Dugan Glass Co., Indiana, PA.

Named by: Hartung, *Opalescent*.

Y.O.P. Circa 1906

Other name: None

Colors made: White, blue and green opalescent, would be rare in canary.

Pieces made: Rose bowl

Reintroduction or Repros: Yes. L. G. Wright Glass Co., New Martinsville, W.Va., made in 1968 the following items: butter dish, celery, compote, creamer, goblet, covered candy, pitcher, plate, berry bowl, spooner, sugar and wine in amber, blue, emerald green and crystal. All colors were frosted. In 1955, a toy lamp and a 10" plate were also in the line. This reproduction bares very little resemblance to the *Cabbage Leaf* shown in fig. 401.

Notes: A very similar variant of this pattern can be seen in fig. 400. Heacock named this other pattern *Winter Cabbage*, since it is not as fully leaved as *Cabbage Leaf*.

CACTUS, FENTON

(See fig. 596)

Maker: Fenton Art Glass Co., Williamstown, W.Va.

Named by: Fenton

Y.O.P. Introduced in 1959—see notes for other dates.

Other name: Desert Tree for their Olde Virginia Glass line.

Colors made: Topaz (canary), blue opalescent, aqua opal, colonial amber, colonial blue, chocolate, colonial pink, custard satin, milk glass and red sunset Carnival.

Pieces made: Basket (six sizes), vase (seven sizes), bonbon, bowl (four sizes), epergne, compote, goblet, nut dish (made from the goblet), salt shaker, cruet, cuspidor (two sizes), pitcher, plate, rose bowl (two sizes), banana bowl, cake stand, candleholder, toothpick, cracker jar, candy dish, candy box, covered butter, cream and sugar.

Reintroduction or Repros: Fenton may reintroduce a pattern or color at any time. If made after 1972, it should be marked with the Fenton logo.

Notes: Topaz was produced in 1959–1960, and again in 1988 (water set) for Levay Distributing Co., Edwardsville, IL. Aqua opal Carnival, blue opalescent, chocolate and red sunset Carnival were produced for Levay in the 1980s. Milk glass was produced from 1959–63. All pieces made after 1972 will be marked either with the Fenton logo or the "OVG" logo. The "OVG" indicates pieces sold through the Olde Virginia Glass line.

Toothpicks in crystal, chocolate (caramel), cobalt, amber, ice blue, marigold, red, and turquoise; Carnival colors of blue, ice blue, marigold, red, white and chocolate were produced by St. Clair Glass of Elwood, IN., in the 1980s.

In 1985, the Summit Art Glass Co. of Rootstown, OH., produced a salt shaker, toothpick and tumbler in amberina, blue-green, cobalt, evergreen, emerald green, green custard, morning glory, milk glass, rubina, vaseline, and watermelon.

An unknown manufacturer, prior to 1975, produced a creamer, salt shaker, sugar shaker toothpick, and tumbler in caramel slag (chocolate). The manufacturer could have been St. Clair.

CACTUS, NORTHWOOD

(See figs. 1288, 1289)

Maker: The Northwood Glass Co., Ellwood City, PA., and Northwood Co., Indiana, PA.

Named by: Peterson

Y.O.P. Circa 1893

Other name: None

Colors made: Two shades of opaque green; cased colors of turquoise, green and pink; opalescent colors of cranberry, canary and blue with the stripe spot mould; transparent amethyst and blue.

Pieces made: Salt shakers

Reintroduction or Repros: None known at this time.

Note: Figure 1288 is printed to show the detail of the design, as the definition of the pattern is obscured by the opalescent stripes. See catalog reprint in *Daisy & Fern*.

CALYX VASE

(See fig. 528)

Maker: Model Flint Glass Co., Findlay, OH.

Named by: Hartung, *Northwood*.

Y.O.P. Circa 1899

Other name: Expanded Stem (Herrick)

Colors made: White, blue and canary opalescent; opaque colors of green, yellow and white.

Pieces made: Vase

Reintroduction or Repros: None known at this time.

Notes: Herrick's name precedes Hartung's by more than ten years. However, *Calyx* has become the more popular and accepted name.

CAMELOT

(See fig. 1285)

Maker: Henry Greener and Co., Sunderland, England.

Named by: Heacock

Y.O.P. Circa 1893, marked with Rd #217749

Other name: None

Colors made: Blue opalescent; others are possible.

Pieces made: Wine glass; others are probable.

Reintroductions/Repros: None known at this time.

CARNELIAN (EVERGLADES)

(See figs. 19-24, 100, 226-227, 428)

Maker: H. Northwood Co., Wheeling, W.Va.

Named by: Original manufacturer's name

Y.O.P. Circa 1903

Other name: Everglades—Peterson, *Glass Salt Shaker*.

Colors made: White, blue, and canary opalescent; limited green opalescent, custard glass, limited purple slag (primarily salt shakers).

Pieces made: Table set, water set, berry set (banana boat shaped), cruet, salt shaker and jelly compote.

Reintroduction or Repros: None known at this time.

Notes: The salt shaker in this pattern has an unusual clambroth effect in the opalescence, which has proven confusing to collectors. The white opalescent looks exactly like clambroth. The canary opalescent shaker appears to be a pale custard glass, but is not. The blue opalescent shakers are illustrated in figure 226.

Heacock originally called this pattern *Everglades*. In the 1982 premiere issue of *The Glass Collector*, Heacock wrote that the original factory name for this pattern was *Carnelian*. Heacock believed original factory names should be used when known. The original manufacturer's name was used in *Harry Northwood, The Wheeling Years 1901-1925*. Thus, the name change for this edition. The stopper is not original.

CAROUSEL

(See fig. 513)

Maker: Jefferson Glass Co., Steubenville, OH.

Named by: Heacock

Y.O.P. Circa 1905

Other name: Jefferson #264

Colors made: White, blue and green opalescent.

Pieces made: Bowls

Reintroduction or Repros: None known at this time.

CARRIAGE

(See fig. 1284)

Maker: Henry Greener & Co., Sunderland, England

Named by: Heacock

Y.O.P. Circa 1890, marked with Rd #150277

Other name: None

Colors made: Blue opalescent; other colors are likely.

Pieces made: Carriage

Reintroductions/Repros: None known at this time.

CASHEWS

(See fig. 455)

Maker: H. Northwood Co., Wheeling, W.Va.

Named by: Joe B. Bell

Y.O.P. Circa 1905

Other name: None

Colors made: White, blue, and green opalescent.

Pieces made: Bowls

Reintroduction or Repros: None known at this time.

Note: Many pieces will have goofus decoration, usually on the underside.

CATALONIAN

(See fig. 1243)

Maker: Consolidated Lamp & Glass Co., Coraopolis, PA

Named by: Original manufacturer's name

Y.O.P. Circa 1927

Other name: Old Spanish and Pattern No. 1100 series.

Colors made: Spanish rose, honey, emerald, jade and amethyst. See note about opalescent.

Pieces made: At least 50 different items were made which included the following: liquor sets, water sets, vases, candlesticks, bowls, cup/saucers, tumblers, goblets, plates, mayonnaise sets, toilet bottles, cigarette boxes, creamers, sugars, puff boxes and ashtrays.

Reintroductions/Repros: McKee Glass Co., Jeanette, PA., introduced a similar line in 1928 and called it *Rebecca*. Morgantown Glass of Morgantown, W.Va., introduced their *El Mexicano* line in 1933.

Note: Following is a quote from *Collecting Glass, Vol. 2*: "This No. 1120, 10 oz. goblet in *Catalonian* is the first reported example of the line in what appears to be white opalescent. The manufacturer, Consolidated Lamp & Glass Co., Coraopolis, PA., is not known to have produced opalescent glass during this period, but this rare goblet indicates they must have experimented with the treatment. A number of items in the mould-blown sculptured ware have an opalescent effect from being cased with a thin layer of translucent 'opaline', but *Catalonian* is a pressed line and must have been refired to create the opalescence."

CENTER HANDLED TRAY

(See figs. 1207, 1227)

Maker: Almost all glass companies in business between the 1920s and the 1960s made these center handled trays. There may even have been a few manufactured in the 1990s.

Note: Center handled trays were made in every color imaginable. The only way to tell who made these trays is to study the shape of the handle. It seems that each company had its own unique design. Figure 1207 (green) was made by Imperial Glass Corp., Bellaire, OH. Figure 1227 was made by Central Glass Co., Wheeling, W.Va.

CHANTICLEER

(See fig. 1250)

Maker: Duncan and Miller Glass Co., Washington, PA.

Named by: Original manufacturer's name. Chanticleer was the name of the rooster in the medieval epic *Reynard the Fox*.

Y.O.P. Circa 1934

Other name: Lalique's Coqs et Plumes (Roosters and Feathers).

Colors made: Green, ruby, blue, amber and crystal in frost or fire polished. It was also made in the light blue opalescent shown in figure 1250, which has been described as a periwinkle blue with just a hint of orchid in it.

Pieces made: Cocktail shaker (32 oz. and 16 oz.), Old Fashion tumbler, cocktail, Martini mixer (32 oz. and 16 oz.), 3" vase crimped or tri-cornered and a 3" crimped vase.

Note: Duncan and Miller probably copied Lalique's Coqs et Plumes, which was introduced around 1932.

CHERRY PANELS

(See fig. 435)

Maker: Dugan Glass Co., Indiana, PA.
Named by: Presznick 2
Y.O.P. Circa 1907
Other name: None
Colors made: White, blue, and canary opalescent; Carnival colors are a possibility.
Pieces made: Vases
Reintroduction or Repros: None known at this time.
Notes: Not made by Millersburg, as previously reported.

CHRISTMAS PEARLS (SEE BEAD AND PANEL)

CHRISTMAS SNOWFLAKE

(See figs. 310, 828, 829, 832, 833)

Maker: The Northwood Co., and reissued by the Dugan Glass Co., Indiana, PA.
Named by: Heacock
Y.O.P. Circa 1895
Other name: Lattice and Daisy (Hartung, *Opalescent*)
Colors made: Cranberry, blue and white opalescent.
Pieces made: Pitcher (two shapes), tumbler, cruet (in white opalescent only).
Reintroduction or Repros: Yes, made by Fenton Art Glass Co., Williamstown, W.Va., for L. G. Wright Glass Co., New Martinsville, W.Va. See text for *Christmas Snowflake, L. G. Wright.*
Notes: The name has been changed because the Hartung name is sometimes confused for the Beaumont syrup, *Daisy in Criss-Cross.* The *Christmas Snowflake* pattern was made with and without the ribbed exterior.

CHRISTMAS SNOWFLAKE, L. G. WRIGHT

(See figs. 934, 935, 1004)

Maker: Fenton Art Glass Co., Williamstown, W.Va., for L. G. Wright, owner of the moulds.
Named by: Original name
Y.O.P. Circa 1980
Other name: None
Colors made: Cranberry and cobalt opalescent.
Pieces made: Pitcher, tumbler, milk pitcher, barber bottle, creamer, cruet, sugar shaker, syrup, spooner, rose bowl (two sizes), wedding bowl, lamp, and basket.
Reintroduction or Repros: This was a reintroduction.
Note: Only the pitcher and tumbler were made in cranberry. See text for *Christmas Snowflake* above. See catalog reprint on page 187.

CHRYSANTHEMUM SWIRL AND VARIANT

(See figs. 243–248, 648 F and L, 707–710, 718–724, 840, 869, 870, 926)

Maker: American Glass Co., Anderson, IN.; Buckeye Glass Co., Martins Ferry, OH.; Northwood Glass Co., Martins Ferry, OH.; Northwood Glass Co., Ellwood City, PA.
Named by: Heacock's variation on a Peterson name.
Y.O.P. Circa 1890
Other name: Chrysanthemum Base Swirl
Colors made: White, blue and cranberry opalescent, sometimes with a satin or speckled finish.
Pieces made: Pitcher, tumbler, berry set, butter dish, covered sugar, creamer, spooner, cruet, syrup, sugar shaker, toothpick, salt shaker, oil lamp, finger bowl, celery vase, mustard, straw holder, custard cup and bar bottle.
Reintroduction or Repros: None known at this time.

This May, 1903, Butler Brothers assortment of decorated pitchers shows that the shape mould used by Northwood on his plain *Christmas Snowflake* pitcher (without ribs) was also used on other types of ware.

Notes: I shall do my best to clarify some of the information written about this pattern. All of the pieces shown in color, with the exception of 648F, 648L, and 840, are identified as manufactured by Northwood in *Harry Northwood, The Early Years 1881-1900.*

If you look closely at the bar bottle (fig. 840), the straw jar (fig. 648F) and the straw jar shown at the right, you will see that the white opalescent stripes slant to the right. All of the identified Northwood pieces have opalescent stripes that slant to the left. In view of this, I feel these two pieces were made by someone other than Northwood. Who made them is a mystery. The stripes on fig. 648L run in the same direction as the other identified Northwood pieces, so I feel reasonably certain that it was also made by them.

Figure 710 is the only piece shown of what Heacock named *Chrysanthemum Swirl Variant*. It is similar in design, but lacks the bulging ribbed base.

This is a highly collectible pattern. It is one of the few cranberry opalescent patterns to have a complete table set.

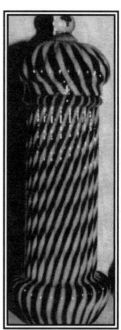

Chrysanthemum Swirl straw jar. Manufacturer uncertain. May be the incorrect top. See text.

Comparison of bases on *Swirl* straw jar and *Chrysanthemum Swirl* straw jar. The one on the left was made by either Hobbs or Beaumont. The one on the right is most likely Northwood.

CLEOPATRA'S FAN
(See fig. 1291)
Maker: Dugan Glass Co., Indiana, PA. Possibly originally by Northwood.
Named by: Heacock
Y.O.P. Circa 1904
Other name: Shell and Leaf Chalice
Colors made: White, blue, and green opalescent.
Pieces made: Vase
Reintroductions/Repros: None known at this time.
Note: There seems to be some confusion in just what to call this pattern. In his 1981 book, *Old Pattern Glass According to Heacock*, the author identified this vase as *Northwood Shell*. In *The Glass Collector, No. 5,* Heacock stated that he no longer believed this was a Northwood pattern and named it *Cleopatra's Fan.* James Measell in

Dugan/ Diamond, The Story of Indiana, Pennsylvania Glass showed a picture of this vase but called it *Leaf Challis*. He also showed a catalog reprint, but that reprint illustrated a picture of *Leaf Challis* shown in this book as figure 397. These are not the same patterns. *Leaf Challis* has four feet on a base; *Cleopatra's Fan* has only three and no base. In view of this I feel, as Heacock also felt, that these are most definitely two different patterns and should carry two different names.

CIRCLED SCROLL
(See figs. 53-62, 575)
Maker: Dugan Glass Co., Indiana, PA.
Named by: Kamm 4
Y.O.P. Circa 1903
Other name: None
Colors made: Blue, green, and white opalescent; later

Carnival colors of marigold and amethyst.

Pieces made: Table set, berry set, water set, cruet, salt shaker and jelly compote.

Reintroduction or Repros: None known at this time.

Notes: *Circled Scroll* in Carnival colors was made in a "swung" vase, which distorts the pattern to the point where it is unrecognizable.

COIN DOT

(See figs. 601, 613, 622, 919, 968, 989, 991, 997, 1043, 1080, 1091, 1092, 1113, 1154–1156, 1189, 1192)

Maker: Fenton Art Glass Co., Williamstown, W.Va.

Named by: Fenton

Y.O.P. 1940s—present

Other name: Victorian name—Windows or Big Windows.

Colors made: White, blue, topaz, green and cranberry opalescent. Other colors are probable.

Pieces made: Water pitcher, tumbler, cruet, barber bottle, rose bowl, hats, vanity set, decanter, candlesticks, covered candy jar, cream/sugar, rose jar, many shapes of vases, bowls, baskets and lamps (many sizes and shapes); others are likely.

Reintroduction or Repros: Fenton may reintroduce a pattern or color at any time. If made after 1972, it should be marked with the Fenton logo.

Note: *This lamp was made by Fenton for L. G. Wright Glass Co. It does not appear that Wright gave this pattern its own name; in view of this, I will just call it by Fenton's name for the pattern. Frank M. Fenton feels that figure 989 is their *Coin Dot* pattern that did not fit the piece. This fairy lamp was made for the auction held by the FAGCA for the 1982 convention. Figures 1154 and 1155 are perfume bottles made for DeVilbiss in the 1940s.

COINSPOT

(See figs. 261, 262, 347, 348, 371–373, 637, 777–782, 784, 787–792, 843–845, 858, 898, 911, 916–918, 928, 1020, 1262)

Makers: Belmont Glass Co., Bellaire, OH (circa 1887) (fig. 262); Phoenix Glass Co., Monaca, PA. (circa 1884); Hobbs, Brockunier & Co., Wheeling, W.Va. (circa 1888); Northwood Glass Co., Martins Ferry, W.Va. (circa 1890); West Virginia Glass Co., Martins Ferry, OH. (circa 1895); Buckeye Glass Co., Martins Ferry, OH. (circa 1889); Beaumont Glass Co., Martins Ferry, OH. (circa 1900); Northwood Glass Co., Wheeling W.Va. (circa 1903) (figs. 261, 347, 348, 371, 373); Jefferson Glass Co., Steubenville (circa 1905) (fig. 637); Dugan Glass Co., Indiana, PA. (circa 1904), Fenton Art Glass Co., Williamstown, W.Va. (circa 1907, named *Dot Optic*).

Named by: Popular nomenclature

Y.O.P. See above

Other name: Polka Dot—Dot Optic,** Spot, Big Spot, Dot and Opal Dot (L. G. Wright's name)

Colors made: White, blue, cranberry, green, rubina, amber, amethyst, amberina and canary opalescent.

Pieces made: Syrup (at least three shapes—ball, ring neck and nine panel); sugar shaker (at least four shapes—ring neck, nine panel, wide waist and bulb shape); cruet (four shapes—Indiana mould, ball, ring neck, Buckeye jug and Phoenix jug); pitcher (at least seven shapes); tumbler, finger bowls, barber bottle, master berry bowl; toothpick (several shapes); water bottle, oil lamps, lamp shades and ice bucket.

Reintroduction or Repros: Yes** See text for *Dot Optic* and *Opal Dot*.

Notes: This is probably the most widely produced pattern of all cranberry opalescent. The majority of all early, handled pieces will have a plain handle. However, there are a few exceptions, so study is suggested when collecting *Coinspot*. The four piece table set is not known in this pattern.

Do not confuse this pattern, which has the opalescent spots, for *Big Windows* or the similarly named *Fenton Coin Dot* (introduced in the 1940s) which has the reverse colored dots on an opalescent background. The cruet in amber opalescent was probably made by Hobbs or Phoenix; the amberina opalescent pitcher was possibly made by Phoenix also.

**Dot Optic (Fenton's name for this pattern) was made by the Fenton Art Glass Co. in the early 1900s, and reintroduced in the 1940s. Fenton has been producing this pattern off and on since the early 1900s, so their glass should not be referred to as a reproduction.

There has been quite a bit of *Coinspot* reproduced in foreign countries, so be careful. The imported pieces are quite easy to identify, as they are very "murky". See catalog reprints in *Erie* and *Old Man Winter* sections.

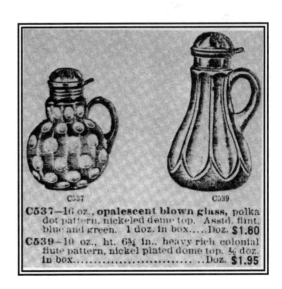

C537—16 oz., opalescent blown glass, polka dot pattern, nickeled dome top. Asstd. flint, blue and green. 1 doz. in box.....Doz. **$1.80**

C539—10 oz., ht. 6¾ in., heavy rich colonial flute pattern, nickel plated dome top. ½ doz. in box.........................Doz. **$1.95**

The Indiana "Ball–shape" syrup is shown here from a 1908 Butler Brothers catalog, indicating that old Northwood moulds from before the National Glass merger were still being used after the factory became the Dugan Glass Co.

Circa 1908 catalog page from Jefferson Glass Co., showing lemonade sets in *Buttons and Braids*, *Opal Swirl* and *Coinspot*. Jefferson discontinued the production of "fancy glass" shortly after this catalog was printed, entering other specialized fields (pressed Krys–Tol lighting ware) after 1909.

This ad appeared in 1902 and was undoubtedly a set produced by Beaumont Glass Co., Martins Ferry, OH.

OPALESCENT GLASS FROM A—Z

COINSPOT AND SWIRL

(See figs. 301, 783, 900)

Maker: The Northwood Co., Indiana, PA., with possible continued production after the National Glass Co. merger.

Named by: Heacock

Y.O.P. Circa 1898

Other name: Swirl and Coin Dot (Taylor)

Colors made: White, blue, and cranberry opalescent.

Pieces made: Syrup jug and cruet.

Reintroduction or Repros: None known at this time.

Note: The syrup is a most common piece in the blue opalescent color. It is extremely rare in cranberry opalescent.

Coinspot And Swirl is a very limited design found only in a syrup and cruet shape. It is unquestionably Northwood, copied by no other manufacturer.

COLLARED REVERSE SWIRL

Maker: Model Flint Glass Works, Albany, IN.

Named by: Uncertain

Y.O.P. Circa 1901

Other name: None

Colors made: White, blue, and canary opalescent; also speckled finish, no cranberry.

Pieces made: Butter dish, creamer, covered sugar, spooner, syrup and toothpick.

Reintroduction or Repros: None known at this time.

Note: The similarity to *Reverse Swirl* and *Chrysanthemum Swirl* is no accident. This is the third pattern made under a patent held by John F. Miller, who managed the Model Flint of Albany, IN., factory and earlier managed the Buckeye and American glass factories. See notes for *Reverse Swirl*. See the following photograph.

Collared Reverse Swirl syrup pitcher, a design introduced by John Miller at Albany, IN.

COLONIAL (FLUTE)

(See fig. 141)

Maker: Westmoreland Speciality Co., Grapeville, PA.

Named by: Original name

Y.O.P. Circa 1912, through part of the 1980s.

Other name: #1776 and Keystone Colonial

Colors made: Crystal, and many of the colors that were in their line at the time they produced the 1776 Colonial.

Pieces made: Water set, condiment set, bowl, tray, cruet, butter dish, plate, novelties and many more; in fact, there were about 50 different items.

Reintroduction or Repros: Westmoreland frequently reintroduced this pattern.

Notes: The illustrated butter dish had Heacock baffled. He identified this butter dish as Northwood's *Flute* with the qualifying statement, "Could this be a Westmoreland product?" It has now been confirmed that it *is* Westmoreland's *Colonial*. Most No. 1776 *Colonial* pieces have a 31–rayed star on the underside of the base.

COLONIAL STAIRSTEPS

(See fig. 570)
Maker: H. Northwood Co., Wheeling, W.Va.
Named by: Heacock
Y.O.P. Circa 1906
Other name: None
Colors made: Crystal and blue opalescent
Pieces made: Toothpick holder, creamer, and sugar.
Reintroduction or Repros: None known at this time.
Notes: The creamer and sugar reportedly have been signed.

CONCAVE COLUMNS (SEE BUCKEYE)

CONTESSA

(See figs. 546, 1280)
Maker: Henry Greener & Co., Sunderland, England.

Greener trademark

Named by: Heacock
Y.O.P. Circa 1890 marked with the Rd #160244
Other name: None
Colors made: Blue, yellow and amber opalescent
Pieces made: Creamer and sugar (two shapes), 7" tall pitcher and novelties
Reintroduction or Repros: None known at this time.
Notes: This is the English version of *Hobnail.* Any opalescent, English or American, from this era should be considered rare. Note the unique thorny handle, peg–like feet, and the band of vine–work around the top. One set of creamer/sugar has a pedestal base, not four-footed. The creamer is 4" tall with the vine design at the base. The open sugar is 4 ³/₄" tall and just over 5" in diameter at the top. It is not unusual to find English pressed glass patterns in both covered and open sugar bowls. Remember, the open sugar is much like, and often confused with, our American jelly compotes.

CORAL

(See fig. 510)
Maker: Probably Jefferson Glass Co., Steubenville, OH.
Named by: Hartung, *Opalescent.*
Y.O.P. Uncertain
Other name: None
Colors made: White, blue, green, and canary opalescent.
Pieces made: Bowls
Reintroduction or Repros: None known at this time.
Notes: Attribution is based on color and pattern characteristics.

CORAL REEF

(See figs. 282, 283, 679, 680, 687a, 914, 1099, 1103)
Maker: Hobbs, Brockunier & Co., Wheeling, W.Va., and Beaumont Glass Co., Martins Ferry, OH.
Named by: John D. Sewell, *Glass Collector's Digest,* 1988.
Y.O.P. Circa 1891
Other name: Seaweed* and Pattern No. 338 for Hobbs, Brockunier.
Colors made: White, blue and cranberry opalescent.
Pieces made: Barber bottles (three shapes), finger bowl, salt shaker and several sizes and types of lamps.
Reintroduction or Repros: None known at this time.
Notes: Unfortunately, this distinctive pattern has been grouped for years with the *Seaweed* pattern. With only a quick glance one can see a decided difference between these two patterns. *Seaweed* has very regular branching with rounded nodules, while *Coral Reef* has very irregular jagged branching. Hopefully, this pattern will soon be known by its own name. See the catalog reprint on the following page.
*See notes for *Seaweed.*

CORONATION

(See fig. 541)
Maker: Greener & Co., Sunderland, England
Named by: Heacock
Y.O.P. Circa 1887
Other name: None
Colors made: Blue opalescent
Pieces made: Pitcher
Reintroduction or Repros: None known at this time.
Notes: English

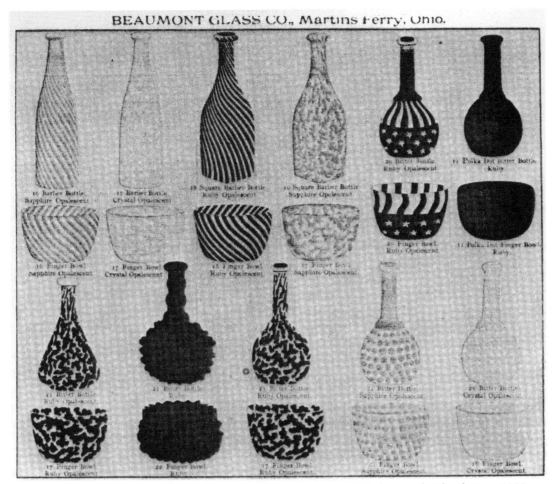

This reprint includes the patterns *Swirl*, *Coral Reef*, *Stars and Stripes*, *Windows*, and *Hobnail*. Circa 1899.

CORN VASE

(See figs. 493, 540, 648D)

Maker: Dugan Glass Co., Indiana, PA.

Named by: Hartung, *Opalescent*

Y.O.P. Circa 1905

Other name: None

Colors made: White, blue, canary, and green opalescent and Carnival (about 1910).

Pieces made: Vases

Reintroduction or Repros: Yes—see fig. 607 and text for *Corn Vase, Repro.*

Notes: See the catalog reprint to the right.

CORN VASE, REPRO

(See fig. 607)

Maker: Unknown, made for L.G. Wright Glass Co., New Martinsville, W.Va.

Named by: Wright

Y.O.P. Circa 1939, with possible production through the mid 1990s.

Other name: Wright, pattern No. 75–1

Colors made: Blue, amber and vaseline.

Pieces made: Vase

Reintroduction or Repros: This is a repro.

Notes: The top of the new vase does not extend into long points as the old one does, and the husks are closed. It

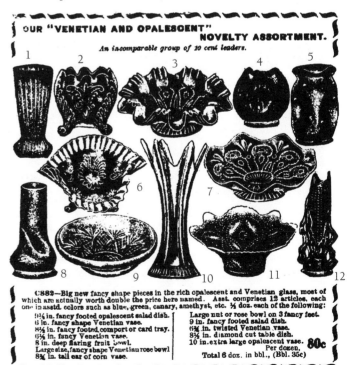

Grouping of Dugan Glass Co. pieces, circa 1905. 1? 2. *Palm and Scroll* 3. *Keyhole* 4. ? 5.? 6. *Palm and Scroll* 7. *Keyhole* 8. ? 9. *Reflecting Diamonds* 10. ? 11. *Wheel and Block* 12. *Corn Vase.*

has been said the husks were "closed" to save costs as they were too hard to produce "open" without a lot of breakage.

CORNUCOPIA, FENTON
(See figs. 1112, 1219, 1223, 1225)
Maker: Fenton Art Glass Co., Williamstown, W.Va.
Named by: Uncertain
Y.O.P.: Circa 1930 to at least the 1950s
Other name: Pattern #950
Colors made: Almost all colors of the era, quite often with an etched pattern.
Pieces made: Candlesticks, usually with a coordinating bowl.
Reintroductions/Repros: Fenton may reintroduce a pattern or color at any time. If made after 1972, the piece should be marked with the Fenton logo.

CORNUCOPIA, NORTHWOOD
(See fig. 478)
Maker: H. Northwood Co., Wheeling, W.Va.
Named by: Presznick 2
Y.O.P. Circa 1905
Other name: None
Colors made: White and blue opalescent; also Carnival*.
Pieces made: Novelties
Reintroduction or Repros: None known at this time.
Note: *Heacock mentions Carnival colors, but no reference is made of any Carnival production of this pattern in *Harry Northwood, The Wheeling Years, 1901-1925.* Therefore, we feel this is not a possibility.

COUNTRY KITCHEN (MILKY WAY)
(See fig. 492, and front cover of book)
Maker: Millersburg Glass Co., Millersburg, OH.
Named by: Manufacturer's original name
Y.O.P. Early 1900s
Other name: Milky Way, Heacock
Colors made: White opalescent, crystal and Carnival.
Pieces made: Bowls, covered butter dish, covered sugar bowl, creamer, spooner, spittoon, swung vases and novelties.
Reintroduction or Repros: None known at this time.
Notes: This may be the only pattern Millersburg ever made in opalescent. Heacock named it *Milky Way.* Many examples of *Country Kitchen* are shown in Marie McGee's book, *Millersburg Glass,* which also identified the previously unknown manufacturer. From this publication we also learned the original name. Thus, the name change for this edition.

CRISS-CROSS, CONSOLIDATED'S
(See figs. 264, 312–314, 693–704, 850, 897, 904, 905)
Maker: Consolidated Lamp & Glass Co., while at Fostoria, OH.
Named by: Heacock
Y.O.P. Circa 1888
Other name: Cable
Colors made: White, cranberry, and rubina opalescent, sometimes with a delicate art–glass satin finish.
Pieces made: Pitcher, tumbler, butter dish, covered sugar, creamer, spooner, finger bowl, berry set, salt shakers, sugar shaker, cruet, syrup, finger bowl, celery vase, mustard, ivy ball and toothpick.
Reintroduction or Repros: None known at this time.
Notes: *Criss–Cross* is considered to be one of the most sought after and highly collectible patterns in cranberry opalescent. The criss-crossing in the pattern is sometimes blurred together or tends to swirl instead of remaining completely vertical.
Criss–Cross is probably the only opalescent pattern made by this company. The butter bases on figures 699 and 703 are different, but both are probably original. This pattern must be considered one of the finest ever produced in opalescent glass.

CROWN JEWELS
(See fig. 543, 544)
Maker: Uncertain
Named by: Heacock
Y.O.P. Circa 1888
Other name: None known at this time
Colors made: Blue opalescent
Pieces made: Water set
Reintroduction or Repros: None known at this time.
Notes: English

CURTAIN CALL
(See fig. 170)
Maker: Possibly McKee and Brothers, Jeanette, PA.
Named by: Heacock
Y.O.P. Circa 1905
Other name: None
Colors made: Known in crystal and very rare in cobalt blue opalescent.
Pieces made: Caster set
Reintroduction or Repros: None known at this time.
Notes: Attribution is based on the stopper to the oil bottle, which is in the McKee *Sunk Honeycomb* pattern. The pattern on the caster set is not shown in the McKee book, but this set probably had such limited production that it was not included in a general catalog.

CURTAIN OPTIC

(See figs. 387, 834, 887, 1194)

Curtain Optic barber bottle made by Fenton for L. G. Wright.

Maker: Fenton Art Glass Co., Williamstown, W.Va.
Named by: Fenton
Y.O.P. Circa 1910 to present
Other name: Blown Opal Drapery, Blown Drapery and pattern No. 350.
Colors made: White, blue, and green opalescent. Ruby was made in 1914; topaz (vaseline) circa 1926.
Pieces made: Pitcher, tumbler and spittoon. A stretch glass guest set was made in topaz opalescent, circa 1926. In recent years, a cruet, milk pitcher, and barber bottle have been produced in cranberry for L. G. Wright Glass Co., New Martinsville, W.Va. In 1987, they made their #2057 vase in French Cream and Provincial Blue opalescent.
Reintroduction or Repros: Fenton may reintroduce a pattern or color at any time. If made after 1972, it should be marked with the Fenton logo.
Note: Following is a quote from a letter I received from Frank M. Fenton dated October 12, 1998: "Now for the drapery patterns. I have been bothered by the various names that are applied to those patterns. Different writers have named the patterns differently and, of course, we didn't name any of those patterns, we just used numbers and descriptions. When we made the item called *Drapery*—this is blown using a spot mould or an optic mould—we called that the *Curtain Optic*, but that was just here in the factory. . . . .the drapery pattern made by Fenton which we call *Curtain* could very well be called Fenton's *Drapery Optic* pattern. That name tells you that it was blown and smooth to the touch just like the *Buttons and Braids*." In view of the fact that the Fenton factory calls this pattern *Curtain,* I feel that this book should do the same. Figure 1194 (fairy lamp) was made for QVC, a program on cable TV in 1992. See catalog reprint in *Buttons and Braids.*

DAFFODILS

(See figs. 390, 638)

Daffodils tumbler by Northwood.

Maker: H. Northwood Co., Wheeling, W.Va.
Named by: Heacock
Y.O.P. Circa 1903
Other name: None
Colors made: White, blue, cranberry, canary and green opalescent.
Pieces made: Pitcher, tumbler and oil lamp (signed).
Reintroduction or Repros: None known at this time.

DAHLIA TWIST

(See fig. 537)
Maker: Jefferson Glass Co., Steubenville, OH.
Named by: Heacock
Y.O.P. Circa 1905
Other name: Jefferson pattern #207
Colors made: White, blue, and green opalescent.
Pieces made: Vase
Reintroduction or Repros: None known at this time.
Notes: This little vase was found in the Jefferson catalog on a page that Kamm failed to reprint in her *Book 7.* See catalog reprint in the *Beaded Fan* pattern section.

DAISY, FENTON

(See figs. 983, 994)
Maker: Fenton Art Glass Co., Williamstown, W.Va.
Named by: Fenton
Y.O.P. 1978—present
Other name: Snowflake
Colors: Cranberry, other colors are probable.
Pieces made: Basket and rose bowl, other pieces are likely
Reintroduction or Repros: Fenton may reintroduce a pattern or color at any time. If made after 1972 it should be marked with the Fenton logo.
Note: I wrote to Frank M. Fenton asking him if *Snowflake* was the correct name for this pattern. His answer was: "I

think we called this *Daisy*." This pattern had a very limited production. Pieces were marked. The rose bowl that was made in the mid–1990s was signed with a capital F in a fancy circle, and has Bill Fenton's signature.

DAISY AND BUTTON, FENTON
(See fig. 590)

Maker: Fenton Art Glass Co., Williamstown, W.Va.**
Named by: Uncertain
Y.O.P. Mid 1950s—present
Other name: None
Colors made: Almost all Fenton colors including crystal, amber, blue, blue opalescent, rose, milk glass, Cape Cod green, Colonial blue, vaseline, royal blue, wisteria, gold and amethyst. Other colors are probable.
Pieces made: Cup, saucer, creamer, sugar, salad plate, hand vase; novelties such as baskets, hats, shoes, perfume, powder jar, fan tray, match holders, ashtrays, etc.
Reintroduction or Repros: Fenton may reintroduce a pattern or color at any time. If made after 1972, it should be marked with the Fenton logo.

This pattern has been reproduced in non–opalescent colors in every shape imaginable by many companies. To name a few: Boyd's Crystal Art Glass Co., Cambridge, OH.; Imperial Glass Corporation, Bellaire, OH.; L. E. Smith Glass Co., Jeannette, PA., and Summit Art Glass Co., Akron, OH.
Notes: **Made for their own line, for L.G. Wright and A & A Importing. This pattern is not known in any old opalescent pieces at this time, except for some English items.

DAISY AND FERN
(See figs. 265, 279–281, 292, 297, 302, 335–338, 351, 361–364, 384, 642, 644–668, 670–676, 842, 854, 860, 861, 888–890, 1034)

Makers: *Buckeye Glass Co., Martins Ferry, OH. (circa 1888); Northwood Glass Co., Ellwood City, PA. (circa 1894); West Virginia Glass Co., Martins Ferry, OH. (circa 1894); Northwood Co., Indiana, PA.; National Glass Co. (circa 1900); Jefferson Glass Co., Steubenville, OH. (circa 1903), Dugan Glass Co., Indiana, PA. (Circa 1904).
Named by: Popular nomenclature
Y.O.P. See above
Other name: None
Colors made: White, blue, green, and cranberry opalescent.
Pieces made: Pitcher (at least three shapes), tumbler, cruet, sugar, creamer, spooner, butter dish, berry set, sugar shaker, syrup (three shapes), toothpick, salt shakers, rose bowl, vase, mustard, night lamp, finger bowl and bitter bottle.
Reintroduction or Repros: Many reproductions—see text for *Daisy & Fern*, *Fenton*. L. G. Wright purchased the moulds for this pattern in the late 1930s and the Fenton Art Glass Co. of Williamstown, W.Va., has been producing this pattern for them into the 1990s. All pieces that are in either the *Northwood Swirl* or *Apple Blossom* mould have never been reproduced. Pieces in the *Melon Rib* mould are probably re-made copies of the pattern, although some old examples do exist. If you wish only to collect the old, beware of all items which have a reeded handle and avoid the pieces which were never originally made (the apothecary jar and lamps, in particular). All pieces in yellow (vaseline) opalescent, and all pieces with a satin finish are new. As far as can be determined, the salt shaker, finger bowl, and toothpick have not been reproduced.

Notes: As far as Heacock could tell, only Northwood made table set items in this pattern and only in his *Ribbed Swirl* mould (fig. 265). The other companies made only water sets and seasoning pieces (syrups, sugar shakers, etc.). Many of the *Daisy and Fern* pieces are made in special shape moulds, i.e. *Apple Blossom*, *Swirl*, *Nine Panel* and *West Virginia Optic*. The ball-shaped pitcher set (see fig. 666) is shown in a November, 1884, *Crockery and Glass Journal*. Northwood apparently retained the moulds or reintroduced the pattern when he opened his own Indiana, PA. factory. After the merger with the National Glass Co. in 1899, production of *Daisy and Fern* was continued (it appeared in a Butler Brothers catalog in 1903) by Dugan Glass Co., Indiana, PA.

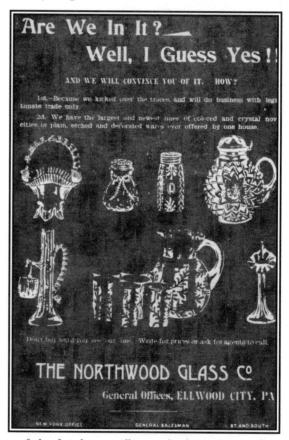

One of the few known illustrated advertisements from the Northwood Co. at Ellwood City, PA. This 1895 ad pictures a lemonade set in *Daisy & Fern* (with six tumblers). Also pictured are three blown glass items reminiscent of English off–hand art glass, salt shakers in the *Bow and Tassel* and *Cactus* patterns, and a syrup in the *Flat Flower* pattern.

DAISY AND FERN (FENTON/WRIGHT)

(See figs. 600*, 605*, 929*, 930*, 956*, 1003*, 1005*, 1023*, 1090*, 1095*, 1098*, 1197*, 1213, 1214*)
Maker: Fenton Art Glass Co., Williamstown, W.Va.
Named by: Original name
Y.O.P. Circa 1940s—present
Other name: Fern (L.G. Wright)
Colors made: Blue, topaz (vaseline) and cranberry, sometimes with a satin finish; other colors are likely.
Pieces made: Pitcher (five sizes and shapes), vases (five shapes), tumbler, ice tea, milk pitcher (two sizes), apothecary jars (six sizes/shapes), barber bottle (two shapes), syrup, creamer, hat, cruet, sugar shaker, pickle caster (two styles), rose bowl (two sizes), candy box, biscuit jar, basket (two sizes), and lamps in many sizes and shapes, including a hurricane lamp.
Reintroduction or Repros: Fenton may reintroduce a pattern or color at any time. If made after 1972, it should be marked with the Fenton logo.
Notes: For many years Fenton made this pattern exclusively for the L. G. Wright Glass Co., New Martinsville, W.Va. Fenton has included this pattern in their regular line and all items made after 1972 were signed. To make it easier for the collector to tell the difference between an L. G. Wright and Fenton piece, Fenton has changed the *Daisy* slightly—Fenton petals will be curved or "wind blown" while L. G. Wright's are straight. See figures 1213 and 1214.
*L. G. Wright called this pattern simply *Fern* but to save confusion I will call it *Daisy and Fern*. See catalog reprints on pages 186 and 187.

DAISY AND GREEK KEY

(See fig. 101)

Davidson trademark

Maker: George Davidson & Co., Gateshead-on-Tyne, England.
Named by: Heacock
Y.O.P. Circa 1890
Other name: None
Colors made: White and blue opalescent.
Pieces made: Only sauces known.
Reintroduction or Repros: None known at this time.

DAISY AND PLUME

(See fig. 413)
Maker: The Northwood Co. and Dugan Glass Co., Indiana, PA.
Named by: Presznick 1
Y.O.P. Circa 1905–1908 for Dugan; earlier for Northwood opalescent pieces.

Other name: None
Colors made: Green, white, and blue opalescent; Carnival colors of marigold, purple, ice blue, green, peach, aqua, peach opalescent and pearl (white).
Pieces made: Bowls and comports.
Reintroduction or Repros: None known at this time.
Note: "Heacock studied this pattern closely, eventually concluding that the Dugan version has at least 80 small beads around each flower, while the Northwood versions have 74 to 76 at most." (*Dugan/Diamond, The Story of Indiana, Pennsylvania Glass*)

DAISY BLOCK ROWBOAT

Maker: Sowerby & Co., Gateshead-on-Tyne
Named by: Sherman Hand
Y.O.P. Circa 1886 through the early 1900s, sometimes marked with Rd 42947.
Other name: Blocked Daisy
Colors made: Primarily in Carnival colors of marigold, amethyst and aqua, as well as plain crystal. Rare in pale green opalescent.
Pieces made: Novelty. This boat was produced in 4", 10", 12", and 15" sizes. It matches the No. 1874 line of pressed tableware.
Reproductions: None known at this time.
Note: This boat is shown on a matching stand. Sowerby opalescent is quite scarce. These boats were made for a long period of time—at least into the 1920s in the Carnival glass.
See the following picture.

Green opalescent *Daisy Block Rowboat*

DAISY DEAR

(See fig. 433)
Maker: Dugan Glass Co., Indiana, PA.
Named by: Joe B. Bell
Y.O.P. Circa 1905
Other name: None
Colors made: White and green opalescent, blue is likely. Carnival colors of amethyst, marigold and peach opalescent.
Pieces made: Bowls
Reintroduction or Repros: None known at this time.
Note: This is an exterior pattern.

DAISY IN CRISS-CROSS

(See figs. 315, 316, 669)
Maker: Beaumont Glass Co., Martins Ferry, OH.
Named by: Taylor
Y.O.P. Circa 1897
Other name: Daisy Syrup (Hartung, *Opalescent*) and Beaumont's Daisy.
Colors made: White, blue, green, and cranberry opalescent.
Pieces made: Syrup and water set, all pieces are rare.
Reintroduction or Repros: None known at this time.
Note: This pattern is difficult to find.

DAISY MAY

Maker: Uncertain. Heacock mused that Dugan Glass Co., Indiana, PA., might be the manufacturer in his 1981 book, *Old Pattern Glass According to Heacock.*
Named by: Heacock
Y. O.P.: Circa 1910
Colors made: White, blue, and green opalescent
Pieces made: Bowls in many shapes
Reintroductions/Repros: None known at this time
Note: If the Dugan attribution is correct, this pattern was probably part of their *Intaglio Ware* line. This should not be confused with the pattern named *Intaglio*. Dugan's *Intaglio* is pressed glass which has a pattern on the outside surface of the piece. The pattern is not raised as is typical in pattern glass; it is below the surface of the glass. See text for *Wilted Flower.*

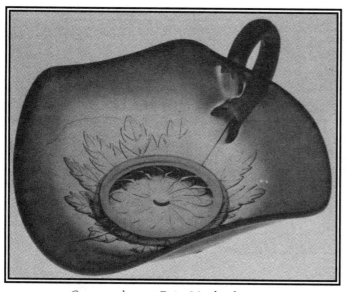

Green opalescent *Daisy May* bonbon.

DESERT GARDEN

(See fig. 432)
Maker: Uncertain
Named by: Heacock
Y.O.P. Uncertain

Other name: None
Pieces made: Bowls
Colors made: White, blue, and green opalescent.
Reintroduction or Repros: None known at this time.
Notes: Maker was unknown in 1975 and is still unknown.

DEVILBISS

(See figs. 979, 1050, 1150–1155, 1157–1164, 1168, 1169, 1231, 1248, 1251)

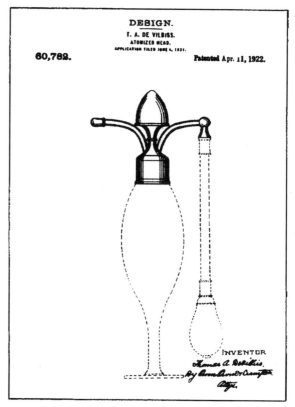

Original *DeVilbiss* atomizer head patent drawing from April, 1922 (Application filed in June, 1921).

Maker etc.: DeVilbiss is not a name for a pattern of glass. In this instance, it is a misnomer. DeVilbiss was a manufacturer of air compressors and, as an interesting side line, they made perfume atomizers. When you hear of someone collecting "DeVilbiss" perfumes, they quite often do not know that DeVilbiss never made a perfume bottle. DeVilbiss commissioned many glass manufacturers to make the perfume bottles on which they would place their atomizers. For quite a while they had American factories making their bottles, then they found that European manufacturers would make them for less money. However, when Hitler overran Europe they found American manufacturers were their only source. At this time, Fenton became a major provider for their glass perfume bottles, fig 326 being one of many. See text for *Pearl.*

DIADEM (SUNBURST-ON-SHIELD)

(See figs. 183-185, 190)

Maker: H. Northwood Co., Wheeling, W.Va.

Named by: Original manufacturer's name

Y.O.P. Circa 1902–1905

Other name: Sunburst–On–Shield, *Kamm 8*

Colors made: White and blue opalescent—no green is known as earlier reported; rare in canary opalescent.

Pieces made: Table set, berry set, breakfast creamer, open sugar, water set, salt shaker, handled nappy, relish tray and cruet.

Reintroduction or Repros: None known at this time.

Notes: Heacock originally called this pattern *Sunburst–On–Shield*. In *The Glass Collector* premiere issue in 1982, he wrote that the original factory name for this pattern was *Diadem*. Heacock believed original factory names should be used when known. The original manufacturer's name was used in *Harry Northwood, The Wheeling Years, 1901-1925*. Thus, the name change for this edition.

DIAMOND AND OVAL THUMBPRINT

(See fig. 526)

Maker: Jefferson Glass Co., Steubenville, OH.

Named by: Hartung, *Opalescent*

Y.O.P. Circa 1904

Other name: Jefferson #228

Colors made: White, blue, and green opalescent.

Pieces made: Vases

Reintroduction or Repros: None known at this time.

DIAMOND LACE

(See figs. 586, 587)

Maker: Fenton Art Glass Co., Williamstown, W.Va.

Named by: Fenton

Y.O.P. Circa 1948 to present

Other name: Vesta, as shown in the first and second editions of this book, and Hobnail in a Square. Pattern No.1948.

Colors made: White, blue, and topaz opalescent; sometimes trimmed with a rose, aqua or emerald green crest; milk glass. New colors are being made such as Springtime green and Burmese.

Pieces made: Epergne (several sizes), bowls, candlesticks, cake plate, vases, covered comport, footed plate and salver.

Reintroduction or Repros: Fenton may reintroduce a pattern or color at any time. If made after 1972, it should be marked with the Fenton logo.

Notes: This is Fenton's rendition of the Victorian pattern *Vesta* and *Hobnail in a Square*. I do not know why Heacock called this pattern *Vesta*. Fenton has always called it *Diamond Lace* as shown in their 1948 catalog. See text for *Vesta*.

See the catalog reprint on the following page.

Canary opalescent *Diadem* handled nappy

Assortment of Fenton's *Diamond Lace,* also shown in a 1950 catalog. This line is a copy of the Victorian *Hobnail–In–Square* or *Vesta* pattern made in Fenton shapes. In 1948, the only colors available were French and blue opalescent.

DIAMOND OPTIC

(See figs. 608, 933, 946, 967, 984, 1044, 1045, 1111, 1215, 1217)

Maker: Fenton Art Glass Co., Williamstown, W.Va., and L. G. Wright Glass Co., New Martinsville, W.Va.

Named by: Fenton

Y.O.P. Circa 1952 to 1980s

Other name: Victorian name—*Bubble Lattice;* also *Lattice*.

Colors made: Cranberry, blue and emerald green, sometimes with a satin finish.

Pieces made: Ivy ball, vase, pitcher, tumbler, finger bowl, lamp, cookie canister. Other items are probable.

Reintroduction or Repros: Fenton may reintroduce a pattern or color at any time. If made after 1972, it should be marked with the Fenton logo.

Notes: Fenton also uses the *Diamond Optic* pattern when making pieces in their "clear" colors, such as figure 1111. It appears to be tangerine, with the opalescence only on the edge of the base and in the bowl. The ivy ball was usually sold with either a crystal satin or emerald green diamond–shaped base.

DIAMOND POINT

(See fig. 521)

Maker: H. Northwood Co., Wheeling, W.Va.

Named by: Hartung, *Opalescent*

Y.O.P. Circa 1906

Other name: None

Colors made: White, blue and green opalescent; Carnival colors of aqua opal, blue, purple, marigold and pearl (white).

Pieces made: Vases

Reintroduction or Repros: None known at this time.

Note: Usually signed with an "N" in a circle. See *Feathers* text for catalog reprint.

DIAMOND POINT AND FLEUR-DE-LIS

(See fig. 463)

Maker: H. Northwood Co., Wheeling, W.Va.

Named by: Presznick 3

Y.O.P. Circa 1906–1908

Other name: None

Colors made: White, blue and green opalescent.

Pieces made: Bowls

Reintroduction or Repros: None known at this time.

Notes: This pattern is frequently found with the "N" in a circle trademark.

DIAMONDS, OPALESCENT

(See figs. 634, 849, 874, 875, 884, 920)

Maker: Uncertain. Possibilities are: Phoenix Glass Co., Monaca, PA., Northwood Glass Co., Martins Ferry, OH., or La Belle Glass Co., Bridgeport, OH.

Named by: Uncertain
Y.O.P. Circa 1888
Other name: None
Colors made: Cranberry, white, blue opalescent (sometimes with a crackle finish) and rubina
Pieces made: Pitchers, tumbler, sugar shaker and cruet.
Reintroduction or Repros: None known at this time.
Notes: This pattern is quite different from most blown opalescent, in that the diamond portion of the pattern is opalized. This is the exact reverse of *Lattice*, which has the diamond work surrounded by opalescence.

Heacock originally attributed this pattern to Hobbs, Brockunier. Neila & Tom Bredehoft make no mention of *Diamonds, Opalescent* in their book, *Hobbs, Brockunier & Co., Glass Identification and Value Guide*, so this attribution is unlikely.

The crackle finish had a very limited production. The opalescence in this pattern is so indistinct that it is seldom sought by opalescent glass collectors.

DIAMOND SPEARHEAD

(See figs. 130, 179, 192, 212, 578)
Maker: National Glass Co. and Dugan Glass Co., Indiana, PA.
Named by: Peterson, *Glass Salt Shakers*
Y.O.P. Circa 1900 for National and 1904 for Dugan.
Other name: Pattern #22, and Pressed Opal Top (Boultinghouse).
Colors made: Crystal and opalescent colors of white, canary, green, sapphire blue and cobalt blue.
Pieces made: Table set, water set, (goblet or tumblers), berry set, toothpick, syrup, mug, celery vase, salt shaker, jelly compote, tankard, individual creamer/sugar, high standard compote, cake plate, water bottle, cup and saucer and wine set.
Reintroduction or Repros: None known at this time.
Notes: The opalescence varies a great deal, from barely anything on the edge to several inches on the larger pieces. Shards unearthed at Indiana, PA.

DIAMOND STEM

(See figs. 532, 1244)
Maker: Model Flint Glass Co., Findlay, OH.
Named by: Hartung, *Opalescent*
Y.O.P. Circa 1903
Other name: None
Colors made: White and canary opalescent.
Pieces made: Vases
Reintroduction or Repros: None known at this time.
Notes: The *Diamond Stem* vase was pulled and flared into several different shapes, and may not be easily recognized from the example illustrated in figure 532.

DIAMOND WAVE

(See fig. 1278)
Maker: Unknown, but most likely English.
Named by: Heacock
Y.O.P. Circa early 1900s or possibly as late as the 1920s
Other name: None
Colors made: Cranberry and amethyst opalescent; others are probable.
Pieces made: Tumbler and covered pitcher; others are likely.
Reintroductions/Repros: None known at this time.
Note: The height of the tumbler is 5" which is typical for an English tumbler.

DOLLY MADISON

(See fig. 138)
Maker: Jefferson Glass Co., Follansbee, W.Va.
Named by: Heacock
Y.O.P. Circa 1907
Other name: Jefferson #271 (*Kamm* 7)
Colors made: Green, blue and white opalescent; crystal and electric blue .
Pieces made: Table set, water set, berry set.
Reintroduction or Repros: None known at this time.
Notes: Due to the late production date of this pattern, the number of table pieces made was considerably minimized. The name was supplied by Heacock because there had been considerable confusion over Jefferson's 251 and 271. The pattern is basically a *Colonial* type pattern, with a touch of class (the flower spray).

DOLPHIN CANDLESTICKS

(See fig. 584)
Maker: Westmoreland Glass Co., Grapeville, PA., for A & A Importing.
Named by: Westmoreland
Y.O.P. 1973-75
Other name: None
Colors made: Medium blue
Pieces made: Candlesticks
Reintroduction or Repros: None known at this time.
Note: Some pieces will be signed.

DOLPHIN COMPOTE

(See figs. 409, 594)
Maker: H. Northwood Co., Wheeling, W.Va.
Named by: Hartung, *Opalescent*
Y.O.P. Circa 1903
Other name: None
Colors made: White, blue and canary opalescent.
Pieces made: Compotes
Reintroduction or Repros: Yes, see figure 594. The L.G. Wright Glass Co., New Martinsville, W.Va., obtained the *Dolphin* mould in 1939 and has had various glass houses produce this item periodically into the 1990s.

Westmoreland was one such manufacturer. Known colors: blue, amberina, vaseline, amber, amethyst and milk glass. Other colors are probable.

Notes: Take care when buying this novelty. It has been heavily reproduced and it is very hard to tell the difference between an old and new piece. See the following catalog reprint.

The assortment comprises ½ doz. each of the following:
7¼-in. Footed Tray Receiver.
Extra Large Rose Bowl.
9½-in. Fancy Salad Dish.
8-in. Footed Card Tray or Jelly Dish
7¼-in. Tall Flaring Vase.
6-in. Large Crackle Vase.
8-in. Deep Scalloped Dish.
(Total 6 doz. in bbl. Sold only by pkg. Bbl. 33c.)
7¼-in. Fancy Flared Dish—Footed.
7¼-in. Fancy Flared Dish.
7-in. Footed Card or Spoon Tray.
Open Sugar, Spoon or Flower Vase.
Fancy Square Cream Pitcher.
Per dozen, 80c

Butler Brothers catalog reprint from 1902. 1. *Button Panels* card receiver 2. *Dolphin* compote 3. Unidentified vase 4. Crackle vase 5. & 7. *Opaline Brocade* 6. *Alaska* creamer.

DOLPHIN, FENTON

(See figs. 1116, 1122, 1127, 1132)
Maker: Fenton Art Glass Co., Williamstown, W.Va.
Named by: Probably Fenton
Y.O.P. Circa 1920s—present
Other name: None
Colors made: Many colors, including: Velva Rose, Florentine Green, Aquamarine, Tangerine, Orchid, Turquoise Opaque, Jade, Rose, Cameo, Ruby, Royal Blue, Ebony, Chinese Yellow, Pekin blue, lilac, blue opalescent, crystal, many engraved.
Pieces made: Many, including: vases, candlesticks, compote, bonbon, bowls, sandwich tray, footed bowls, candy jar and double handled plate.

Reintroductions/Repros: Fenton may reintroduce a pattern or color at any time. If made after 1972, the piece should be marked with the Fenton logo.

DOLPHIN, MODEL FLINT

(See figs. 410, 1264–1267)
Maker: Model Flint Glass Co., Findlay, OH.
Named by: Model Flint
Y.O.P. Circa 1902
Other name: None
Colors made: White, blue and canary opalescent; crystal.
Pieces made: Novelties
Reintroduction or Repros: None known at this time
Notes: This novelty is made in both a card tray and a vase. The vase is shown in the original National Glass catalog reprinted in Marcelle Bond's *The Beauty of Albany Glass.*

DOLPHIN PETTICOAT CANDLESTICKS

(See fig. 411)
Maker: The Northwood Co., and Dugan Glass Co., Indiana, PA.
Named by: Lee, *Early American Pressed Glass*
Y.O.P. Circa 1903
Other name: Pattern No. 565
Colors made: White, blue, and canary opalescent.
Pieces made: Candlesticks
Reintroduction or Repros: None known at this time.
Notes: Shards unearthed at the Indiana, PA., factory dump. See the catalog reprint on the following page.

OPALESCENT GLASS FROM A—Z

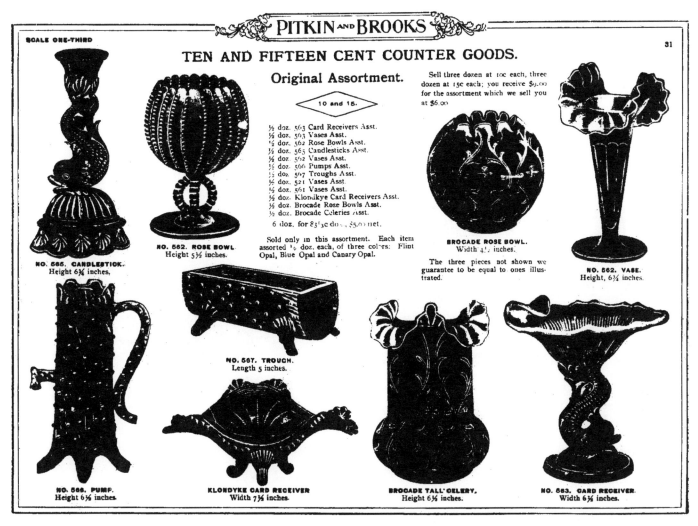

SCALE ONE-THIRD

31

TEN AND FIFTEEN CENT COUNTER GOODS.

Original Assortment.

10 and 15.

Sell three dozen at 10c each, three dozen at 15c each; you receive $9.00 for the assortment which we sell you at $6.00

½ doz. 563 Card Receivers Asst.
½ doz. 563 Vases Asst.
½ doz. 562 Rose Bowls Asst.
½ doz. 565 Candlesticks Asst.
½ doz. 562 Vases Asst.
½ doz. 566 Pumps Asst.
½ doz. 567 Troughs Asst.
½ doz. 521 Vases Asst.
½ doz. 561 Vases Asst.
½ doz. Klondkye Card Receivers Asst.
½ doz. Brocade Rose Bowls Asst.
½ doz. Brocade Celeries Asst.

6 doz. for 83⅓c doz., $5.00 net.

Sold only in this assortment. Each item assorted ⅙ doz. each, of three colors: Flint Opal, Blue Opal and Canary Opal.

The three pieces not shown we guarantee to be equal to ones illustrated.

NO. 565. CANDLESTICK.
Height 6¾ inches.

NO. 562. ROSE BOWL
Height 5½ inches.

BROCADE ROSE BOWL.
Width 4½ inches.

NO. 562. VASE.
Height, 6¾ inches.

NO. 566. PUMP.
Height 6½ inches.

NO. 567. TROUGH.
Length 5 inches.

KLONDYKE CARD RECEIVER
Width 7½ inches.

BROCADE TALL CELERY.
Height 6½ inches.

NO. 563. CARD RECEIVER
Width 6½ inches.

Pitkin and Brooks 1900 Catalog showing No. 565 *Dolphin Petticoat*. No. 562 *Opal Open*. *Brocade* Rose Bowl (*Opaline Brocade* or *Spanish Lace*). No. 562 *Lorna*. No. 566 and 567 *Pump and Trough*. *Klondyke*. *Brocade*. No. 563 *Dolphin* card receiver.

DOT OPTIC—OPAL DOT

(See figs. 592, 938, 961, 988, 1002, 1042, 1062, 1109, 1142, 1150–1152, 1190, 1218, 1224, 1229)

Maker: Fenton Art Glass Co., Williamstown W.Va., for L.G Wright Glass Co., New Martinsville, W.Va.

Named by: Fenton

Y.O.P. Circa 1907—present

Other name: Victorian name for other companies: Coinspot; L.G. Wright name: Opal Dot

Colors made: White, blue, topaz, green, amethyst and cranberry opalescent.

Pieces made: Baskets, pitchers (several styles including a tankard), tumblers, perfume bottles, hat, vases, sugar, creamer, cruet, fairy light, sugar shaker, pickle caster, finger bowl and lamps; others are likely.

Reintroduction or Repros: Fenton may reintroduce a pattern or color at any time. If made after 1972, it should be marked with the Fenton logo.

Notes: Heacock called this *Thumbprint*. *Thumbprint* is made from the same spot mould but becomes *Dot Optic*

when the opalescent treatment is added and the dots become white. Figure 1224 must be quite rare as I have never seen any other piece of *Dot Optic* with the Blue Ridge coloring. Figures 1150–1152 are perfumes made for DeVilbiss in the 1940s. See catalog reprints on pages 186 and 187, *Buttons and Braids*, and *Wide Rib* sections.

DOUBLE GREEK KEY

(See figs. 140, 206-207)

Maker: Nickel Plate Glass Co., Fostoria, OH., with continued production by U. S. Glass Co.

Named by: Lee, *Victorian Glass*

Y.O.P. Circa 1892

Other name: None

Colors made: Blue and white opalescent; crystal.

Pieces made: Pressed: table set, berry set, water set, celery vase, pickle tray. Blown: salt shaker, mustard, toothpick and syrup.

Reintroduction or Repros: None known at this time. See the following picture.

Very rare syrup pitcher in blue opalescent *Double Greek Key*.

DOUBLE WEDDING RING OPTIC

(See fig. 1123)
Maker: Fenton Art Glass Co., Williamstown, W.Va.
Named by: Fenton
Y.O.P. Circa 1985
Other name: Pattern #2323GO
Colors made: Green opalescent (shinny and satin finish)
Pieces made: Bowl
Reintroductions/Repros: Fenton may reintroduce a pattern or color at any time. This piece is marked with the Fenton logo.

DOVER DIAMOND

Maker: Unknown
Named by: Heacock
Y.O.P. Circa 1892; sometimes marked with Rd 193365
Other name: None
Colors made: Unknown
Pieces made: Individual creamer, others are likely.
Reintroductions/Repros: None known at this time.

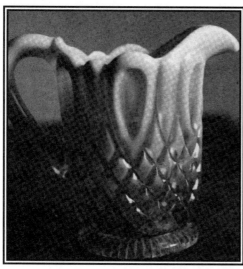

Dover Diamond individual creamer.

DRAGON AND LOTUS

Maker: Fenton Art Glass Co., Williamstown, W.Va.
Named by: Popular nomenclature
Y.O.P. Circa 1910
Other name: Pattern No. 1656
Colors made: White opalescent, custard and Carnival colors of marigold, amethyst, blue, green, very rare vaseline opalescent, red, ice green and ice blue. Other colors are possible.
Pieces made: Bowls and plates
Reintroduction or Repros: None known at this time, but Fenton may reintroduce a pattern or color at any time. Any items produced after 1972 will be marked.
Notes: Very rare in opalescent.

Excerpt from the 1915 Fenton catalog No. 1656 *Dragon and Lotus* bowl.

DRAGONLADY

(See fig. 480)
Maker: Unknown
Named by: Heacock
Y.O.P. Uncertain
Other name: None
Colors made: White, blue, and green opalescent.
Pieces made: Rose bowl and possibly novelties.
Reintroduction or Repros: None known at this time.

DRAPERY, BLOWN OPAL

(See figs. 822, 823)
Maker: National Glass Co., operating Northwood Glass Works, Indiana PA.; Jefferson Glass Co., Steubenville OH.; Coudersport Glass Co.; and Fenton Art Glass Co., Williamstown, W.Va.
Named by: Hartung, *Opalescent*
Y.O.P. Circa 1900–1910
Other name: Blown Opal Drapery
Colors made: White, blue, green, and cranberry opalescent.
Pieces made: Pitcher, tumbler, and barber bottle.
Reintroduction or Repros: Yes—by Fenton Art Glass Co., Williamstown, W.Va,. for L.G. Wright Glass Co., New Martinsville, W.Va. They made a pitcher and barber bottle in cranberry from an optic mould owned by L.G. Wright.

Notes: *Drapery* has been made by Fenton since 1907 and is still in their line today; be prepared to find it in many colors and shapes. Any piece made after 1972 will be marked. Fenton prefers to call this pattern *Curtain Optic,* so have listed it that way also. See *Curtain Optic* text for more information.

DRAPERY, NORTHWOOD'S
(See figs. 111-118)
Maker: H. Northwood Co., Wheeling, W.Va.
Named by: Hartung, *Northwood*
Y.O.P. Circa 1905
Other name: None
Colors made: Blue and white opalescent. Sometimes decorated with heavy gold on the vertical ribs as well as the rims of bowls.
Pieces made: Table set, water set, berry set and perhaps novelties.
Reintroduction or Repros: None known at this time.
Notes: The pattern must be referred to as *Drapery, Northwood* or *Opalescent Drapery* to avoid confusing with the earlier Sandwich pattern of the same name. Usually signed with "N" in a circle.

DRIFTWOOD AND SHELL
(See fig. 1277)
Maker: Burtles, Tate and Co.,Manchester, England.
Named by: Heacock
Y.O.P. Circa 1885. The Rd #39807 appears on the back of the yellow wall pocket.
Other name: None
Colors made: Blue, yellow. Others are probable.
Pieces made: Wall pocket and whimseys
Reintroductions/Repros: None known.

DUCHESS
(See fig. 200)
Maker: Riverside Glass Co., Wellsburg, W.Va.
Named by: Heacock
Y.O.P. Circa 1903
Other name: None
Colors made: Blue, canary, and white opalescent; emerald green with gold; crystal, with frosted panels and enamel decoration. Also amethyst–flashed crystal with satin panels.
Pieces made: Water set, table set, berry set, toothpick, cruet, lamp shade (illustrated).
Reintroduction or Repros: None known at this time.
Notes: The *Duchess* pattern is so strikingly beautiful that it is sad so little of it can be found, especially in opalescent. The emerald green pieces are more easily found, and are uncannily similar to *Empress,* a Riverside pattern. The stopper to the *Duchess* cruet is much like one used on the *Esther* cruet, also a Riverside pattern.

ELLIPSE AND DIAMOND
(See fig. 879)
Maker: Unknown
Named by: Heacock
Y.O.P. Circa 1890
Other name: None
Colors made: Cranberry opalescent
Pieces made: Pitcher
Reintroduction or Repros: None known at this time
Note: This pattern is similar to *Honeycomb and Lattice,* but has alternating series of ellipses and diamonds, making it unique.

ELLIPSES
Maker: Beaumont Glass Co., Martins Ferry OH.
Named by: Uncertain
Y.O.P. Circa 1901
Other name: Pattern No. 106
Colors made: Crystal, rose–flashed crystal, and white opalescent.
Pieces made: Butter dish, spooner, creamer, sugar and mug; other pieces are likely.
Note: This pattern was never documented in opalescent until 1982 in Heacock's, *The Glass Collector,* No. 2. See the following picture.

Beaumont Glass Co.'s *Ellipses*

ENCORE (JEWEL AND FLOWER)
(See figs. 25-29, 228, 229, 377, 503)
Maker: H. Northwood Co., Wheeling, W.Va.
Named by: Original manufacturer's name
Y.O.P. Circa 1905
Other name: Jewel and Flower (*Kamm 8*)
Colors made: White, blue and canary opalescent, decorated with gold.
Pieces made: Water set, table set, berry set, cruet and salt shaker.
Reintroduction or Repros: None known at this time.
Notes: In more than one case it has been noted that a butter base, other than the one illustrated, was used.

However, the base illustrated is obviously the more "original" of the two. The other is simple in design with a scalloped rim, and was not opalized.

Heacock originally called this pattern *Jewel and Flower*. In his premiere issue of *The Glass Collector* in 1982, he wrote that the original factory name for this pattern was *Encore*. Heacock believed original factory names should be used when known. The original manufacturer's name was used in *Harry Northwood, The Wheeling Years, 1901-1925*. Thus, the name change for this edition.

"I wish all good things to the Northwood Co. for calling everything by names. They have a decided talent in this direction and are likely to spring four upon you at one blow. *Encore* is the name of the new line of opalescent tableware. The line comes in canary, blue and flint opalescent undecorated, and in the three colors decorated in ruby and gold. A rather queer effect is produced by the gold and ruby decoration on blue and canary opalescent." (*China, Glass and Lamps,* January 16, 1904)

ENGLISH, UNNAMED
(See figs. 1235, 1237, 1238, 1241)

Unfortunately, Heacock knew nothing definitive about these pieces in 1985 when he pictured them in *Collecting Glass, Vol. 2,* and nothing has come to light since. Following is what he said at that time: "These four light weight mould–blown items in green opalescent are probably English. Whereas the color of vaseline (greenish yellow) opalescent is common in English opalescent, a true green is quite rare. The only items in blown green opalescent shown in Manley (figs. 203, 224) are suggested as Stevens and Williams and a firm which Mr. Manley told me was their chief competitor (and copier of ideas)—W.H., B. & J. Richardson. All of this type of blown opalescent English glass, sometimes with applied rigaree (as in figure 1235) is neatly categorize in America as 'Stourbridge' glass. However, Manley warns collectors of specimens which may look English, but are actually 'foreign'. I am certain by this he must mean from the European continent. No pattern names, further classification or dates are being offered at this time, as my knowledge on European blown opalescent is much too limited."

ERIE (BEADED OVALS IN SAND)
(See fig. 567)

Maker: Dugan/Diamond Glass Co., Indiana, PA.
Named by: Original manufacturer's name
Y.O.P. Circa 1906–16
Other name: Beaded Ovals in Sand (Heacock)
Colors made: Apple green, blue and crystal—rare in opalescent colors of white blue and green.
Pieces made: Water set, table set, berry set, cruet, salt and pepper, toothpick, and a tiny ruffle–edged nappy.

Reintroduction or Repros: None known at this time.
Notes: An extremely rare pattern in opalescent colors. Heacock originally called this pattern *Beaded Ovals in Sand.* In his series *The Glass Collector, Collecting Glass,* he began advising the reader of the original manufacturer's names. Heacock believed original factory names should be used when known. The original factory name is used in *Dugan/Diamond, The Story of Indiana, Pennsylvania Glass.* Thus, the change for this edition. See the following catalog reprints.

Sugar shakers, syrup jugs and condiment sets as shown in the 1907 Dugan catalog. Note the original pattern names—*Erie (Beaded Ovals in Sand)* and *National (S–Repeat). Coinspot* is also shown. Courtesy of Steve Jennings.

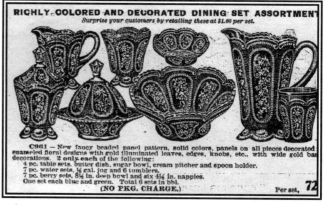

This nice assortment of decorated *Erie (Beaded Ovals in Sand)* items in blue and green was shown in a Mid–Spring, 1906 Butler Brothers catalog.

ERIE WITH HOLLY

(See catalog reprint with *Lattice and Daisy*)
Maker: Dugan Glass Co., Indiana, PA.
Named by: Elmore—see note
Y.O.P. Circa 1916
Other name: Beaded Ovals and Holly
Colors made: White and blue opalescent; others are likely.
Pieces made: Table set
Reintroductions/Repros: None known at this time.
Note: The original manufacturer's name for the basic pattern was *Erie (Beaded Ovals in Sand)*. With the addition of Holly, it seems to follow that the name should be *Erie with Holly*. See catalog reprint in the *Lattice and Daisy* section.

EVERGLADES (SEE CARNELIAN)

EYE DOT

(See figs. 589, 932, 941, 942, 944, 945, 951, 1079, 1102, 1193, 1195, 1198)
Maker: Fenton Art Glass Co., Williamstown, W.Va., for L.G. Wright Glass Co., New Martinsville, W.Va., owner of the moulds.
Named by: L.G. Wright
Y.O.P. Circa 1940s–1980s
Other name: Victorian name: Polka Dot
Colors made: Cranberry and blue opalescent, sometimes with a satin finish.
Pieces made: Barber bottle, tumbler, lamps, cruet, creamer, rose bowl, finger bowl and lamp.
Reintroduction or Repros: This was a Wright reintroduction.
Note: See text for *Polka Dot*. Figure 1102 (barber bottle) may be old as there is a strange scar on the bottom which could be a pontil mark. Then again, it could just be a manufacturer's flaw. Figures 1195 and 1198 (lamps) are made using the *Beaded* and the *Eye Dot* optic moulds. See catalog reprint on page 186.

EYE DOT AND DAISY

(See catalog reprint on page 187)
Maker: Fenton Art Glass Co., Williamstown W.Va., for L.G. Wright Glass Co. New Martinsville W.Va.
Named by: L.G. Wright
Y.O.P. Circa 1980s
Other name: Daisy and Eye Dot; Victorian name was Floral Eyelet.
Colors made: Blue opalescent
Pieces made: Pitcher and tumbler.
Reintroductions or Repros: This is a Wright reintroduction. See notes for *Floral Eyelet*.

FAN

(See figs. 127-128, 445)
Maker: Dugan Glass Co., Indiana, PA.
Named by: Hartung, *Northwood*
Y.O.P. Circa 1906
Other name: None
Colors made: White, blue, green opalescent; custard, emerald green, royal blue and Carnival glass colors of marigold, purple and peach opalescent.
Pieces made: Table set, berry set, water set, gravy boat and assorted novelties.
Reintroduction or Repros: None known at this time.
Notes: The illustrated novelty in figure 445, sometimes called a gravy boat, is signed with a "D–in–a–Diamond" mark. See the following catalog reprint.

Fan pattern in the 1907 Dugan catalog. Courtesy of Steve Jennings.

FAN AND FILE

(See figs. 623, 624)
Maker: Westmoreland Glass Co., Grapeville, PA.
Named by: Westmoreland
Y.O.P. See notes
Other name: Flattened Diamond and Starburst
Colors made: Many colors.
Pieces made: Child's punch set, covered butter, open sugar, creamer, covered sugar, banana stand and cake plate. All of these are child size.
Reintroduction or Repros: None known at this time.
Notes: This pattern was first introduced in 1920. The emerald green opalescent was made in 1975 for Levay, and again in 1979 in many colors. This pattern was brought back again in 1982, 1983 and 1984.
Fan and File was never made in old opalescent glass. Some pieces will be signed.

FANCY FANS

(See fig. 851)
Maker: The Northwood Glass Co., Ellwood City, PA. is a possibility.
Named by: Heacock
Y.O.P. Circa 1893
Other name: None
Colors made: Cranberry and blue opalescent. Also milk glass.
Pieces made: Cruet, salt shaker, sugar shaker, covered sugar, and oil night lamp.
Reintroduction or Repros: None known at this time.
Note: In the book, *Harry Northwood, The Early Years 1881-1900*, James Measell states that Northwood was probably the manufacturer of this interesting pattern, but more research is needed.

Polka Dot sugar bowl from the *Fancy Fans* shape mould

FANCY FANTAILS

(See fig. 474)
Maker: Jefferson Glass Co., Steubenville, OH.*
Named by: Heacock
Y.O.P. Circa 1905
Other name: None
Colors made: White, blue, green, and canary opalescent, sometimes with a cranberry border.
Pieces made: Bowls
Reintroduction or Repros: None known at this time.
Notes: *In the first and second editions of this book, Heacock attributed this pattern to Northwood. *Fancy Fantails* does not appear in *Harry Northwood, The Early Years, 1881–1900* or *Harry Northwood, The Wheeling Years, 1901–1925* so this attribution is not likely. Best guess is Jefferson, based on the cranberry edging which is a typical Jefferson treatment.

FEATHER OPTIC

(See fig. 987)
Maker: Fenton Art Glass Co., Williamstown, W.Va.
Named by: Fenton
Y.O.P. Circa 1982
Other name: None
Colors made: Cranberry, other colors are possible
Pieces made: Fairy light, other pieces are possible.
Reintroduction or Repros: Fenton may reintroduce a pattern or color at any time. If made after 1972, the piece should be marked with the Fenton logo.
Note: This fairy light was made for the FAGCA auction at their 1982 convention.

FEATHERS

(See fig. 523)
Maker: H. Northwood Co., Wheeling, W.Va.
Named by: Hartung, *Opalescent*
Y.O.P. Circa 1906
Other name: None
Colors made: White, blue and green opalescent; Carnival colors of marigold, purple, green and ice blue.
Pieces made: Vases, often "swung"
Reintroduction or Repros: None known at this time.
Note: Carnival pieces are usually signed. See the catalog reprint on the following page.

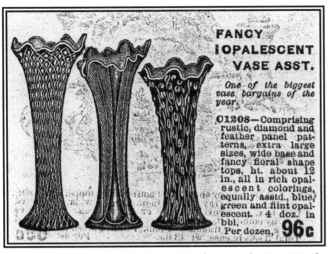

Northwood's *Diamond Point*, *Feathers* and *Tree Trunk*. Opalescent vases from the Butler Brothers' April, 1906 catalog.

Pieces made: Pitcher (four styles), tumbler, butter dish, creamer, sugar, spooner, berry set, sugar shaker (two styles), syrup, cruet, salt shaker, mustard, celery vase, finger bowl, toothpick and barber bottles (two styles).

Reintroduction or Repros: Yes—by Fenton Art Glass Co., Williamstown, W.Va. See text for *Fenton, Fern.*

Note: Special shape moulds were: West Virginia's *Optic*, Beaumont's *Square-top pitcher* and *Melon Rib* barber bottle.

Trade Quote:
"The illustrated catalogue of the West Virginia Glass Co., of Martins Ferry, Ohio, is now ready and an examination of its pages reveals a wealth of beauty in color and design...No. 204 there are oils, toothpick, molasses can, celery, salts, sugar sifter, blown set, nappies, bowls, tumblers, finger bowl, gal. pitcher, in ruby optic, crystal optic, ruby opalescent and crystal opalescent." (*China, Glass & Lamps,* January 31, 1894)

FERN, FENTON
(See fig. 1081)
Maker: Fenton Art Glass Co.
Named by: Fenton
Y.O.P. Circa 1952 and again in 1989. Other years are possible.
Other name: Pattern #1720
Colors made: Cranberry and blue opalescent (also satin finish), Persian Blue, 1989.
Pieces made: Cruets (two sizes), and vase.
Reintroduction/Repros: Fenton may reintroduce a pattern or color at any time. If made after 1972, the piece should be marked.

FERN, OPALESCENT
(See figs. 291, 295, 344–346, 564, 794, 795, 797–802, 872, 873, 909, 910, 1038–1040, 1048, 1100)
Makers: West Virginia Glass Co., Martins Ferry, OH., (designed by Beaumont) circa 1894 (Kamm 5, page 89); Beaumont Glass Co., Martins Ferry, OH circa 1898; Model Flint Glass Co., Findlay, OH, and Albany, IN, (no cranberry production) circa 1903; both Model Flint and West Virginia Glass joined the National Glass Co. during 1899–1900.
Named by: Heacock
Y.O.P. See above
Other name: Blue Opal (Kamm); Fern Sprays (Hartung, *Opalescent*)
Colors made: White, blue and cranberry opalescent. Yellow opalescent by Model Flint.

The line called *Blue Opal Ware* is in West Virginia's *Opalescent Fern* pattern. The creamer has an unusual open pouring spout. From an 1894 Montgomery Ward catalog.

Assortment of *Opalescent Fern* from an 1894 Montgomery Ward catalog.

FINECUT AND ROSES

(See figs. 180, 446)
Maker: Jefferson Glass Co., Steubenville, OH. and H. Northwood Co., Wheeling W.Va.*
Named by: Hartung, *Opalescent*
Y.O.P. Circa Jefferson—uncertain. H. Northwood Co., circa 1908.
Other name: Jefferson's #249 or Floral and Diamond Point
Colors made: Opalescent colors of white and blue; custard (sometimes with a nutmeg decoration); Carnival colors of marigold, ice blue, green, blue, purple, dark amber and aqua opalescent.
Pieces made: Three footed rose bowl and card receiver.
Reintroduction or Repros: None known at this time.
Notes: *Originally made by Jefferson in opalescent, later production in Carnival and custard glass by Northwood. It has baffled researchers for years how the moulds were transferred from Jefferson to Northwood. These two companies were serious competitors for over 20 years, both specializing in the same type of glass (except for Carnival—Jefferson never made any). Sometimes the Northwood Carnival pieces were marked with the "N" in circle trademark. The interior may be plain or it may be adorned with the pattern *Fancy*.

FISHSCALE AND BEADS

(See catalog reprint with *Lattice and Daisy*)
Maker: Dugan Glass Co., Indiana, PA.
Named by: Heacock

Y.O.P. Circa 1916
Other name: None
Colors made: White and blue opalescent.
Pieces made: Bowls
Reintroductions/Repros: None know at this time.

FISH–IN–THE–SEA VASE

(See figs. 525, 647)
Maker: Uncertain
Named by: Heacock
Y.O.P. Uncertain
Other name: None
Colors made: White, blue, and green opalescent, sometimes with goofus decoration on the base.
Pieces made: Novelty vases
Reintroduction or Repros: None known at this time.
Notes: The worn decoration in goofus tends to make one lean towards Northwood as the manufacturer.

FLOATING SNOWFLAKE

(See figs. 1168, 1169, 1240)
Maker: Fenton Art Glass Co., Williamstown, W.Va. for the DeVilbiss Co. of Toledo, OH.
Named by: Elmore
Y.O.P. Circa 1940s
Other name: None
Colors made: White, blue, and green opalescent
Pieces made: Perfume
Reintroductions/Repros: None know at this time.

FLORADINE

(See figs. 287, 288, 907, 908)
Maker: Dalzell, Gilmore & Leighton Co., Findlay, OH.
Named by: Manufacturer
Y.O.P. Circa 1889
Other name: Findlay Onyx, Rose Onyx, Onyx all are misnomers. This pattern was never meant to be called Onyx. Onyx is an entirely different type of glass.
Colors made: Cranberry usually with a satin finish and Autumn Leaf.
Pieces made: Butter dish, covered sugar, creamer, spooner, mustard, pitcher, toothpick, celery vase, sugar shaker, syrup, salt shaker, vases, pickle caster, berry bowl, sauce, finger bowl, cruet and tumbler.
Reintroduction or Repros: None known at this time.
Notes: Everything written as to what this pattern should be named is very confusing. Following are two journal quotes and an analysis upon which this name change has been based:
"Dalzell...shows a magnificent assortment of ware...But what we want to call special attention to are their new lines of colored ware. The first of them, which they call FLORADINE ware, is in two colors, ruby and autumn leaf, with the patterns elegantly traced on the exterior. The effect is extremely rich. In this they make sets, bottles, jugs, celeries, molasses cans, finger bowls,

sugar dusters, 8" bowls and several other articles. The other, the *Onyx* ware is still more beautiful and there is nothing in glass on the market to surpass it. The colors of this are onyx, bronze and ruby and the pieces are all white interior lined. Like the *Floradine*, the pattern is impressed on the exterior in graceful forms and only for the shining surface the ware would look more like fine china than glass." (*Pottery and Glassware Reporter*,1889)

"The Dalzell, Gilmore & Leighton Co. opened the new year with some of the handsomest novelties ever produced in the country, which are destined to have an immense run. Among these is something entirely new, being ruby and opalescent, with raised figures of flowers and leaves, producing an effect of great beauty, but which is simply indescribable. It is a great relief to those who have grown tired of seeing polka dot and plain knobs. A patent has been applied for to cover the method of production and the new process is capable of a large variety of forms and designs that must necessarily render it the best selling thing in tableware." (*Crockery and Glass Journal*, January 1, 1889)

"The Dalzell firm saw *Floradine* and *Onyx* as separate lines, so collectors should not lump them together under the term 'Onyx'. U.S. Patent #402090 was held by George W. Leighton and assigned to the firm. The specification, however, details the making of glass with a metallic luster (Onyx) not an opalescent effect (Floradine)." (James Measell and Don E. Smith, *Findlay Glass*)

FLORAL EYELET

(See fig. 871)
Maker: Probably: Northwood Co., National Glass Co., and Dugan Glass Co. all at the Indiana, PA., factory.
Named by: Uncertain
Y.O.P. Circa 1898
Other name: None
Colors made: White, blue, and cranberry opalescent.
Pieces made: Pitcher and tumbler
Reintroductions/Repros: Yes, by Fenton Art Glass Co. for L.G. Wright Glass Co., New Martinsville, W.Va. They produced a water set in blue opalescent. Wright's name for this pattern was *Eye Dot and Daisy*.
Notes: The attribution is based on the reproductions produced by L.G. Wright Glass Co. These were probably made from original moulds Mr. Wright acquired in Indiana, PA. Original production must have been limited as the pattern is rare today. No mention is made of *Floral Eyelet* in *Harry Northwood, The Early Years 1881-1900*, *Harry Northwood, The Wheeling Years 1901-1925* or *Dugan/Diamond, The Story of Indiana, Pennsylvania, Glass*. See the following picture.

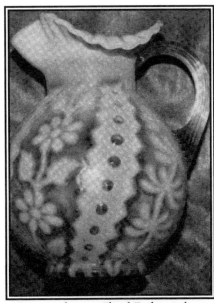

Blue opalescent reproduction *Floral Eyelet* pitcher, which L.G. Wright Glass Co. called *Eye Dot And Daisy*.

FLOUNCES

(See fig. 1157)
Maker: Fenton Art Glass Co., Williamstown, W.Va., for DeVilbiss.
Named by: Elmore
Y.O.P. Circa 1940s
Colors made: White, blue, and Topaz opalescent
Pieces made: Perfume
Reintroductions/Repros: None

FLUTED BARS AND BEADS

(See figs. 451, 539)
Maker: Jefferson Glass Co., Steubenville, OH.
Named by: Heacock
Y.O.P. Circa 1904
Other name: Fluted Opaline Rose Bowl
Colors made: White, blue, green and canary opalescent.
Pieces made: Rose bowls and novelties
Reintroduction or Repros: None known at this time.
Notes: The name of the pattern has been changed from Presznick's earlier name as it does little to describe the pattern, and this novelty was formed into shapes other than rose bowls.

FLUTED SCROLLS (SEE KLONDYKE)

FLUTED SCROLLS WITH VINE

(See fig. 529)
Maker: The Northwood Co., Indiana, PA.
Named by: Heacock
Y.O.P. Circa 1899
Other name: None
Colors made: White, blue, and canary opalescent. Green would be rare.

Pieces made: Novelties and vase.
Reintroduction or Repros: None known at this time.

FROSTED LEAF AND BASKETWEAVE
(See figs. 95–98, 142)

Frosted Leaf and Basketweave swung vase.

Maker: H. Northwood Co., Wheeling W.Va.
Named by: Heacock
Y.O.P. Circa 1905
Other name: None
Colors made: Blue and canary opalescent, possibly white and crystal.
Pieces made: Table set, covered butter, "swung" vase and rose bowl.
Reintroduction or Repros: None known at this time.

GOLFING
(See fig. 1263)
Maker: Unknown
Named by: Elmore
Y.O.P. Uncertain
Other name: None
Colors made: Blue opalescent
Pieces made: Ashtray
Reintroductions/Repros: None known at this time.
Note: Around the edges are golfing items like balls, clubs, bags, tees, and goal flags. This 7" ashtray was previously unlisted and may have been a special order item.

GONTERMAN HOB
(SEE ADONIS HOBNAIL)

GONTERMAN SWIRL
(SEE ADONIS SWIRL)

GRACE DARLING ROWBOAT
(See figs. 644, 1279)
Maker: Edward Bolton. See note below.
Named by: Popular nomenclature
Y.O.P. Circa 1885

Other name: The pattern is Daisy and Button
Colors made: White, blue, and yellow opalescent and crystal.
Pieces made: Novelties, others are probable.
Reintroductions/Repros: Yes—see Daisy and Button, Fenton.
Note: This 11" boat is marked with two different registration numbers—Rd 23527 and Rd N 39414. The first number appears in the base, the second at the back just below the rim. Also on the inside base are the words GRACE DARLING BOAT. The name GRACE DARLING appears again (without the BOAT) at the back of the boat above the second Rd number. Both of these numbers date the design from 1885.

According to Raymond Notley in a May, 1982, article published in the H.O.A.C.G.A. (Carnival glass) newsletter, the *Grace Darling Rowboat* was made by Edward Bolton of the Oxford Lane Glassworks, Warrington. Lancashire. The example pictured in his story appears to be crystal. Grace Darling was the 23-year-old daughter of a lighthouse keeper, who rowed with him through choppy seas to rescue clinging survivors of a steamer wrecked off the shores of Northeast England. This occurred in 1838 and the heroic deed of this young girl made headlines all over Europe. Grace died four years later of consumption.

It is believed that Hobbs, Brockunier & Co., Wheeling W.Va., copied this boat as their No. 101 Yacht celery. It is a near perfect match. Figure 644 is English but Hobbs, Brockunier also made an item very much like this and called it #101 crown oval. Hobbs, Brockunier is not known for the production of opalescent glass in the *Daisy and Button* pattern. All of their production of this pattern is believed to have been in non–opalescent glass.

Hobbs' No. 101 "Bun Tray"

GRAPE

(See fig. 883)

Maker: Probably Fenton Art Glass Co., Williamstown W.Va., for L.G. Wright, New Martinsville, W.Va.

Named by: L.G. Wright

Y.O.P. Probably the 1960s or 1970s

Other name: Vineyard was the name given by Heacock in the first edition of this book. He did not offer any information about this piece.

Colors: Amethyst, amber, with blue and green a possibility; cranberry opalescent.

Pieces made: Decanter, vase and bowls in several sizes including a rose bowl.

Reintroduction or Repros: This was a Wright reintroduction.

Note: The decanter in cranberry opalescent would be considered scarce or rare.

GRAPE AND CABLE

(See figs. 491, 1246)

Maker: H. Northwood Co., Wheeling, W.Va. and Fenton Art Glass Co., Williamstown, W.Va.

Named by: Presznick 4

Y.O.P. Circa 1908

Other name: Grape and Thumbprint, for pieces having the added thumbprints.

Colors made: Known only in white and canary opalescent, custard glass, and Carnival colors of marigold, amethyst, green, blue, ice blue, ice green and red.

Pieces made: Hatpin holder, tumbler, pitcher, cologne, pin tray, spooner, butter dish, sugar, creamer, breakfast creamer and sugar, footed berry, berry, master berry, punch bowl, punch cup, fernery, humidor, centerpiece bowl, two–handled nappy (also single handled), plate (six-sided and round), cracker jar, orange bowl (two styles), humidor, banana boat, footed covered and open compote, ice cream set, candlesticks, liqueur set (tiny shot glasses and handled decanter), sweetmeat, puff jar, tiny perfume and dresser tray.

Reintroduction or Repros: In 1968, Fenton made a Carnival *Grape and Cable* with *Thumbprint* tobacco jar for Rose Presznick. In 1971, they produced it in Blue Marble; in 1974 in Blue Satin; in 1990 they produced in Red Carnival the #9059 bowl and #9074 basket. They produced the tobacco jar again in 1999 in Spruce Green.

Notes: *Grape and Cable* was made in a complete table service. The bowl shown in fig. 491 was made by Fenton and is an orange bowl, not a punch bowl. However, only the orange bowl has been reported in opalescent, so it should really be considered an experimental piece—a novelty. Fenton only made bowls (four sizes and shapes), plates, baskets and spittoons. Northwood pieces are usually signed with "N" in a circle.

GRAPE AND CHERRY

(See fig. 416)

Maker: Unknown

Named by: Hartung, *Carnival 7*

Y.O.P.

Other name: None

Colors made: White, blue opalescent and Carnival marigold; other colors are possible.

Pieces made: Bowls

Reintroduction or Repros: None known at this time.

GRAPEVINE CLUSTER

(See fig. 497)

Maker: H. Northwood Co., Wheeling, W.Va.

Named by: Heacock

Y.O.P. Circa 1905

Other name: None

Colors made: White, canary, and blue opalescent; purple slag.

Pieces made: Novelties

Reintroduction or Repros: None known at this time.

GREEK KEY AND RIBS

Northwood *Greek Key* with rayed center.

Maker: H. Northwood Co., Wheeling, W.Va.

Named by: Heacock

Y.O.P. Circa 1905

Other name: Greek Key

Colors made: White, blue, and green opalescent; rare in canary; Carnival colors of marigold and green.

Pieces made: Novelties

Reintroduction or Repros: None known at this time.

Notes: The name of this pattern has been changed from *Greek Key* for two reasons. First, there are too many patterns with this same name and it creates confusion when advertising in trade papers. Second, this pattern was made in two variants and each should have a different name.

GREEK KEY AND SCALES

(See fig. 417)

Maker: H. Northwood Co., Wheeling, W.Va.
Named by: Heacock
Y.O.P. Circa 1905
Other name: Greek Key
Colors made: White, blue, and green opalescent. Also Carnival colors.
Pieces made: Bowls
Reintroduction or Repros: None known at this time.
Notes: See notes for the *Greek Key and Ribs* pattern.

HAND VASE

(See figs. 621, 1165–1167)

Maker: Fenton Art Glass Co. Williamstown, W.Va.
Named by: Popular name
Y.O.P. 1940s and 1970s
Other name: None
Colors made: White, blue, and topaz opalescent; milk glass and Carnival colors.
Pieces made: Vase
Reintroduction or Repros: Yes—crystal with ruby stain.
Notes: Carnival made in 1970s. Fenton may reintroduce a pattern or color at any time. If made after 1972, it should be marked with the Fenton logo.

HEART—HANDLED OPEN O'S

(See fig. 402)

Maker: H. Northwood Co., Wheeling, W.Va.*
Named by: Heacock
Y.O.P. Circa 1906
Other name: None
Colors made: White, blue and green opalescent.
Pieces made: Novelties
Reintroduction or Repros: None known at this time.
Notes: This novelty is called a basket. *This pattern is not mentioned in either *Harry Northwood, The Early Years, 1881-1900* or *Harry Northwood, The Wheeling Years, 1901-1925*, so the attribution is doubtful.

HEART OPTIC

(See figs. 981, 992, 1230)

Maker: Fenton Art Glass Co., Williamstown, W.Va.
Named by: Fenton
Y.O.P. Circa 1950
Other name: None
Colors made: White, cobalt, peaches 'n cream, sapphire blue and cranberry, other colors are probable.
Pieces made: Perfume (several styles), hat, vase, cruet and fairy light, other pieces are likely.
Reintroductions/Repros: Fenton may reintroduce a pattern or color at any time. If made after 1972, it should be marked with the Fenton logo.
Note: White opalescent was made in 1950; cranberry opalescent in 1978 for the convention auction; cobalt (hat) in 1985 for FAGCA members; peaches 'n cream (hat), and sapphire blue (cruet) in 1986 for FAGCA members; cranberry in the 1990s as a Valentine Day promotion, made only throughout the month of February. Frank M. Fenton states that in 1950 the price for a small perfume bottle in white opalescent without a stopper was $4.50 per dozen.

HEARTS AND CLUBS

(See fig. 408)

Maker: Jefferson Glass Co., Steubenville, OH.
Named by: Heacock
Y.O.P. Circa 1905
Other name: Jefferson pattern #274
Colors made: White, blue, and green opalescent.
Pieces made: Novelties
Reintroduction or Repros: None known at this time.
Notes: This discovery was found on one of the pages of the Jefferson catalog which Kamm did not reprint.

HEARTS AND FLOWERS

(See fig. 454)

Maker: H. Northwood Co., Wheeling, W.Va.
Named by: Hartung *Carnival 2*
Y.O.P. Circa 1908
Other name: None
Colors made: White and blue opalescent; Carnival colors of iridescent custard and milk glass, marigold clambroth, ice green, ice blue, blue, green and aqua opalescent.
Pieces made: Novelties, plates, bowls and compote.
Reintroduction or Repros: None known at this time.

HEATHERBLOOM

(See fig. 421)

Green opalescent *Heatherbloom* vase.

Maker: Jefferson Glass Co., Steubenville, OH.
Named by: Heacock
Y.O.P. Circa 1905
Other name: Jefferson pattern #268
Colors made: White, blue, and green opalescent.

Pieces made: Vases

Reintroduction or Repros: None known at this time.

Notes: Figure 427 is a "swung" vase which distorts the pattern. Above is a picture of a *Heatherbloom* vase which has not been swung and shows the interesting pattern.

HERRINGBONE OPALESCENT

(See figs. 290, 307, 308, 648H, 876, 877, 882, 885)

Maker: Uncertain. Possibly Phoenix Glass Co., Monaca, PA., while Northwood was there.

Named by: Heacock

Y.O.P. Circa 1888–1902

Other name: None

Colors made: White, blue, and cranberry opalescent.

Pieces made: Pitcher, tumbler, cruet and rare syrup.

Reintroduction or Repros: None known at this time.

Notes: This pattern was also made without the ribbed effect (see fig. 885). In Heacock's *Book 2*, he believed this pattern was made by Hobbs, Brockunier and Co., and in *Book 9* he thought it was Northwood who made this pattern. In *Hobbs, Brockunier & Co., Glass Identification and Value Guide* the Bredehoft's made no mention of this pattern and it was not mentioned in *Harry Northwood, The Early Years* or *The Wheeling Years*. Hopefully, a catalog showing this interesting *Herringbone* pattern will turn up so we will finally know who produced this wonderful pattern.

HILLTOP VINES

(See fig. 430)

Maker: H. Northwood Co., Wheeling, W.Va.

Named by: Heacock

Y.O.P. Circa 1906–1908

Other name: None

Colors made: White, blue, and green opalescent.

Pieces made: Novelties

Reintroduction or Repros: None known at this time. See the picture below.

Hilltop Vines compote from a 1906 Butler Brothers ad.

HOBNAIL, FENTON

(See figs. 615, 616, 620, 954, 1077, 1078, 1089, 1131, 1170–1173, 1175, 1186)

Maker: Fenton Art Glass Co., Williamstown, W.Va. They also made some pieces for the L.G. Wright Glass Co., New Martinsville, W.Va., in 1937.

Named by: Fenton

Y.O.P. Circa 1930s—present

Other name: None

Colors made: White, blue, green, topaz, plum, cranberry, amethyst and almost every other color in the Fenton line.

Pieces made: Pitchers, tumblers, cruets, vases, bowls, plates, vanity sets, sugar, creamer, baskets, compotes, salt/pepper, candlesticks, candy jars, ash trays, bonbon, nappies, condiment sets, cake plate, jam set, mayonnaise set, decanter, shoes, hats, cup and saucer, etc., etc.

Reintroduction or Repros: Fenton may reintroduce a pattern or color at any time. If made after 1972, it should be marked with the Fenton logo.

Notes: Almost every glass company of the era had a *Hobnail* pattern in their line and it was made in every color. Figure 1186 (lamp) was assembled by a lamp manufacturer in upstate New York in the 1950s or 1960s. They used a mini vase, perfume, two plates and 14 prisms. The bowl shade was added by the collector. I know of at least three of these unique lamps.

HOBNAIL AND PANELED THUMBPRINT

(See figs. 99, 628–631)

Maker: H. Northwood Co., Wheeling W.Va.

Named by: Heacock

Y.O.P. Circa 1905

Other name: Dew Drop

Colors made: Canary, white, and blue opalescent.

Pieces made: Table set, berry set, water set.

Reintroduction or Repros: None known at this time.

Notes: The tumblers in this pattern have no thumbprints at the base to distinguish them. They have nine rows of hobs (fig. 169 has eight), and the distinctive circle in the base.

HOBNAIL, FOUR—FOOTED

(See fig. 156)

Maker: La Belle Glass Co., Bridgeport, OH.

Named by: Lee, *Early American Pressed Glass.*

Y.O.P. Circa 1887

Other name: Dewdrop

Colors made: Canary and white opalescent, deep blue, plain crystal, canary and blue.

Pieces made: Table set.

Reintroduction or Repros: None known at this time.

Notes: This pattern was made while Harry Northwood was the "designer and metal maker."

See the *Hobnail, Four—Footed* advertisement on the following page.

Ad featuring *Hobnail Four–Footed* in *Crockery and Glass Journal*, July 29, 1886. Note the various colors listed.

HOBNAIL, 3–FOOTED
(SEE OVER–ALL HOB)

HOBNAIL, (BLOWN*)

(See figs. 158-159, 320–334, 816–821, 863, 903, 953, 955, 1010–1016, 1026, 1027, 1255)

Maker: Hobbs, Brockunier & Co., Wheeling, W.Va., with continued production by U.S. Glass Co. and La Belle Glass Co., Bridgeport, OH.
Named by: Popular nomenclature
Y.O.P. Circa 1886 to 1892
Other name: Dewdrop, Pineapple, and Nodule
Colors made: White, blue, cranberry, Rubina, vaseline, Rubina verde opalescent; cased colors of pink, white, mauve etc. (probably by La Belle).
Pieces made: Water set, table set, berry set (square shape), cruet, syrup, waste bowl (finger bowl), five sizes of water pitchers, water bottle, barber bottle, celery vase, lamp shades, vase, bride's basket in frame and water tray.

Reintroduction or Repros: Yes—see *Hobnail, Fenton*. From 1930 to 1939 Czechoslovakian reproductions were imported for the American market. These pieces were blown and have a pontil scar which was never subjected to the workman's polishing wheel.
Notes: Heacock originally stated that the *Hobnail* pattern made by Hobbs, Brockunier was blown, and described the polished pontil mark in the first two editions of *Book 2*. In *Book 9* he printed the following quote from *Pottery and Glassware Reporter*, August 26, 1886: "Hobbs, Brockunier & Co., of Wheeling...Their No. 323 (Dew Drop—Hobnail) opalescent pressed ware is very attractive and they claim a patent on it."

Why Heacock continued to believe this pattern was blown, after seeing it described as "pressed ware" (except in the case of cranberry, which must always be mould blown) is not understood. To further back up the fact that this was pressed ware the Bredehoft's stated in their book, *Hobbs, Brockunier & Co., Glass Identification and Value Guide*: "Dew Drop (hobnail) is a pressed, not blown, pattern. Much confusion has arisen over this, but the patent (No. 343,133) clearly states that the pattern is pressed and careful examination of pieces will reveal mould lines still present and smooth interior surfaces." In view of this perhaps all of the hobnails should be grouped together.

The five pitchers, shown here in diminishing order of height, should be referred to as: a lemonade, water, milk, individual milk, and "miniature" water pitcher.

Thanks to Mr. and Mrs. Ed Sawicki, the existence of the toy water set in Hobb's *Hobnail* has been discovered. They advised that this piece, which most people considered the toothpick holder, was actually a toy–sized tumbler. The Sawicki's sent a copy of an old Hobbs Glass Co. catalog to substantiate their claim. The miniature water pitcher is barely 5" tall. This miniature set was only known in the *Francis Ware* decoration (see fig. 333).

When it is confirmed from undiscovered catalog reprints of all companies that they called *Hobnail* by the name *Dew Drop,* the name in this book will be changed. See notes for other *Hobnail* patterns.
*Figure 1010 is probably English and figures 1011–1016 are likely of Czechoslovakian origin.
See the *Blown Hobnail* catalog reprint below.

HOBNAIL–IN–SQUARE (SEE VESTA)

HOBNAIL, NORTHWOOD, BEAUMONT*
(See figs. 167–168)
Maker*:* H. Northwood Co., Wheeling, W.Va., and Beaumont Glass Co., Martins Ferry, W.Va.
Named by: Heacock
Y.O.P. Circa 1903
Other name: None
Colors made: White, blue, and canary opalescent; other colors are possible.
Pieces made: Table set, water set, berry set, celery, individual creamer and sugar (open) and mug.
Reintroduction or Repros: Yes—see figures 615, 616, 620 and text for *Hobnail, Fenton.* Imperial Glass Co., Bellaire, OH., made Hobnail in the 1920s, 1930s, 1960s and 1970s. Colors were crystal, amber, Ritz Blue, Stiegel Green, Rose Marie, ruby, black, Sea Foam. Opalescent colors: Harding Blue, Moss Green and Burnt Almond (amber). Pieces included: Plates (both round and square), tumbler (at least three sizes), pitcher (two styles), compotes, vase, goblet, sherbet, ivy ball (footed and hanging), bowls, cologne and puff box, plus many more. Many other companies have made *Hobnail.*
Notes: According to Lee's *Early American Pressed Glass,* plate 84, the tumbler to this pattern has nine rows of hobs.
*Northwood or Beaumont name must be included to avoid confusion.

Assortment of Hobbs, Brockunier & Co.'s No. 323 *Blown Hobnail.* Circa 1888 catalog.

HONEYCOMB, FENTON AND WRIGHT

(See figs. 602, 936, 937, 939, 940, 943, 947–949, 963, 993, 999, 1001, 1083, 1084, 1087, 1093, 1191, 1196)

Maker: Fenton Art Glass Co., Williamstown, W.Va., for L.G. Wright Glass Co., New Martinsville, W.Va.

Named by: L.G. Wright

Y.O.P. 1950s—present

Other name: Victorian name: Windows; Fenton name: Window Pane.

Colors made: Blue and cranberry, other colors are likely. Sometimes made with a satin or pearl finish.

Pieces made: Pitcher, tumbler, milk pitcher, syrup, creamer, cruet, vase, bowl, finger bowl, epergne, fairy light and lamps (many styles).

Reintroduction or Repros: Fenton may reintroduce a pattern at any time. If made after 1972, it should be marked with the Fenton logo.

Note: See catalog reprint on page 186.

HONEYCOMB AND CLOVER

(See fig. 137)

Maker: Fenton Art Glass Co., Williamstown, W.Va.

Named by: Presznick

Y.O.P. Circa 1909

Other name: Honeycomb and Four Leaf Clover

Colors made: White, blue, and green opalescent, crystal, emerald green and Carnival colors.

Pieces made: Water set, table set, berry set and assorted novelties (bowls).

Reintroduction or Repros: None known at this time, but Fenton may reintroduce a pattern or color at any time. If made after 1972, it should be marked with the Fenton logo.

HONEYCOMB, OPALESCENT

(See figs. 268, 635, 803, 881, 892, 924, 1126)

Maker: Uncertain*

Named by: Heacock

Y.O.P. Circa 1889

Other name: Bulbous Spot Resist (Taylor)

Colors made: Cranberry, white, blue, green, Blue Amberina, rainbow and amber opalescent (this color is typical of Phoenix, as is the reeded handle).

Pieces made: Pitcher, tumbler, cracker jar, barber bottle (two styles), small juice pitcher, oil lamp and syrup.

Reintroduction or Repros: Yes—see text for Honeycomb, Fenton.

Notes: The unusual color seen in figure 635 can also be found in a variant of the *Windows* pattern. The pitcher illustrated has an unusual greenish caste at the top, undoubtedly a reaction from the chemicals in the glass when heated.

*Heacock originally attributed *Honeycomb, Opalescent* to Hobbs, Brockunier & Co. In the Bredehoft's book, *Hobbs, Brockunier & Co., Glass Identification and Value*

Guide, there is no mention of this pattern. It is possible that someone else made this pattern. In *Book 9*, Heacock attributed *Honeycomb* to Hobbs, Phoenix and Northwood at Indiana, PA. This pattern is not mentioned in *Harry Northwood, The Early Years* or *The Wheeling Years*. In *Dugan/Diamond, The Story of Indiana, Pennsylvania Glass* a *Honeycomb* rose bowl is shown, but no reference is made as to production of other shapes. Maybe Dugan did make this pattern, but it is only a guess. Hopefully, a catalog showing this interesting *Honeycomb* pattern will turn up so we will finally know who made it. I purchased a *Honeycomb* water set while traveling in England in 1988; perhaps the original manufacturer was English. Figure 1126 (pitcher) is an unusual grayed–blue shading down to a rich amber color with a polished pontil.

See the following pictures.

Rare green *Opalescent Honeycomb* oil lamp, possibly English. The fount fits inside a hollowed vase base.

Honeycomb. Unusual two-part oil lamp in green opalescent.

HORSE CHESTNUT

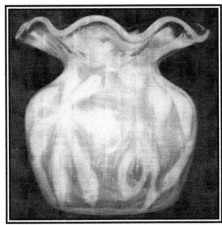

Horse Chestnut yellow opalescent vase.

Maker: Richardsons of Wordsley, England. Moulds were sold to Thomas Webb and Sons at Stourbridge around 1936.
Named by: Uncertain
Y.O.P. Circa 1916
Other name: None
Colors made: Yellow opalescent; others are likely.
Pieces made: Vases
Reintroductions/Repros: None known at this time.
Note: This pattern is similar to *Poinsettia*. Do not confuse the two.

IDYLL

(See figs. 149, 199, 378, 552)
Maker: Jefferson Glass Co., Follansbee, W.Va.
Named by: Hartung, *Opalescent*
Y.O.P. Circa 1907
Other name: Jefferson #251 (Kamm 7)
Colors made: White, blue, and green opalescent, crystal, apple green and blue. Sometimes decorated with gold.
Pieces made: Water set, table set, berry set, toothpick, cruet, salt shaker (these last three were sometimes grouped in a set on a tray); berry sauces were made in both 4" and 6" diameters.
Reintroduction or Repros: None known at this time.
Notes: Take care not to confuse this *Idyll* pattern with a Carnival pattern vase which Hartung inadvertently gave the same name.

INSIDE RIBBING

(See fig. 1253)
Maker: Beaumont Glass Co., Martins Ferry, OH.
Named by: Uncertain
Y.O.P. Circa 1899
Other name: None
Colors made: Vaseline opalescent; others are likely.
Pieces made: Miniature creamer; others are likely.
Reintroductions/Repros: None known at this time.

Note: Heacock was very tentative about this name and attribution in *Collecting Glass, Volume 2,* where he first pictured this tiny little creamer. Therefore, this information is doubtful.

INTAGLIO

(See figs. 45-49, 51-52, 134, 216, 1290)
Maker: The Northwood Co., and Dugan Glass Co., Indiana, PA.
Named by: Original manufacturer's name
Y.O.P. Circa 1898
Other name: Flower Spray & Scrolls
Colors made: White, blue, and canary opalescent; emerald green with gold; custard glass with blue or green decoration.
Pieces made: Tumbler, pitcher, butter dish, spooner, sugar, creamer, berry set (look like compotes), cruet, salt shakers, jelly compote, assorted novelty shapes.
Reintroduction or Repros: None known at this time. See catalog reprints in the *Button Panels, Old Man Winter,* and *Opaline Brocade* sections.

INVERTED FAN AND FEATHER

(See figs. 39-44, 606)

Inverted Fan and Feather sets from a 1909 Butler Brothers catalog. Note that these were available only in emerald green and opalescent blue. The other opalescent colors and pink slag were made in 1900–1901.

Maker: The Northwood Co., National Glass Co. and Dugan/Diamond Glass Co., Indiana, PA.
Named by: Warman's Milk Glass Addenda
Y.O.P. Circa 1899–1906
Other name: Fan and Feather
Colors made: Flint, green, blue, and canary opalescent, custard, green with gold and pink slag.
Pieces made: Table set, water set, berry set, rose bowl; rare in cruet, salt shaker, jelly compote, punch bowl, cups, toothpick, and novelties such as: ladies spittoon and pulled vases.
Reintroduction or Repros: Yes. In 1965 the St. Clair Glass Works, Inc. of Elwood, IN., produced toothpicks

in amberina, custard, pink slag and the Carnival colors of cobalt, ice blue, marigold and white.

In 1985, the Summit Art Glass Co. of Rootstown, OH., produced a toothpick, covered sugar, salt shaker and tumbler in decorated custard and contemporary colors. There is some question if the tumbler was ever actually produced, but it was shown in their catalog.

Notes: This pattern was designed by Mr. Northwood himself around 1900. Reportedly, *Inverted Fan & Feather* was featured at the Pan American Exposition in Buffalo, NY, in 1902.

Occasionally, salt shakers are found with Northwood's signature in block letters. The name is usually indistinguishable, as the letters are all backwards (a mould maker's error?) and often only a few letters are readable. The novelties in this pattern are not reproductions. They are circa 1910–1920. See catalog reprint in the *Buckeye* section.

IRIS (IRIS WITH MEANDER)
(See figs. 139, 155, 224-225)
Maker: Jefferson Glass Co., Steubenville, OH.
Named by: Kamm 6
Y.O.P. Circa 1903
Other name: Iris with Meander, Fleur–de–Lis and pattern #197.
Colors made: Flint, blue, canary, and green opalescent; rare in amber opalescent, crystal, blue, apple green and amethyst with gold.
Pieces made: Table set, water set, berry set (two sizes of sauces), toothpick, salt shaker, cruet, jelly compote, tall vase, pickle dish and plate.
Reintroduction or Repros: None known at this time.
Notes: The amber opalescent was experimental. The green opalescent is rare in anything except the toothpick and berry set. The stopper is not original. See the catalog reprint on the following page, showing the original name as *Iris*.

JACKSON
(See figs. 104, 230, 404, 571)
Maker: The Northwood Co., with continued production by Dugan Glass Co., Indiana, PA.
Named by: Uncertain
Y.O.P. Circa 1898
Other name: Fluted Scrolls with Flower Band and Klondyke.
Colors made: White, blue, and canary opalescent; custard glass; novelties in green opalescent. Also amethyst Carnival.
Pieces made: Table set, water set, berry set, cruet, mini epergne, candy dish and salt shaker.
Reintroduction or Repros: None known at this time.
Notes: This pattern is exactly the same as *Klondyke,* with a band of embossed flowers added to the plain space between the "ringed" areas. These flowers are sometimes "gold" decorated. The dictionary meaning of *embossed* is:

"to decorate or cover with designs, patterns, etc., raised above the surface."

See the black and white picture below which shows the embossed flowers somewhat more clearly than the color photos.

Jackson rose bowl in very rare amethyst Carnival. It is the only one known.

JACQUELINE
(See figs. 1069–1071)
Maker: Fenton Art Glass Co., Williamstown, W.Va.
Named by: Fenton named this pattern in honor of Mrs. John F. (Jacqueline) Kennedy.
Y.O.P. Circa 1961, and again in 1993 and 1994
Colors: Wild rose, powder blue, apple green, yellow, blue and pink opaline, ruby. Others are probable. Cranberry opalescent was not made until 1993 and 1994. These pieces were made for the FAGCA and are so marked.
Pieces made: Vases, pitcher, creamer and sugar, salt and pepper.

JEFFERSON SPOOL
(See fig. 535)
Maker: Jefferson Glass Co., Steubenville, OH
Named by: Heacock
Y.O.P. Circa 1905
Other name: None
Colors made: White, blue, green, and canary opalescent.
Pieces made: Novelties
Reintroduction or Repros: None know at this time.

JEFFERSON WHEEL
(See fig. 403)
Maker: Jefferson Glass Co., Steubenville, OH
Named by: Hartung, *Opalescent*
Y.O.P. Circa 1905–1908
Other name: Jefferson pattern #260 and Wheel and Gate
Colors made: White, blue, and green opalescent.
Pieces made: Bowls
Reintroduction or Repros: None known at this time.

JERSEY SWIRL
(See fig. 593)
Maker: Unknown, for L.G. Wright Glass Co., New Martinsville, W.Va.*

IRIS

PLAIN ♦ COLORED ♦ OPALESCENT

The Jefferson Glass Co.
Geo. Mortimer, Vice-Pres.
G. Grant Fish, Treas. & Gen'l Mgr.
Steubenville, Ohio
See our display Pittsburg, Pa., Monongahela House, Geo. Mortimer

An assortment of the *Iris* pattern (*Iris with Meander*).

Named by: Original name
Y.O.P. Circa 1956 to 1990s
Other name: Pattern No. 35, Windsor Swirl, and Swirl.
Colors made: Amber, amethyst, amberina, blue, blue opalescent, crystal, green, green satin, ruby, vaseline and vaseline opalescent.
Pieces made: Compote (four styles), goblet, plate, (two sizes), salt dip (two sizes), sauce dish, and wine.
Reintroduction or Repros: This is a reintroduction.
Notes: *L.G. Wright had many companies make their glass at various times during their history. This makes it almost impossible to tell who made what, when. My best guess is Westmoreland or Imperial.

JEWEL AND FAN
(See fig. 431)
Maker: Jefferson Glass Co., Steubenville, OH.
Named by: Heacock
Y.O.P. Circa 1904
Other name: Jefferson pattern #125
Colors made: White, blue and green opalescent; rare in canary.
Pieces made: Bowls
Reintroduction or Repros: None known at this time.

JEWEL AND FLOWER (SEE ENCORE)

JEWELLED HEART (SEE VICTOR)

JEWELS AND DRAPERY
(See figs. 444, 527)
Maker: H. Northwood Co., Wheeling, W.Va.
Named by: Heacock
Y.O.P. Circa 1907
Other name: None
Colors made: White, blue, green, and aqua opalescent.
Pieces made: Bowls and vases.
Reintroduction or Repros: None known at this time.

JOLLY BEAR
(See fig. 484)
Maker: Jefferson Glass Co., Steubenville, OH., and H. Northwood Co., Wheeling, W.Va.
Named by: Presznick 3
Y.O.P. Circa 1908
Other name: None
Colors made: White, blue, and green opalescent.
Pieces made: Bowl, water set, and plate.
Reintroduction or Repros: None known at this time.
Notes: The water set with the "dancing" group of bears was made only in Carnival glass and is extremely rare. Rare in a plate.

KEYHOLE
(See fig. 426)
Maker: Dugan Glass Co., Indiana, PA.
Named by: Heacock
Y.O.P. Circa 1904
Other name: None
Colors made: White, blue, and green opalescent; Carnival colors of marigold, purple, and peach opalescent.
Pieces made: Bowls
Reintroduction or Repros: None known at this time.
Notes: In Carnival glass *Keyhole* is used as an exterior pattern with *Raindrops* being the interior.
See catalog reprint in the *Corn Vase* pattern section.

KISMET
(See figs. 1268–1270, 1274, 1275)
Maker: Model Flint Glass Co., Albany, IN.
Named by: McKee
Y.O.P. Circa 1895–1902
Other name: Broken Pillar and Reed and No. 909.
Colors made: Crystal, amber, blue, green, gold flash and Maiden's Blush; white, canary and blue opalescent.
Pieces made: Bonbon, bowl, butter dish, salver, celery vase, celery tray, cologne, compote, creamer, custard cup, soap dish, footed jelly, oil bottle, pitcher (two sizes), plate, salt shaker, spooner, sugar bowl, syrup, toothpick, tray, tumbler and vase (four sizes).
Reintroductions/Repros: None known at this time.

KLONDYKE (FLUTED SCROLL)
(See figs. 102–3, 105–10, 231)
Maker: The Northwood Co., and Dugan Glass Co., Indiana PA.
Named by: Original manufacturer's name
Y.O.P. From 1898 to 1900s
Other name: Fluted Scroll, Kamm 2
Colors made: Blue, white, amber and canary opalescent, custard; also made in crystal; rare in green opalescent.
Pieces made: Table set, water set, berry set, cruet, salt shaker, a tiny two piece epergne, round covered jewel or puff tray (sometimes called a quarter-pound butter dish), assorted ruffled-edge novelties in bowls, and card receivers.
Reintroduction or Repros: Yes. A master berry bowl in cobalt blue by Boyd's Crystal Art Glass, Cambridge, OH. Pieces are usually marked with a "B" in a diamond trademark.
Notes: The salt shakers and tumblers in *Klondyke* are the same as those used with the *Alaska* pattern. There is a distinct enamel decoration used on both of these patterns and this is the only characteristic which will tell these pieces apart. If it has an enameled band of daisies, it is *Klondyke*. If it has a band of tiny Forget-Me-Nots with ivy leaves, then it is *Alaska*. All salt shakers and tumblers in emerald green belong to the *Alaska* pattern, as *Klondyke*

was not made to any degree in that color. A "sister" pattern was made, named *Jackson*. See text for *Jackson*.

Heacock originally called this pattern *Fluted Scrolls*. In his series *The Glass Collector, Collecting Glass*, he began advising the reader of the original manufacturer's names. Heacock believed original factory names should be used when known. The original factory name is used in *Harry Northwood, The Early Years, 1881–1900*. Thus, the name change for this edition. See catalog reprint in the *Dolphin Petticoat*, and *Button Panels* sections.

LADY CAROLINE

Lady Caroline pattern

Maker: Uncertain, but most likely English.
Named by: Heacock
Y.O.P. Circa 1991
Other name: None
Colors made: Blue and yellow opalescent
Pieces made: Breakfast and individual–size creamer and sugar (sometimes with a crimped top), baskets and novelties.
Reintroduction or Repros: None known at this time.
Note: No large table items of any type are known; no Rd number has been reported.

LADY CHIPPENDALE
(See figs. 549, 1293)

Maker: George Davidson & Co., Gateshead-on-Tyne, England.

Davidson trademark.

Named by: Heacock
Y.O.P. Circa 1990. Sometimes marked with the Rd #176566
Other name: Chippendale
Colors made: Blue and yellow opalescent.
Pieces made: Table set, compote, basket, and novelties
Reintroduction or Repros: Yes—by Fenton Art Glass Co., Williamstown, W.Va. It was produced from 1965–72 in their *Colonial* colors of blue, pink, amber, green, and orange. Unfortunately, no Fenton name is listed but it was their pattern No. 1939.

LATTICE (BUBBLE LATTICE & OPAL)
(See figs. 293, 341, 342, 349, 365, 366, 382, 640, 742, 744, 745, 747, 750–753, 758–760, 847, 878, 891, 906, 1022, 1030, 1031, 1041)

Maker: Buckeye Glass Co., Martins Ferry, OH., Northwood Glass Co., Martins Ferry, OH., Northwood Glass Co., Ellwood City, PA., Northwood Co., Indiana PA., and possibly continued production by National Glass Co. and Dugan Glass Co., Indiana, PA.
Named by: Heacock
Y.O.P. Circa 1889
Other name: Plaid (Hartung), and Bubble Lattice (Peterson), Diamond Optic and Quilted Opal.
Colors made: White, blue, cranberry, rubina and canary opalescent, sometimes with a satin finish.
Pieces made: Pitcher (three shapes), tumbler, berry set, butter dish, covered sugar, creamer, spooner, finger bowl, celery vase, cruets (four shapes), sugar shaker (two shapes), syrup, toothpick, finger bowl, salt shakers, bride's basket, lamp shades and bowls.
Reintroduction or Repros: Yes, by Fenton Art Glass Co. and for L.G. Wright Glass Co., circa the 1950s through the 1990s. Fenton calls this pattern *Diamond Optic* and L.G. Wright calls it *Quilted Opal*. Pieces made: tumbler, finger bowl, vases, ivy ball and cruet in cranberry, emerald green, and blue. Other pieces and colors are probable, as Fenton may reintroduce a pattern or color at any time. Any piece in Fenton's line after 1972 will be marked.
Notes: Heacock attributed this pattern to Hobbs, Brockunier & Co. In their book, *Hobbs, Brockunier & Co., Glass Identification and Value Guide*, the Bredehoft's made no mention of *Lattice*, so this attribution is questionable.

The following journal quote makes a case for the fact that Northwood did make this pattern: "Capt. S.C. Dunlevy has a beautiful exhibit of the goods manufactured by the Northwood Glass Co., of Martins Ferry, at the Monongahela House. They are chiefly blown lead goods and comprise tableware, water sets, flower holders, molasses cans, shades, gas globes, water bottles, finger bowls, hall globes, tumblers, casters, oil bottles, salt, pepper and oil cruets, and a general line of fancy glassware. The colors are most exquisite and include effects in satin finish, diamond, rib, spot, etc. This company's works are now in operation." (*Pottery and Glassware Reporter*, February 9, 1888)

Heacock also mentioned Phoenix Glass Co., Monaca, PA., and La Belle Glass Co., Bridgeport, OH., as other possible manufacturers.

Figure 760 is made in the *Ribbed Pillar* mould and figure 758 is in the *Quilted Phlox* mould, both known Northwood shapes. See text for *Diamond Optic*.

LATTICE AND DAISY

Maker: Dugan Glass Co., Indiana, PA.
Named by: Uncertain
Y.O.P. Circa 1916
Other name: None
Colors made: White and blue opalescent; Carnival colors of marigold, blue and purple.
Pieces made: Water set and berry set.
Reintroductions/Repros: None known at this time
See catalog reprint below.

LATTICE MEDALLIONS

(See fig. 465)
Maker: H. Northwood Co., Wheeling, W.Va.
Named by: Hartung, *Opalescent*
Y.O.P. Circa 1907
Other name: None
Colors made: White, blue, and green opalescent.
Pieces made: Bowls
Reintroduction or Repros: None known at this time.
Note: Occasionally some pieces will be signed.

LAURA

(See fig. 481)
Maker: Dugan/Diamond Glass Co., Indiana, PA.
Named by: Rose Presznick
Y.O.P. Circa 1910
Other name: Single Flower Framed
Colors made: White and blue opalescent; also Carnival.
Pieces made: Bowls
Reintroduction or Repros: None known at this time.

LEAF AND BEADS

(See fig. 498)
Maker: H. Northwood Co., Wheeling, W.Va.
Named by: Hartung, *Opalescent*
Y.O.P. Circa 1906–1908
Other name: None
Colors made: White, blue, and green opalescent; custard glass and Carnival colors of aqua opalescent, green, blue and purple/amethyst.

Dugan Glass Co., Indiana, PA.,opalescent assortment. Butler Brothers, 1916 catalog. 1. *Lattice & Daisy* 2. *Stork and Rushes* 3. *New York (Beaded Shell)* 4. *National (S–Repeat)* 5. *??* 6. *Windflower* 7. *Erie with Holly* 8. *Fishscale & Beads* 9. *Mary Ann* 10. *Fishscale & Beads*.

Pieces made: Bowls

Reintroduction or Repros: None known at this time.

Notes: The rose bowls in this pattern were made with two different bases. One had three open branch–like feet, as shown in figure 498, and one had a short pedestal base. When made in Carnival colors, *Leaf and Beads* was used as an exterior pattern with a plain interior or with the patterns *Stippled Rays*, *Fine Ribs* or *Floral Ribs*. The edge of the bowl may have 30 points, 15 rounded scallops (most often seen), or just eight gentle scallops. Some pieces will be signed with the "N" in a circle trademark.

LEAF AND DIAMONDS
(See fig. 487)

Maker: H. Northwood Co., Wheeling, W.Va.
Named by: Hartung, *Opalescent*
Y.O.P. Circa 1906
Other name: None
Colors made: White and blue opalescent; scarce in green opalescent; white sometimes goofus decorated.
Pieces made: Bowls
Reintroduction or Repros: None known at this time.

LEAF AND LEAFLETS
(See fig. 485)

Maker: H. Northwood Co., Wheeling, W.Va.
Named by: Heacock
Y.O.P. Circa 1908
Other name: None
Colors made: White, blue, and green opalescent. The white opalescent was frequently decorated with goofus.
Pieces made: Bowls
Reintroduction or Repros: None known at this time

LEAF CHALICE
(See fig. 397)

Maker: The Northwood Co., National Glass Co., and Dugan Glass Co., Indiana, PA.
Named by: Hartung, *Opalescent*
Y.O.P. Circa 1899–1904
Other name: None
Colors made: White, blue, canary. Rare in green opalescent and non–opalescent amethyst.
Pieces made: Novelties
Reintroduction or Repros: None known at this time.

LEAF MOLD
(See figs. 369, 648C)

Maker: Northwood Glass Co., Martins Ferry, OH.
Named by: Taylor
Y.O.P. Circa 1890
Other name: None
Colors made: Rare experimental color of cranberry stained and opalescent stripes; also made in cased *Vasa Murrhina* spatter (pink and white), canary with cranberry and white spatter (possibly called Yellowine, frosted and shiny), frosty camphor–like crystal, blue, cranberry and lime-green, deep cranberry and opaque colors of white, blue and pink.

Pieces made: Water set, table set, berry set, syrup, sugar shaker, celery vase, salt shakers, cruet, jam jar, toothpick holder, perfume bottle, rose bowl and fairy lamp.

Reintroduction or Repros: None known at this time.

Note: The *Leaf Mold* finial is the same as the finial found on the *Parian Swirl* pieces. The pitcher may have a crystal or colored handle.

LEAF TIERS (OVERLAPPING LEAVES)
(See fig. 437)

Two examples of *Leaf Tiers*.

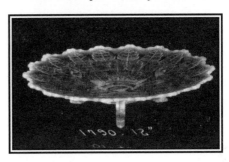

Maker: Fenton Art Glass Co., Williamstown, W.Va.
Named by: Uncertain
Y.O.P. Circa 1914 to present
Other name: Overlapping Leaves, Joe B. Bell and pattern No. 1790.
Colors made: White, blue and green opalescent, amethyst (c.1933); Carnival colors of marigold, green, blue and purple (c.1914); Mandarin red (c.1934); milk glass (c.1934); Persian Pearl stretch glass (c.1932); other colors are very likely.
Pieces made: Cake plate, spooner, butter dish, sugar, creamer, pitcher, tumbler, bowl (many shapes), berry set, lamp shade; other pieces are likely.
Reintroduction or Repros: Fenton may reintroduce a pattern or color at any time. If made after 1972, it should be marked with the Fenton logo.
Notes: The feet on this unusual cake platter are shown in the picture above. Fenton has called this pattern *Leaf Tiers* for years, thus the name change for this edition.

LIGHTERS

(See figs. 1145–1149)

Maker: Unknown, but the white opalescent lighters are marked "Made in France", "Depose", and the lighter inserts are marked "Evans". The blue and pink opalescent lighters are unmarked.

Y.O.P. Circa 1950s or 1960s

LINCOLN INN

(See fig. 1249)

Maker: Fenton Art Glass Co., Williamstown, W.Va.

Named by: Original manufacturer's name.

Y.O.P. Circa 1928

Other name: Pattern #1700

Colors made: Ruby, royal blue, crystal, rose, two shades of green, aquamarine. Rare colors of black, jade, orchid, amber, and green opalescent which was probably experimental.

Pieces made: Goblet, sherbet, wine, juice, footed tumbler, footed ice tea, pitcher, highball, tumbler, finger bowl/under plate, cup/saucer, salt/pepper, fruit saucer, creamer, sugar, bread/butter plate, 12" plate, 8" plate, oval compote, footed nut, footed mint, cereal bowl, olive dish, bonbons and compotes.

Reintroductions/Repros: Fenton may reintroduce a pattern/color at any time. The water set was reproduced in Carnival purple in 1982 for Levay Distributing Co. as a limited edition, and they produced it again in blue stretch for their 90th birthday.

Note: *Lincoln Inn* is a pressed copy of a blown crystal stemware set by Val-Saint-Lambert, Belgium. Some of the original design was found in the Fenton archives.

LINED HEART

(See fig. 530)

Maker: Jefferson Glass Co., Steubenville, OH.

Named by: Hartung, *Opalescent*

Y.O.P. Circa 1906–1908

Other name: None

Colors made: White, blue, and green opalescent.

Pieces made: Vases

Reintroduction or Repros: None known at this time.

Notes: The taller version of this pattern loses its heart–like characteristic, and is not as easily recognized when found.

LINKING RINGS

Maker: George Davidson & Co., Gateshead-on-Tyne, England.

Named by: Heacock

Y.O.P. Circa 1896 sometimes marked with Rd #237038

Other name: None

Colors made: Blue opalescent, others are probable.

Pieces made: Bowl, tumbler, and pitcher.

Reintroductions/Repros: None known at this time

Note: A long band of ribbing can be found above and below the "linking rings" on the pitcher.

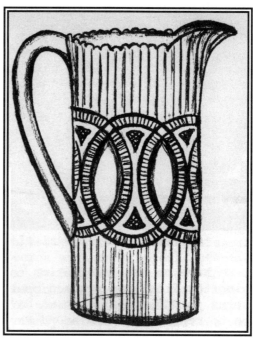

Linking Rings water pitcher.

LITTLE NELL

(See fig. 422)

Maker: Uncertain

Named by: Heacock

Y.O.P. Circa early 1900s

Other name: None

Colors made: White, blue, and green opalescent.

Pieces made: Vases

Reintroduction or Repros: None known at this time.

LORDS AND LADIES

Maker: George Davidson & Co., Gateshead-on-Tyne, England.

Named by: Heacock

Y.O.P. Circa 1896, sometimes marked with Rd #285342 or 285312.

Other name: None

Colors made: Yellow and blue opalescent; others are likely.

Pieces made: Quarter pound covered butter, open salt, and 3" high creamer, open sugar and creamer; others are probable.

Reintroductions/Repros: None known at this time.

Note: The butter dish is quite small by American standards. In *The Glass Collector*, No. 6, Heacock stated: "Dugan copied the design around 1905 in his *Reflecting Diamonds* novelty bowl, made at Indiana, PA."

See the following picture.

Lords & Ladies small covered butter.

LORNA
(See fig. 531)
Maker: Model Flint Glass Co., Findlay, OH., and Albany, IN; and The Northwood Co., and Dugan Class Co., Indiana, PA.
Named by: Heacock
Y.O.P. Circa 1896
Other name: None
Colors made: White, blue, and canary opalescent.
Pieces made: Vase
Reintroduction or Repros: None known at this time.
Notes: Shards of this vase have been dug up at the Albany plant site. See catalog reprint in *Dolphin Petticoat* section.

LUSTRE FLUTE
(See figs. 381, 632, 633)

Lustre Flute assortment (Fall, 1908 Butler Brothers catalog).

Maker: H. Northwood Co., Wheeling, W.Va.
Named by: Kamm 4
Y.O.P. Circa 1908
Other name: English Hob Band (Presznick 2) and Waffle Band)
Colors made: White, blue opalescent and Carnival colors; other opalescent colors would be rare. A small creamer and sugar are known in emerald green. Crystal and emerald green can be found with marigold iridescence.
Pieces made: Water set, berry set, table set, vases bonbon, crimped nappy and custard cups.
Reintroduction or Repros: None known at this time.
Note: Usually signed with the "N" in a circle.

MANILA (WREATH AND SHELL)
(See figs. 70-79, 83-87, 553, 648 E and G)
Maker: Model Flint Glass Co., Albany, IN.
Named by: Herrick
Y.O.P. Circa 1899–1903
Other name: Wreath and Shell, Shell and Wreath, and pattern No. 905
Colors made: White, blue, green and canary opalescent, sometimes decorated with flowers; crystal and crystal with gold, amber, teal and possibly opaque colors.
Pieces made: Water set, table set, berry set, celery vase, toothpick holder, rose bowl, ladies spittoon, cracker jar, salt dip and novelties.
Reintroduction or Repros: None known at this time.
Notes: See the catalog reprint on the following page.

MANY LOOPS
(See fig. 504)
Maker: Jefferson Glass Co., Steubenville, OH.
Named by: Hartung, *Opalescent*
Y.O.P. Circa 1908
Other name: Jefferson #247
Colors made: White, blue, and green opalescent.
Pieces made: Bowls
Reintroduction or Repros: None known at this time.

MANY RIBS
(See fig. 534)
Maker: Model Flint Glass Co., Albany IN.
Named by: Heacock
Y.O.P. Circa 1900
Other name: None
Colors made: White, canary and blue opalescent.
Pieces made: Vase
Reintroduction or Repros: None known at this time.
Note: Heights may vary as this is a swung vase.

MAPLE LEAF CHALICE
(See fig. 452)
Maker: H. Northwood Co., Wheeling, W.Va.
Named by: Heacock
Y.O.P. Circa 1903
Other name: None
Colors made: White, blue, green, and canary opalescent; purple slag.
Pieces made: Novelties
Reintroduction or Repros: None known at this time.
Notes: This pattern is constantly being confused for the *Leaf Chalice*, but they are obviously not the same, only vaguely similar.

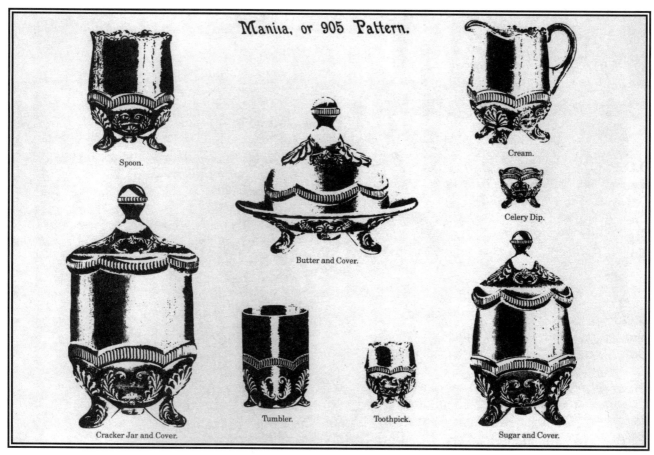

Manila pieces shown in the National Glass Co.'s 1899 Model Flint Glass Works Catalog. National featured this pattern by Model Flint's factory number, 905.

MAPLE LEAF, NORTHWOOD & DUGAN

(See figs. 211, 429, 645)

Maker: The Northwood Co., with continued production by Dugan/Diamond, Indiana, PA.

Named by: Kamm 5

Y.O.P. Circa 1898 and Dugan 1903

Other name: Diamond's Maple Leaf

Colors made: Opalescent white, blue and green (known only in jelly compote), emerald green, cobalt blue and custard sometimes with gold decorations. Carnival colors of amethyst, blue, purple and marigold by Dugan only.

Pieces made: Only the jelly compote has been reported in opalescent. The other colors were made in a water set, table set, berry set, salt shaker, cruet and toothpick.

Reintroduction or Repros: Yes—in 1972 by L.G. Wright Glass Co. of New Martinsville, W.Va. Pieces made: Creamer, covered sugar, butter dish, compote, tumbler, pitcher, spooner, toothpick and salver in crystal, cobalt and ruby, which sometimes struck as amberina. In 1974, five pieces were made in Carnival glass. In 1984, all nine pieces were made in green opalescent; several pieces were made in cobalt and ruby, which sometimes struck as amberina. These nine items were reportedly made from the original moulds. Wright also produced, from a new mould, a goblet in amber, blue, crystal (plain and frosted), green and amethyst.

Note: The berry set pieces are quite often called compotes because they are on footed stems. See catalog reprint in the *New York* section.

MARY ANN

(See fig. 1130 and catalog reprint with *Lattice and Daisy*)

Maker: Dugan Glass Co., Indiana, PA.

Named by: Uncertain

Y.O.P. Circa 1916

Other name: None

Colors made: White and blue opalescent, amber, and Carnival colors of marigold, amethyst and purple.

Pieces made: Vase only

Reintroductions/Repros: None known at this time.

Note: This nicely designed vase was named after the sister of Thomas and Alfred Dugan. Her full name was Fanny Mary Ann Dugan. She was born September 23, 1873, in England and died July 16, 1951. See the pictures on the following page.

Both of these *Mary Ann* vases in marigold Carnival glass were made at the Dugan plant; the one on the left has ten scallops on its top rim, while the other has eight.

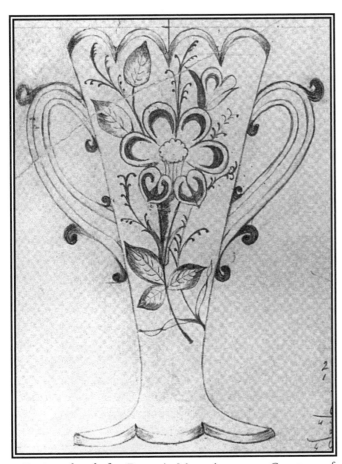

Design sketch for Dugan's *Mary Ann* vase. Courtesy of Steve Jennings.

MAY BASKET
Maker: Jefferson Glass Co., Follansbee, W.Va.
Named by: Heacock
Y.O.P. Circa 1906
Other name: Pattern No. 87
Colors made: White, blue, and green opalescent.
Pieces made: Basket
Reintroductions/Repros: None known at this time. See the following picture.

Jefferson's opalescent *May Basket*.

MEANDER
(See fig. 501)
Maker: Jefferson Glass Co., Steubenville, OH., and H. Northwood Co., Wheeling, W.Va.
Named by: Hartung, *Opalescent*
Y.O.P. Jefferson uncertain; Northwood circa 1908
Other name: Jefferson pattern #233
Colors made: White, blue, and green opalescent; Northwood Carnival colors of marigold, blue, purple, green, and ice blue.
Pieces made: Bowls
Reintroduction or Repros: None known at this time.
Notes: Moulds were mysteriously transferred to Northwood around 1908, as was the pattern used in Carnival production. Pieces made by Northwood are quite often marked with the "N" in a circle.

MELON WITH SPRIG (PANELED SPRIG)
(See figs. 557, 1256)
Maker: Northwood Glass Co., Martins Ferry, OH., Northwood Co., and Dugan Glass Co., Indiana, PA.
Named by: Original manufacturer's name was just Melon. The words "with Sprig" have been added to avoid confusion with all the other patterns named "Melon".
Y.O.P. Circa 1892; later by Dugan
Other name: Paneled Sprig and Vine
Colors made: Known only in white opalescent; colored

opalescent would be very rare. Plain colors, without the lattice design, were made in cranberry, apple green, amethyst, blue, crystal, milk glass and Rubina. Rare with a speckled finish.

Pieces made: Opalescent version known only in cruet, toothpick and salt shakers; cranberry and Rubina made in a water set, table set, berry set, cruet, sugar shaker, salt shaker, and syrup jug. The other colors are only known in the "seasoning service".

Reintroduction or Repros: Yes—by Fenton Art Glass Co., Williamstown, W.Va., for L.G. Wright Glass Co., New Martinsville, W.VA. Pieces made: cruets and salt shakers in cranberry, peach blow, blue (light and dark) overlay, amber overlay, rose and amethyst overlay. Wright called this pattern *Vine*.

Note: Heacock called this pattern *Paneled Sprig*. He believed original manufacturer's names should be used when known. In *Harry Northwood, The Early Years, 1881–1900*, an advertisement reprint shows that this pattern was named *Melon*. Thus, the name change for this edition. This ad also calls a sugar shaker a "sugar duster". See ad reprint below.

SUGAR DUSTERS

The finest we can buy. For powdered sugar. Ornamental, useful and economical articles, for which there is now a steady demand.

MELON.   ACORN.

"Melon" Sugar Duster—Here is something to retail at popular prices. Opal glass, handsomely embossed and decorated in green and gold. A graceful shape standing 4½ inches high. Metal tops. 1 doz. in box. Price........ per doz., $1 25

Acorn Sugar Duster—A new, low square design in opal glass with fancy embossed surface and rich decorations in colors and gold on all four sides. Metal tops. Height, 4 inches. 1 doz. in box.
Price .. ..per doz., $1 25

Melon With Sprig pattern.

MIKADO, NORTHWOOD (BLOOMS AND BLOSSOMS)

(See fig. 520)

Maker: H. Northwood Co., Wheeling, W.Va.
Named by: Original manufacturer's name
Y.O.P. Circa 1905
Other name: Blooms & Blossoms, Heacock; Flower and Bud, Petterson.
Colors made: Green, white, and blue opalescent. Color stained crystal pieces were decorated with ruby stain and gold—each of the flowers was carefully shaded with red, yellow-green, and either blue or light purple. A few pieces, such as a handled nappy, have been seen in blue. Emerald green is another possibility.
Pieces made: Novelties in opalescent. Table set, berry set, salt shaker, cruet, and olive dish were made in the decorated crystal.
Reintroduction or Repros: None known at this time.
Notes: Sometimes signed with an "N" in a circle. Heacock initially called this pattern *Blooms & Blossoms*. In his series *The Glass Collector, Collecting Glass*, he began advising the reader of the original manufacturer's names. Heacock believed original factory names should be used when known. The original factory name was used in *Harry Northwood, The Wheeling Years, 1901–1925*. Thus, the name change for this edition. The word "Northwood" should be included to avoid confusion with a U.S. Glass pattern with the same name.

MILKY WAY (SEE COUNTRY KITCHEN)

MINIATURE EPERGNE

(See fig. 468)

Maker: Uncertain
Named by: Heacock
Y.O.P. Uncertain
Other name: None
Colors made: Blue and canary opalescent.
Reintroduction or Repros: None known at this time.

MINIATURES BY FENTON

(See figs. 1174–1185, 1254)

Maker: Fenton Art Glass Co., Williamstown, W.Va.
Named by: Elmore
Y.O.P. Circa 1942—present
Other name: Pattern 37
Colors made: The early colors were white, blue, and topaz opalescent, aqua crest, gold crest, and crystal crest.

In 1981, Fenton made a basket, hand vase, and 2" toothpick holder in purple stretch.

In 1984, Fenton made vases (two 4" styles and two 2" styles) in Velva Rose stretch glass for Levay Distributing Co.

In 1984 and 1985, Fenton made baskets for Zeta Todd in plum opalescent, ruby snowcrest, cobalt w/crystal crest, and black w/transparent peach colored crest. In 1986, they made flame crest.

The National Fenton Glass Society (NFGS) has had Fenton produce baskets and vases to help support their building fund in the following colors:

Baskets, 1995—Burmese, iridized ruby, spruce green, and cobalt iridized.

1996—Blue Burmese, satin Burmese, iridized Carnival, mulberry blue iridized, and accidental orange. The orange resulted from an attempt to reproduce Mandarin red—the batch turned out to be a translucent orange.

1997—Satin Blue Burmese, Mandarin red, cobalt blue, milk glass slag. Vases: Honey gold and Stiegal green.

1998—Ruby (heart crimp) and black (flared).

Pieces made: Creamer, basket and vase (round, square, tulip, ruffled and oval).

Reintroductions/Repros: Fenton may reintroduce a pattern or color at any time.

MOON AND STAR

(See figs. 588, 611)

Maker: Unknown, for L.G. Wright Glass Co., New Martinsville, W.Va., plus many more discussed below.

Named by: Original name

Y.O.P. Circa 1938–1990s

Other name: Based upon the 1880s pattern, Palace.

Colors made: Amber, blue (and satin), crystal, green (and satin), milk glass, pink (and satin), amethyst, amberina, and ruby (and satin), vaseline (and satin) and vaseline opalescent; possibly others.

Pieces made: Spooner, creamer, covered sugar, covered stemmed jelly, covered butter, covered compote (four sizes), wine, decanter, salt/pepper, sugar shaker, relish (three sizes), nappy, juice glass, tumbler, ice tea, console set, pitcher, salver, toothpick and lamps, etc. There are more than 50 different items.

Reintroduction or Repros: The items shown are reintroductions.

Notes: L.G. Wright had many companies make their glass at various times of their history, making it virtually impossible to tell who made what, when. Best guess: Westmoreland, Imperial or Indiana Glass.

Other Companies: In the 1960s the L. E. Smith Glass Co., Mount Pleasant, PA., made at least 100 different pieces in amber, amethyst Carnival, amberina, blue, blue opalescent, brown, crystal, cranberry rose opalescent, green, mint green opalescent and ruby.

In the late 1980s to the early 1990s, Weishar Enterprises, Wheeling, W.Va., produced a miniature banana stand, bowl, candleholder, pitcher, plate and tumbler in crystal, crystal Carnival, cobalt, cobalt Carnival, pink, and pink Carnival. Other companies probably produced this pattern also.

NAILSEA TYPE*

(See figs. 1035, 1036, 1110, 1117, 1119)

Maker: See notes

Named by: Popular name

Y.O.P. Circa 1880s

Other name: See notes.

Colors made: Cranberry and white opalescent. See notes.

Pieces made: See notes.

Notes: *Nailsea is really a misnomer in that it is not the name of a pattern of glass, but the name of a glass factory and an area in Somerset, England.

There were several factories in this area, such as the Nailsea Glass House, and a factory in Rockwardine. The name Nailsea, or a better term "Nailsea type", glassware includes three types: flecked glassware, festooned glassware, and colored (pale green) or clear glassware with simple white filigrana decoration. Some items made were: fairy lamps, flasks, witches balls, walking sticks, rolling pins, pole–heads etc. As you can see, the word "Nailsea" covers a broad spectrum of glassware—not just stunning fairy lamps.

NATIONAL (S—REPEAT)

(See figs. 67, 132, 1236)

Maker: National Glass Co., with continued production by Dugan Glass Co., Indiana, PA.

Named by: Original manufacturer's name.

Y.O.P. Circa 1903 to 1910

Other name: S-Repeat and Sea Foam, Hartung 3

Colors made: Opalescent blue, green, and white (limited); crystal, apple green, blue and amethyst—sometimes gold decorated. A few pieces were made in Carnival colors of white, marigold, and purple.

Pieces made: Table set, water set, berry set, toothpick, cruet set, wine decanter, wine glass, celery vase (only the first three sets are known in opalescent), salt shaker, cruet set on tray, punch bowl, cups, jam jar, and compote.

Reintroduction or Repros: Yes, but none in opalescent. L.G. Wright Glass Co. reproduced National (S-Repeat) in milk glass, amethyst, green, blue, ruby, crystal and amber. Wright called this pattern the "S" pattern. Pieces made: Cruet, goblet, plate, sherbet, toothpick, wine, plate and cup.

In 1974 and 1978, Kanawha Glass Co. of Kanawha, W.Va., produced a toothpick in crystal, amber, azure, and milk glass. In 1985, the Summit Art Glass Co. of Akron, OH., also produced a toothpick in amberina, blue–green, chocolate, coral iridized, cobalt blue, evergreen, first frost, morning glory and rubina.

Notes: Heacock originally called this pattern S–Repeat. In his series The Glass Collector, Collecting Glass, he began advising the reader of the original manufacturer's names. Heacock believed original factory names should be used when known. The original name is used in *Dugan/Diamond The Story of Indiana, Pennsylvania, Glass.* Thus, the name change for this edition. See catalog reprint in the *Erie* (which shows the original name) and *Lattice and Daisy* sections. See reprints below.

National (S–Repeat) water sets from a May, 1903, Butler Brothers catalog. (Note: "amethyst or wine ruby" refer to the same color, not different colors.)

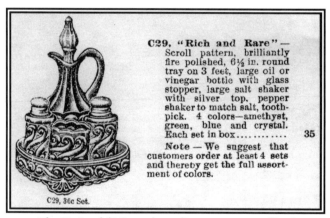

The *National (S–Repeat)* condiment sets were offered in four colors in this 1907 Butler Brothers catalog.

NAUTILUS (ARGONAUT SHELL)
(See figs. 136, 144, 154, 619*, 627)
Maker: The Northwood Co., and Dugan Glass Co., Indiana, PA.
Named by: Original manufacturer's name
Y.O.P. Circa 1898 to 1910
Other name: Argonaut Shell, Kamm 4
Colors: Blue and white opalescent, novelties in canary opalescent, custard, Carnival colors of marigold, purple and peach opalescent.
Pieces made: Water set, table set, berry set, cruet, salt and pepper, novelty dishes, toothpick (only in custard), jelly compote.
Reintroduction or Repros: Yes. *Figure 619 is a rein-

troduction. The L.G. Wright Glass Co., had produced a tumbler, berry set, toothpick, salt and pepper, jelly compote, butter, creamer and sugar in blue opalescent, custard, chocolate and crystal. Wright called this pattern *Argonaut.* The crystal and opalescent toothpicks found today are all Wright reproductions, circa 1970 or later.

L.G. Wright had many glass companies produce their glass at various times throughout their history, making it virtually impossible to tell who made what, when. Best guess: Fenton, Paden City, Westmoreland or Imperial.

Westmoreland Glass Co., Grapeville, PA., produced chocolate glass for Wright in the 1980s. There were seven pieces of *Argonaut Shell* (covered sugar bowl, creamer, stemmed jelly, plus four more), flat iron, hen on nest, stove, large covered turtle, three wheel cart, hoot owl relish and covered rabbit. Many of these pieces were also made in green. These pieces were sometimes signed with an underlined, oddly shaped "W" within a circle.
Notes: Heacock originally called this pattern *Argonaut Shell.* In his series *The Glass Collector, Collecting Glass,* he began advising the reader of the original manufacturer's names. Heacock believed original factory names should be used when known. The original name was used in *Harry Northwood, The Early Years, 1881–1900.* Thus, the name change for this edition. Script Northwood signature was sometimes used. See catalog reprint in the *Buckeye* section.

NETTED ROSES
(See fig. 419)
Maker: H. Northwood Co., Wheeling W.Va.
Named by: Hartung, *Opalescent*
Y.O.P. Circa 1906
Other name: None
Colors made: Blue and white opalescent, sometimes goofus decorated.
Pieces made: Bowls
Reintroduction or Repros: None known at this time.
Note: Occasionally pieces will be signed.

NEW YORK (SHELL)
(See figs. 145, 193, 208, 558)

"Etruscan" assortment from a Butler Brothers catalog. 1. *Wreathed Cherry* 2. *Grapevine Lattice* 3. ? 4. *Maple Leaf* 5. *Vining Twigs* 6. and 7. *New York (Shell)* 8. ? 9. *Fisherman* mug 10. ?

Maker: Dugan Glass Co., Indiana, PA.
Named by: Kamm 7
Y.O.P. Circa 1903
Other name: Shell, Kamm 7; Beaded Shell.
Colors made: White, green and blue opalescent, crystal, apple green, electric blue, canary yellow and Carnival colors of amethyst, blue, marigold, purple and pearl.
Pieces made: Table set, water set, berry set, cruet, toothpick, salt shakers, compote, cruet set on tray, and mug. The tray is *National/S–Repeat.*
Reintroduction or Repros: Yes—by Moser, Cambridge, OH.
Notes: Heacock originally called this pattern *Shell.* In his series *The Glass Collector, Collecting Glass,* he began advising the reader of the original manufacturer's names. Heacock believed original factory names should be used when known. The original factory name was used in *Dugan/Diamond, The Story of Indiana Glass.* Thus, the name change for this edition. Only the Carnival pieces will be signed.
See catalog reprint in the *Lattice and Daisy* section.

NORTHERN STAR
(See fig. 508)
Maker: Fenton Art Glass Co., Williamstown, W.Va.
Named by: Hartung, *Carnival*
Y.O.P. Circa 1910
Other name: None
Colors made: White, blue, and green opalescent; marigold Carnival glass.
Pieces made: Bowls, chop plate, and card tray.
Reintroduction or Repros: None known at this time. However, Fenton may reintroduce a pattern or color at any time. If made after 1972, the piece should be marked with the Fenton logo.
Notes: The large chop plate illustrated is a flattened out mould for a master berry bowl; the berry bowl is found more frequently in this pattern.

OCEAN SHELL
(See fig. 395)
Maker: H. Northwood Co., Wheeling, W.Va.
Named by: Hartung, *Opalescent*
Y.O.P. Circa 1903
Other name: None
Colors made: White, blue, and green opalescent; purple slag (originally called "mosaic" glass).
Pieces made: Novelties
Reintroduction or Repros: None known at this time.

OLD MAN WINTER
(See fig. 210)
Maker: Jefferson Glass Co., Steubenville, OH.
Named by: Heacock
Y.O.P. Circa 1906–1908
Other name: Jefferson—patterns #135 and #91*

Colors made: White and blue opalescent.
Pieces made: Small baskets—#135 with no feet and large basket #91, footed.
Reintroduction or Repros: None known at this time.
Notes: Heacock named this pattern *Old Man Winter* due to its resemblance to an iceberg illustrating the main features of a man's face, and also because the production date coincides with Byrd's discovery of the North Pole. The baskets usually have a patent date embossed under the rim of the base. See the catalog reprint on the following page.

OPALINE BROCADE (SPANISH LACE)
(See figs. 270, 271, 303, 317–319, 343, 354, 392, 569, 641, 648 B and I, 649–663)
Maker: Possibly made first in England; later by the Northwood Co., National Glass Co., and Dugan Glass Co., Indiana, PA.
Named by: Original manufacturer's name. It seems that there were two original manufacturer's names for this pattern. The name appeared as *Brocade* in the Pitkin and Brooks advertisements. It appeared as *Opaline Brocade* in advertisements by G. Sommers and Co. and National Glass Co. Perhaps Northwood called this pattern *Brocade,* and National and Dugan changed the name to *Opaline Brocade*? I am using the name *Opaline Brocade* because James Measell chose to use that name in his books on Northwood and Dugan/Diamond.
Y.O.P. Circa 1899-1908
Other name: Brocade, Queen's Lace (Taylor), Spanish Lace (popular name).
Colors made: White, blue, canary, and cranberry opalescent. Very rare in green.
Pieces made: Pitcher, tumbler, butter dish, covered sugar, creamer, spooner, berry set, syrup jug, sugar shaker, celery vase, salt shakers, finger bowl, bride's basket, miniature bride's basket, barber bottle, wine decanter, cracker jar, perfume bottle, cruet, miniature lamp, water bottle, jam jar, vases and rose bowls of all sizes and shapes. The bride's basket, jam jar, and cracker usually had silver attachments.
Reintroduction or Repros: Yes—by Fenton Art Glass Co., Williamstown, W.Va. See text for Spanish Lace, Fenton.
Notes: Heacock originally called this pattern *Spanish Lace.* In his series *The Glass Collector, Collecting Glass,* he began advising the reader of the original manufacturer's names. Heacock believed original factory names should be used when known. The original factory name is used in *Dugan/Diamond, The Story of Indiana Glass* and *Harry Northwood, The Early Years, 1881–1900.* Thus, the name change for this edition.

The base on the cranberry opalescent butter is always white opalescent. The top can be blown, but the base can

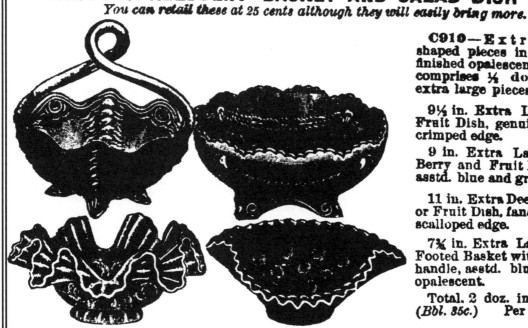

FANCY OPALESCENT BASKET AND SALAD DISH ASST.

You can retail these at 25 cents although they will easily bring more.

C910—Extra large fancy shaped pieces in beautiful full finished opalescent ware. Asst. comprises ½ doz. each of 4 extra large pieces as follows:

9½ in. Extra Large Salad or Fruit Dish, genuine ruby color, crimped edge.

9 in. Extra Large and Deep Berry and Fruit Bowl on 4 feet, asstd. blue and green opalescent.

11 in. Extra Deep Footed Salad or Fruit Dish, fancy crimped and scalloped edge.

7¾ in. Extra Large and Deep Footed Basket with fancy rustic handle, asstd. blue and green opalescent.

Total, 2 doz. in bbl.
(Bbl. 35c.)   Per dozen, **$1.75**

Grouping of Jefferson pieces. Further proof that Jefferson made *Swag with Brackets* is shown here. The footed basket is the larger version of the *Old Man Winter* basket, which has no feet. The blown ruffle–edge bowls are in the *Buttons & Braids* and *Coinspot* patterns.

Opaline Brocade and *Intaglio* items in a National Glass Co. catalog, circa 1901.

only be pressed. It is not possible to "press" a true cranberry color.

Journal Quote: "Harry Northwood, the glassmaster, is present himself in Room 62 and assisted by a staff of salesmen, has been kept busy showing buyers his handsome new lines. The trade has annually come to look to Northwood for blown and pressed lines of glassware which in design, finish, and conception, are of a higher artistic merit than the ordinary or general run of glassware pattern, and Harry has never disappointed the trade in this respect, and this year is no exception to the rule. This year, three original lines are shown, each distinct from the other, which are briefly described as Intaglio, in ivory and gold, and green and gold; Opaline Brocade, in four colors including pink and Venetian, in enamel colors and gold, and in three colors, ruby, blue and green." (*China, Glass and Lamps*, January 12, 1899) See the catalog reprints in *Dolphin Compote* and *Dolphin Petticoat*.

Extremely rare *Opaline Brocade* wine decanter.

Unusual yellow opalescent vase. This is not our American version of the pattern, it is the English original.

1899 Pitkins and Brooks ad shows the name of this pattern as *Brocade*. Note the original stopper in the cruet, which appears to be a pressed faceted stopper.

OPAL OPEN

(See fig. 495)

Maker: The Northwood Co., and Dugan Glass Co., Indiana, PA.

Named by: Hartung, *Opalescent*

Y.O.P. Circa 1899–1906

Other name: Beaded Panel, *Presznick 2*

Colors made: White, blue, green, and canary opalescent.

Pieces made: Rose bowl

Reintroduction or Repros: Yes. The L.G. Wright Co. started reproducing this pattern in 1939 and was still having it produced as late as 1995. Pieces made: Ivy ball (two sizes), compote (flared and crimped), small compote and candleholder. Colors made: Amber, green, blue, amethyst, ruby, crystal (circa 1990), Stormy Blue and Sparkling Ruby lustre (circa 1995).

Notes: There are no known reproductions in opalescent glass. See catalog reprint in the *Dolphin Petticoat* section.

OPAL DOT (SEE DOT OPTIC)

OPAL RIB (SEE RIB OPTIC)

OPAL SWIRL

(See figs. 931, 959, 960, 996, 998, 1000, 1082, 1094)

Maker: L.G. Wright, New Martinsville, W.Va., owned the shape moulds and Fenton Art Glass Co., Williamstown, W.Va., owned the optic moulds. Fenton made the majority of this type of glass for Wright.

Named by: Wright

Y.O.P. Circa 1950s through the 1980s and possibly into the 1990s.

Other name: Swirl and Spiral

Colors made: Cranberry, blue, and vaseline opalescent.

Pieces made: Epergne, cruet (two styles), lamp (many styles), pitcher (many styles), barber bottle, syrup, sugar shaker, tumbler, vases, pickle caster, and finger bowl. Other items are probable.

Reintroduction or Repros: This was a Wright reintroduction.

Note: See text for *Swirl, Opalescent* and *Spiral*. See catalog reprint on page 186.

OPEN O'S

(See fig. 518)

Maker: The Northwood Co., and Dugan Glass Co., Indiana, PA.

Named by: Hartung, *Opalescent*

Y.O.P. Circa 1903

Other name: None

Colors made: White, blue, green, and canary opalescent.

Pieces made: Novelties

Reintroduction or Repros: None known at this time.

Notes: Shards found at the Indiana, PA., plant site.

ORANGE TREE (OPALESCENT)

(See fig. 595)

Maker: Fenton Art Glass Co., Williamstown, W.Va.

Named by: Popular nomenclature

Y.O.P. Circa 1970s. This pattern was first introduced by Fenton in 1911 in Carnival colors.

Other name: None

Reintroduction or Repros: Fenton may reintroduce a pattern or color at any time, as they did with this one. Any piece made after 1972 should be marked with the Fenton logo.

Colors made: Blue opalescent; blue, pink, green, custard, Burmese with a satin finish, rosalene and Carnival colors.

Pieces made: Rose bowl, and bowls.

Notes: Blue opalescent was possibly made for A & A Importing. This pattern was not originally made in opalescent glass.

OVER—ALL HOB

(See figs. 160, 165, 169, 561, 1259)

Maker: Nickel Plate Glass Co., Fostoria, OH.

Named by: Kamm 5

Y.O.P. Circa 1892

Other name: Hobnail 3–Footed

Colors made: White, blue, and canary opalescent; amber, blue, and crystal.

Pieces made: Water set, water tray, table set, berry set, toothpick, celery vase, mug, finger bowl, and unfooted salt dip.

Reintroduction or Repros: None known at this time.

Notes: Production on this pattern was probably continued by U.S. Glass after they took over the plant in 1892. Sometimes the berry set is triangular in shape.

OVERLAPPING LEAVES (SEE LEAF TIERS)

PALISADES

(See figs. 441, 453)

Maker: Dugan Glass Co., Indiana, PA.

Named by: Hartung, *Opalescent*

Y.O.P. Circa 1903

Other name: Lined Lattice, when produced in Carnival colors.

Colors made: White, blue, green, and canary opalescent. Carnival colors of peach opalescent, marigold, amethyst, blue and pearl.

Pieces made: Novelties and swung vase.

Reintroduction or Repros: None known at this time.

PALM BEACH
(See figs. 119-126)

Blue opalescent *Palm Beach* very rare 8" plate.

Maker: U.S. Glass Co., Glassport, PA.
Named by: Lee, *Victorian Glass*
Y.O.P. Circa 1905 (in opalescent)
Other name: Pattern #15119
Colors made: Blue, canary opalescent, crystal, decorated crystal. Carnival colors of marigold, purple, and white.
Pieces made: In opalescent: table set, water set, berry set, finger bowl (or larger sauce dish), jelly compote, handled nappy, 8" plate and wine. Some of these pieces were produced in Carnival colors.
Reintroduction or Repros: None in opalescent. In 1955, U.S. Glass produced this pattern again in milk glass.
Pieces made: Bowls (three sizes), butter dish, creamer, sugar, olive dish, pickle dish, pitcher, sauce dish, vase and tumbler.

PALM AND SCROLL
(See fig. 425)
Maker: H. Northwood Co., Wheeling, W.Va., and Dugan Glass Co., Indiana, PA.
Named by: Hartung, *Opalescent*
Y.O.P. Circa 1905–1908
Other name: None
Colors made: White, blue, and green opalescent.
Pieces made: Bowls and novelties.

Reintroduction or Repros: None known at this time.
Notes: This pattern has been incorrectly attributed to the Jefferson Glass Co. See catalog reprint in the *Corn Vase* pattern section.

PANACHE
(See figs. 1158–1160, 1248)
Maker: Fenton Art Glass Co., Williamstown W.Va. for DeVilbiss Co., Toledo, OH.
Named by: Elmore
Y.O.P. Circa 1940s
Other name: None
Colors made: White, blue, green, and vaseline opalescent.
Pieces made: Perfume
Reintroductions/Repros: None known at this time
Note: This perfume bottle was designed to accommodate a glass stopper or atomizer.

PANEL GRAPE
(See figs. 603, 604)
Maker: See notes
Named by: L.G. Wright and Westmoreland
Y.O.P. Wright, 1940s to 1990s; Westmoreland, 1970s until their closing.

Other name: Paneled Grape is the name used by Westmoreland.

Colors made: Many colors, see below.

Pieces made: Goblets (several sizes), compote, sugar, creamer, tort plate, punch set, bowl, pitcher, plate, cup, saucer, cake stand, epergne, jardiniere, canape set, sauce boat, vase, tumblers (several sizes), candlesticks, salt/pepper, cruet, novelties and many more.

Notes: There is a great deal of confusion as to who made which pieces in this pattern. Westmoreland made a very extensive line of this pattern in many colors. In her book, *Westmoreland Glass 1950–1984*, Lorraine Kovar states: "Westmoreland did not make this pattern for L.G. Wright." L.G. Wright has been having this pattern made for them for many years in amber, blue, crystal, green, amethyst, ruby and blue opalescent. Possible makers: Fenton, Imperial, or Indiana Glass. Judging by the color shown in this photo, my best guess would be that Fenton made the blue opalescent pieces.

PANELED HOLLY

(See figs. 68, 69, 90, 379)

Maker: H. Northwood Co., Wheeling, W.Va.

Named by: Kamm 2

Y.O.P. Circa 1905

Other name: None

Colors made: White and blue opalescent (the white with red and green decoration, and the blue with gold decoration), emerald green with gold, crystal with red and gold decoration. Carnival colors of marigold and green.

Pieces made: Water set, table set, berry set, novelty bowls, and salt shaker.

Reintroduction or Repros: None known at this time.

Notes: There has been considerable confusion over the purpose of the spooner to this set. Many refer to it as an open sugar. However, a covered sugar was made, but has been so seldom seen that many doubt its existence. So many creamers and spooners have been found (yet they are far from common) that it is likely they were sold as a pair by the barrel with the spooner serving as an open sugar. All other pieces to this pattern are very rare. Pieces are usually marked with the "N" in a circle.

PANELED SPRIG, OPALESCENT (SEE MELON WITH SPRIG)

PEACOCK

(See figs. 609, 610)

Maker: Westmoreland Glass Co., Grapeville, PA., for A & A Importing.

Named by: Uncertain

Y.O.P. Circa 1973–1975

Other name: None

Colors made: Blue opalescent, possibly other colors.

Pieces made: Covered cream and covered sugar.

Reintroduction or Repros: None known at this time.

PEACOCK, FENTON

(See fig. 1287)

Maker: Fenton Art Glass Co., Williamstown, W.Va. Possibly originally by Northwood, Wheeling, W.Va.

Named by: Uncertain

Y.O.P.: Carnival glass in 1915, opalescent and other colors in the 1930s. They have brought this pattern back periodically ever since.

Other name: Peacock Garden, pattern #791

Colors made: Marigold Carnival, cameo with a stretch finish, white opalescent, Mandarin red, Mongolian green, Periwinkle blue, crystal, crystal satin, milk glass, and some contemporary colors.

Pieces made: Vases, flared and cupped in 6", 8", and 10" sizes.

Reintroduction/Repros: Fenton may reintroduce a pattern or color at any time.

Note: This vase in cameo stretch is very rare and could possibly be an experimental piece, as there are no records showing this item was ever in their line.

PEACOCKS ON A FENCE

(See fig. 214)

Maker: H. Northwood Co., Wheeling, W.Va.

Named by: Variation of *Presznick 1*

Y.O.P. Circa 1908

Other name: Northwood's Peacocks

Colors made: White, blue, and cobalt blue opalescent; custard glass and Carnival colors.

Pieces made: Bowls

Reintroduction or Repros: None known at this time.

Notes: Only the ruffle–edged bowl has been reported in opalescent. However, an ice cream set is known in the custard and Carnival colors and it is possible that they are available in opalescent as well. See the reprint below.

Mid–spring 1912 Butler Brothers catalog. Note the *Peacocks on a Fence* bowl, second from right, bottom row.

PEARL FLOWERS

(See fig. 450)

Maker: H. Northwood Co., Wheeling, W.Va.

Named by: Hartung, *Opalescent*

Y.O.P. Circa 1904

Other name: Beaded Flower Rosette (*Presznick 2*)
Colors made: White, blue, and green opalescent.
Pieces made: Novelties
Reintroduction or Repros: None known at this time.

PEARLS
(See figs. 979, 1153)
Maker: Fenton Art Glass Co., Williamstown, W.Va., for DeVilbiss.
Named by: Uncertain
Y.O.P. Circa 1940s
Other name: None
Colors made: Cranberry and possibly white opalescent.
Pieces made: Perfume
Reintroduction or Repros: None known at this time.
Note: See text for *DeVilbiss.*

PEARLS AND SCALES
(See fig. 477)
Maker: Jefferson Glass Co., Steubenville, OH.
Named by: Heacock
Y.O.P. Circa 1904
Other name: None
Colors made: White, blue, green, and canary opalescent, often with the distinguishable cranberry stained border.
Pieces made: Bowls, compotes, and novelties.
Reintroduction or Repros: None known at this time.

PEERLESS
Maker: Model Flint Glass Co., Albany, IN.
Named by: Original manufacturer's name
Y.O.P. Circa 1896
Other name: None
Colors made: Amber, blue, canary, crystal, green, and canary opalescent.
Pieces made: Bowl (many sizes), finger bowl, handled bowl, square bowls (three sizes), salver, celery, compote, cordial, wine, cracker dish, creamer, sugar, cruet, punch cup, decanter (two sizes), footed fruit bowl, handled nappy, three cornered and round olive, salt dip, pitcher, plate, rose bowl, salt shaker, saucer, shot glass, spooner, toothpick, tray (two shapes), tumbler, vases, wine bottle, and toy set consisting of an open salt, pepper, cruet and small tray.
Reintroduction or Repros: None known at this time.
Note: With the many colors and wide variety of pieces made, *Peerless* must have been produced until National closed the Model Flint plant. See reprint on the following page.

PIASA BIRD
(See figs. 440, 524)
Maker: Uncertain
Named by: Heacock
Y.O.P. Uncertain
Other name: Old Man of the Sea, and Demonic
Colors made: White and blue opalescent.
Pieces made: Bowls and novelties

Reintroduction or Repros: None known at this time.
Notes: The name is pronounced Pi-A-Saw. Some sources believe this line is English. The pattern is found on vases, rose bowls, and lady's spittoons but rarely on bowls. The bowl illustrated in figure 440 is very similar to the *Admiral* (*Flora*) novelty bowl in color and shape, which makes us lean toward Beaumont as its manufacturer. Also, the *Piasa Bird* is an American Indian legendary creature; a picture has been included to illustrate this uncanny similarity of features. That resemblance led Bill Heacock to name the pattern *Piasa Bird*.

Piasa Bird

PICCADILLY
(See fig. 542)
Maker: Sowerby & Co., Gateshead-on-Tyne, England.

Sowerby trademark

Named by: Heacock
Y.O.P. Circa 1880
Other name: #1173
Colors made: Green opalescent, and opaque colors.
Pieces made: Novelties
Reintroduction or Repros: None known at this time.
Notes: Sowerby was one of the few English firms capable of producing both pressed and blown wares.

PINEAPPLE AND FAN, HEISEY
(See fig. 436)
Maker: A.H. Heisey Glass Co., Newark, OH.
Named by: Kamm 2
Y.O.P. Circa 1898
Other name: Heisey #1255
Colors made: Crystal, ruby-stained, emerald green, some custard souvenirs; rare experimental pieces in opalescent glass.
Pieces made: Novelties in opalescent
Reintroduction or Repros: None known at this time.
Notes: Heisey's *Prison Stripe* and *Peerless* patterns also underwent rare opalescent glass production.

PLAIN AND SIMPLE
(See fig. 1234)
Maker: Unknown
Named by: Elmore
Y.O.P. Uncertain
Other name: None
Colors made: Green opalescent; others are likely.

Above is a portion of a page illustrating *Peerless* from National's 1900-1902 Export catalog No. 2. From the Library and Archives Division, Historical Society of Western Pennsylvania, Pittsburgh, PA.

Pieces made: Vase
Reintroductions/Repros: None known at this time.
Note: Unfortunately, Heacock knew nothing definitive about this swung vase in 1985 when he pictured it in *Collecting Glass, Vol. 2,* and nothing has come to light since.

PLAIN PANELS

(See fig. 1233)
Maker: Dugan Glass Co., Indiana, PA.
Named by: Uncertain
Y.O.P. Circa 1912
Other name: None
Colors made: White, blue, and green opalescent; Carnival colors are probable.
Pieces made: Vases
Reintroductions/Repros: None known at this time.
Note: Attribution is based on the fact that *Plain Panels* looks as though it was made from the same shape mould as *Pulled Loop,* a known Dugan shape.

PLAIN PATTERN

(See figs. 1282, 1283)
Maker: Model Flint Glass Co., Albany, IN
Named by: Original manufacturer's name
Y.O.P. Circa 1900
Other name: Pattern No. 21
Colors made: Crystal and blue opalescent
Pieces made: Berry set (round and square), bowl (several sizes), finger bowl, cup, saucer, and salt shaker.
Reintroductions/Repros: None known at this time

Note: Identifying this pattern is not easy as many companies offered "plain" ware during this time frame.

PLUME PANELS

Maker: Fenton Art Glass Co., Williamstown, W.Va.
Named by: Popular nomenclature
Y.O.P. Circa 1914
Other name: None
Colors made: Carnival colors of red, marigold, green, blue, violet, white and green opalescent (blue is very probable).
Pieces made: Only vases are known
Note: This pattern was unlisted in green opalescent until 1982. See picture on the following page.

PLUME TWIST

(See figs. 1161, 1251)
Maker: Unknown manufacturer for DeVilbiss Co., Toledo, OH.
Named by: Elmore
Y.O.P. Circa 1940s
Other name: None
Colors made: White and vaseline opalescent
Pieces made: Perfume
Reintroductions/Repros: None known at this time.
Note: This piece is a mass produced, machine-made bottle. DeVilbiss sometimes turned to cheaper methods to get some of their bottles produced. It is a shorter "twisted" copy of the similar "Malines" perfume bottle by Rene Lalique. Fenton did make a copy of the Lalique bottle. See text for *Plumes and Spaces.*

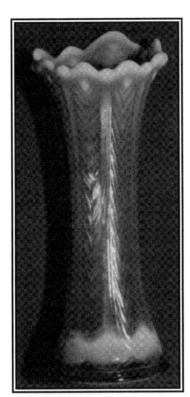

Green opalescent *Plume Panels* swung vase.

Rene Lalique *Malines* vase.

PLUMES AND SPACES
(See fig. 1231)
Maker: Fenton Art Glass Co., Williamstown, W.Va.
Named by: Elmore
Y.O.P.: Circa 1940s
Other name: Malines
Colors made: White opalescent
Pieces made: Perfume
Reintroductions/Repros: None known at this time.
Note: This is Fenton's rendition of Rene Lalique's perfume bottle called *Malines*. As you can see, they are very similar. See sketch above.

POINSETTIA LATTICE
(See fig. 447)
Maker: H. Northwood Co., Wheeling, W.Va.
Named by: Presznick 3
Y.O.P. Circa 1907
Other name: Christmas Bowl
Colors made: White, blue, and canary opalescent; custard with nutmeg and blue decoration; Carnival colors of green, blue, purple, ice blue and aqua opalescent.
Pieces made: Bowls in many shapes.
Reintroduction or Repros: None known at this time.

POINSETTIA, OPALESCENT
(See figs. 266, 267, 272, 273, 360, 386, 393, 824, 827, 835)

Northwood's *Poinsettia* pitcher with *Swirl* and *Coinspot* motif pitchers in the 1906 Lyon Brothers catalog.

Maker: H. Northwood Co., Wheeling, W.Va.
Named by: Heacock
Y.O.P. Circa 1902
Other name: Big Daisy
Colors made: Cranberry, blue, white, and green opalescent; rare in canary; Rubina; later production in marigold Carnival.
Pieces made: Pitcher, tumbler, bride's bowl, sugar shaker and syrup.
Reintroduction or Repros: None known at this time.
Notes: The water pitcher was made in three different shapes. The tumblers can be found in both blown and pressed glass. The bride's bowl was made to be placed in a silver–plated holder, but was advertised without the holder in early wholesale catalogs. Both the syrup and sugar shaker are extremely rare.
Journal Quote: "There is a real novelty in the lemonade set shown here from the Northwood factory. This set and some new molasses cans are among the newest things on the display tables of Frank Miller, the New York representative of H. Northwood & Company. The lemonade set referred to has a jug of graceful shape, but it is the decoration which at once attracts the eye. Its flower and

foliage seem to stick right out, although the relief is not high. The effect is secured by the opalescent tint of the relief, which upon the various backgrounds of canary, flint, blue, and pink is most striking. It is certainly a novelty and shows that Mr. Northwood knows how to produce original effects. Still, he usually did do that. The molasses cans have nothing new in the shapes, but they are revivals of one of the best selling shapes we ever had and made as the Northwood factory is making them, in dainty colors, why shouldn't they sell better than ever they did?" (*China, Glass & Lamp*, November 15, 1902)

POLKA DOT
(See figs. 352, 560, 793, 804–806, 851, 852, 927, 1019, 1086)

Polka Dot salt shaker, sugar shaker, and toothpick holder by West Virginia Glass Co., Martins Ferry, OH.

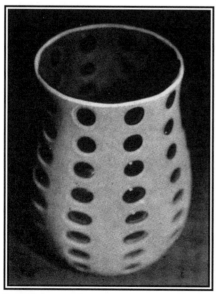

Polka Dot celery vase by West Virginia Glass. The shape mould used on this piece is the same one used on their *Optic* line.

Maker: West Virginia Glass Co., Martins Ferry, OH., and Northwood Glass Co., Ellwood City, PA., and probably Indiana, PA.
Named by: Heacock
Y.O.P. Circa 1894
Other name: Spot Resist
Colors made: White, blue, and cranberry opalescent.
Pieces made: Syrup, sugar shaker (two different shapes for both), salt shaker, toothpick, cruet, finger bowl, barber bottle, oil lamps (several sizes), celery vase, pitcher and tumbler.
Reintroduction or Repros: Yes—by the Fenton Art Glass Co., Williamstown, W.Va. Fenton made this pattern for many years for the L.G. Wright Glass Co., but they called it *Eye Dot*. Pieces made: Tumbler, barber bottle, small bowls, small pitcher and cruet in cranberry and blue opalescent.
Note: There are many reproductions in this pattern! Some use the identical mould and others are redesigned under the heading "technically not reproductions". Both provide great confusion to the collector. The old *Polka Dot* water pitchers, cruets, barber bottles, and finger bowls have polished pontils. Reproductions of these items do not have this identifying mark. The old salt shakers, sugar shakers and syrups do not have pontil scars.

The tumbler is by far the hardest to discern. Like the shakers and syrup, it will have a slightly rolled upper rim (often missing if chips have been polished out). The best guide to the new and old is the weight. Old tumblers are "thin walled" and light in weight. The toothpick has not been reproduced. Figure 851 is made in the *Fancy Fans* mould—see text for *Fancy Fans* and *Eye Dot*.

POLKA DOT (FENTON)
(See figs. 614, 971, 972, 974–977, 1061, 1075)
Maker: Fenton Art Glass Co., Williamstown, W.Va.
Named by: Fenton
Y.O.P. Circa 1955–56
Other name: Victorian name *Baby Coinspot*
Colors made: Cranberry opalescent, Jamestown blue (1958–59), Ruby Overlay (cranberry 1956–66); other colors are likely.
Pieces made: Sugar shaker, creamer, butter dish (has clear twig finial and milk glass open looped base), rose bowls, vases, salt/pepper shakers, cruet, footed ivy ball, water set, basket, and bowl.
Reintroduction or Repros: Fenton may reintroduce a pattern or color at any time. If made after 1972, the piece should be signed with the Fenton logo.

POPPY BY TIFFIN
(See fig. 1292)
Maker: U.S. Glass Co.
Named by: Uncertain

Y.O.P. Circa 1930s, but it is possible the opalescent colors were made much earlier.

Other name: Pattern No. 16255, 8" vase, and No. 16256 5" vase.

Colors made: Shiny or satin colors of black, pink, green, blue, canary yellow, and blue opalescent.

Pieces made: Vases

Reintroductions/Repros: None known at this time.

Note: The No. 16256 vase appeared in black satin in *The Glass Outlook,* a 1924 U. S. Glass Co. monthly sales brochure.

POPSICLE STICKS
(See fig. 516)

Maker: Jefferson Glass Co., Steubenville, OH.

Named by: Heacock

Y.O.P. Uncertain

Other name: Jefferson pattern #263

Colors made: White, blue, and green opalescent.

Pieces made: Bowls and novelties

Reintroduction or Repros: None known at this time.

Notes: Made in several variations. See catalog reprint in the *Astro* pattern section.

PRINCE WILLIAM

Maker: George Davidson & Co. Gateshead-on-Tyne, England.

Named by: Heacock

Y.O.P. Circa 1893, sometimes marked with Rd #217752.

Other name: None

Colors made: Blue opalescent; other colors are likely.

Pieces made: Creamer, open sugar, pitcher, tumbler, tray and 11" oval plate.

Reintroductions/Repros: None known at this time.

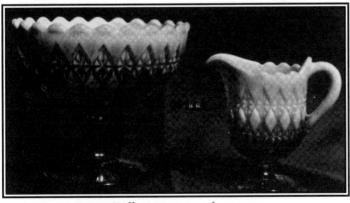

Prince William sugar and creamer.

PRINCESS DIANA
(See fig. 1276)

Maker: George Davidson and Co., Gateshead–on–Tyne, England

Named by: Heacock, for Princess Diana. Heacock's statement in *The Glass Collector* No. 5, Winter, 1983: "We are honoring the mother of the future King of England by naming this full table line *Princess Diana*."

Y.O.P. Circa 1890

Other name: 1890 Suite.

Colors made: White, yellow, and blue opalescent; other colors are possible.

Pieces made: Oval plate (four sizes), crimped plate (four sizes), oval crimped dish (four sizes), round crimped dish (four sizes), jug, butter dish, open sugar, creamer, covered biscuit jar with underplate, water set (pitcher, tumbler and tray), compote with silverplate base and salad bowl.

Reintroductions/Repros: None known at this time.

Note: Note that some pieces have a section of melon ribbing below the diamonds and fans.
See the catalog reprint on page 216.

PULLED LOOP
(See fig. 1104)

Maker: Dugan Glass Co., Indiana, PA.

Y.O.P. Circa 1912

Other name: Pattern #1030–R

Colors made: White, blue, green opalescent and Carnival colors of marigold, blue, pearl Iris, peach opal.

Pieces made: Swung vases

Reintroductions/Repros: None known at this time.

PUMP AND TROUGH
(See figs. 203-204)

Maker: H. Northwood Co., Wheeling, W.Va.

Named by: Common usage

Y.O.P. Circa 1907

Other name: None

Colors made: White, blue, and canary opalescent; possibly green and emerald green.

Pieces made: Novelties

Reintroduction or Repros: Yes. As early as 1939, the L.G. Wright Glass Co. began producing *Pump and Trough*. Colors made: green, amber, blue opalescent, and purple slag (made by Imperial). Other colors are possible.

Notes: Some of the original *Pumps and Troughs* were signed "Northwood" in script. Do not depend upon the signature to determine authenticity, however, as not all were signed. The original *Pump* had a scalloped top edge; the reproduction looks as though the top was sawed off so that the collector would have no problem telling the difference. The *Trough* is another story—they are very similar. Use caution when purchasing them separately. See catalog reprint in *Dolphin Petticoat* section.

QUADRUPLE DIAMONDS
(See fig. 1260)

Maker: Unknown, but probably English.

Named by: Heacock

Y.O.P. Circa early 1900s

Other name: None

Colors made: Cranberry and blue at the top blending to a pale vaseline at the bottom. It is made in a process similar to that used to make rubina verde.

Pieces made: Rose bowl, tumbler; others are likely.
Reintroductions/Repros: None known at this time.

QUEEN'S CROWN

Maker: Uncertain
Named by: Heacock
Y.O.P. Circa 1898, sometimes marked with Rd #320124
Other name: None
Colors made: Yellow and blue opalescent; other are likely.
Pieces made: Oval dish, open sugar or compote; other pieces are probable.
Reintroductions/Repros: None known at this time.

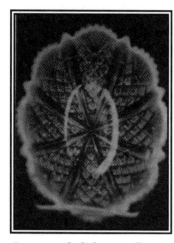

Queen's Crown oval dish in yellow opalescent. This is a "look–alike" to *Princess Diana*.

QUILTED PILLOW SHAM

Maker: Uncertain
Named by: Heacock
Y.O.P. Uncertain
Other name: None
Colors made: Vaseline opalescent; others are likely.
Pieces made: Butter dish, creamer, jelly dish in metal holder, others are probable.
Reintroductions/Repros: None known at this time.
Note: Following is a quote from *The Glass Collector, No. 6*: "The unique shape, the hobnail feet in the base of the butter, the scalloped foot on the base of the creamer, the unusual added "skirt" with scalloped edge around the body of each piece, as well as the raised quilted pattern, all combine to present an attractive package. I am calling it *Quilted Pillow Sham*, based on the obvious shape, design and ornamental skirt."
See the following picture.

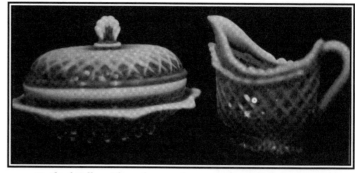

Quilted Pillow Sham butter (or sugar) and creamer.

QUILTED PINE CONE

(See fig. 1239)
Maker: Fenton Art Glass Co., Williamstown, W.Va. for the DeVilbiss Co.of Toledo, OH.
Named by: Elmore
Y.O.P. Circa 1940s
Other name: Design #43
Colors made: White, blue, and green opalescent
Pieces made: Perfume
Reintroductions/Repros: None known at this time.
Note: Shown below is a design drawing found in a scrapbook of design ideas kept by Frank L. Fenton (1880-1948), father of Frank M. Fenton. The majority of the clippings in this scrapbook include glass and china lines from the circa 1930-1945 years, some from which Mr. Fenton received inspiration for designing Fenton items.

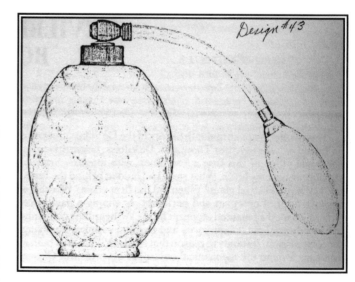

Design drawing for the *Quilted Pine Cone* (design #43) perfume.

RAYED HEART

Maker: Dominion Glass Co., Canada, but probably originally made by Jefferson Glass Co., Follonsbee, VA., and Toronto, Canada.

Named by: Uncertain

Y.O.P. Circa 1907 for Jefferson and circa 1913 for Dominion.

Other name: None

Colors made: Crystal and green opalescent; others are likely.

Pieces made: Goblet and compote; others are probable.

Reintroductions/Repros: None known at this time.

Green opalescent *Rayed Heart* compote.

REFLECTING DIAMONDS

(See fig. 405)

Maker: Dugan Glass Co., Indiana, PA.

Named by: Heacock

Y.O.P. Circa 1905

Other name: None

Colors made: White, blue, and green opalescent.

Pieces made: Bowls

Reintroduction or Repros: None known at this time.

Notes: Attribution of this pattern is based on the 1905 Butler Brothers catalog. See catalog reprint in *Corn Vase* pattern section. Pieces will sometimes be marked with the "Diamond–D" mark.

REFLECTIONS

(See fig. 438)

Maker: Dugan Glass Co. (later Diamond Glass), Indiana, PA.

Named by: Heacock

Y.O.P. Circa 1908

Other name: None

Colors made: White, blue, and green opalescent.

Pieces made: Bowls

Reintroduction or Repros: None known at this time.

Notes: This bowl is signed with the Diamond–D trademark.

REGAL, NORTHWOOD'S

(See figs. 131, 143, 148)

Maker: H. Northwood Co., Wheeling W.Va.

Named by: Hartung, *Opalescent*

Y.O.P. Circa 1906

Other name: Blocked Midriff, Peterson, *Glass Salt Shakers 1,000 Patterns*.

Colors made: White, green, and blue opalescent, crystal and emerald green.

Pieces made: Table set, water set, berry set, salt shaker and cruet.

Reintroduction or Repros: None known at this time.

Notes: *Regal* was not the most ideal choice for this pattern, since there were already two others known by that name. Thus, the word "Northwood" should follow this pattern when identifying. Occasionally signed with an "N" in a circle.

This assortment of Northwood's *Regal*, shown in Butler Brothers Mid–Spring, 1907 catalog, mentions green and flint opalescent "with extra wide burnt–in gold band decorations."

REVERSE DRAPERY (BOGGY BAYOU)

(See figs. 424, 473)

Maker: Fenton Art Glass Co.,Williamstown, W.Va.

Named by: Fenton

Y.O.P. Circa 1907

Other name: Cut Arcs, for Carnival collectors

Colors made: White, blue, amethyst, and green opalescent. Carnival colors of marigold, blue, amethyst and pearl.

Pieces made: Bowls and vases of many heights and shapes.

Reintroduction or Repros: None known at this time. Fenton may reintroduce a pattern or color at any time.

Note: Excerpt from a letter I received from Frank M. Fenton, October 12, 1998: "Now for the *drapery* patterns. I have been bothered by the various names that are applied to those patterns. Different writers have named the patterns differently and, of course, we didn't name any of those patterns, we just used numbers and descriptions. Northwood had a *Drapery* pattern that was distinctive and was made in Opalescent glass as well as Carnival glass. His drapes curved downwards. Fenton has a very similar pattern in pressed pieces where the curves curve up instead of down, and that's probably the reason for the *Reverse Drapery* name. Some people who have written about these patterns call the one *Northwood's Drapery* and the other *Fenton's Drapery*. The *Reverse Drapery* and the *Fenton's Drapery* patterns are the same. They are pressed pieces with a substantial ridge and bar between the swags. They can be called either *Reverse Drapery* or *Fenton's Drapery*. Bill's [Heacock] name of *Boggy Bayou* just doesn't seem to belong in the naming category. Yet, since he was the first one to recognize that pattern and name it, it seems to have stuck with some of the Carnival glass people. We have used the term *Boggy Bayou* on only one piece in the Museum, and I am planning to change the label on that piece to *Reverse Drapery* or *Fenton's Drapery*."

REVERSE SWIRL

(See figs. 233, 234, 238–242, 278, 286, 298, 309, 566, 636, 705, 706, 711–717, 841)

Maker: Buckeye Glass Co., Martins Ferry, OH., (circa 1888) and Model Flint Glass Co., Findlay, OH., Albany, IN. Model Flint joined the National Glass Co., in 1899–1900.*

Named by: Heacock

Y.O.P. Circa 1888 to 1902*

Other name: Ribbon Swirl

Colors made: White, blue, cranberry (not at Model Flint) and canary opalescent, sometimes with a satin finish; opaque colors and speckled colors of white, canary, blue and cranberry.

Pieces made: Pitcher, tumbler, butter dish, covered sugar, creamer, spooner, berry set, cruet, toothpick, sugar shaker, syrup jug, mustard, water bottle, finger bowl, salt shaker, custard cup, celery vase, miniature lamp, lamp shades; oil and vinegar cruet set on a metal holder (the mustard, cruet, salt and pepper are often found in three different colors in one set).

Reintroduction or Repros: None known at this time.

Notes: *Originally made by the Buckeye Glass Co., under the guidance of Harry Northwood. Later production by the Model Flint Glass Co. which was managed by John F. Miller. Miller had previously worked at Buckeye and patented the process used on this pattern.

The finials on figures 246, 249, 309 and 643 are identical and of common origin. The name *Reverse Swirl* seems to refer to the fact that the opalescent swirls go in one direction and the swirled ribs in the glass go in the other. The stoppers are not original.

In his book *Albany Glass/Model Flint Glass Co. of Albany, Indiana*, Ron Teal states that many Albany moulds were moved to the Dugan Glass Co. of Indiana, PA. The *Reverse Swirl* moulds were among this group, so it is very likely that production was continued by Dugan. This pattern is not mentioned in the Heacock/Measell/Wiggins book, *Dugan/Diamond, The Story of Indiana, Pennsylvania Glass*.

Journal Quote: "The new opalescent set of the Buckeye Glass Co. is a daisy [a Victorian term meaning a beauty, not a flower]. It is just out and ready for the spring trade, and all the dealers who have seen it have ordered freely. The number is 528 (Reverse Swirl) and there are four colors of it, canary, blue, crystal, and ruby. In the same goods, casters and water sets will be made. The Buckeye is getting there in good shape." (*Pottery and Glass Reporter*, January 5, 1888)
See the following pictures.

Two sizes of *Reverse Swirl* water bottles, made by the Model Flint Glass Co.

The caster set is Buckeye in the *Reverse Swirl* pattern with a blue cruet, yellow mustard, and cranberry shakers. The tankard pitcher is *Chrysanthemum Swirl* by Northwood. Note the swirls angle in the opposite direction.

RIBBED COINSPOT AND FINE RIBBED COINSPOT

(See figs. 785, 786, 846, 912, 923, 1021)
Maker: Northwood Glass Co., Martins Ferry, OH.
Named by: Uncertain
Y.O.P. Circa 1888
Other name: None
Colors made: White, blue, and cranberry opalescent.
Pieces made: Tumbler, sugar, creamer, pitcher, syrup, salt shaker and celery.
Reintroduction or Repros: None known at this time.
Note: Very limited items have surfaced in this pattern. The finial of the sugar bowl lid is identical to the sugar finial in the *Ribbed Opal Rings* pattern. One would assume that the remainder of the table set (spooner and butter dish) exists. *Fine Ribbed Coinspot* is created by using the *Coinspot* spot mould with the mould used for the *Christmas Snowflake* pieces (much smaller ribs). See figure 828.

Ribbed Coinspot creamer in cranberry opalescent.

RIBBED OPAL LATTICE

(See figs. 236, 237, 339, 340, 743, 746, 748, 749, 754–757, 895, 901, 1096, 1097, 1226)
Maker: *Probably Hobbs, Brockunier Co., Wheeling, W.Va., Buckeye Glass Co., Martins Ferry, OH., or Northwood Glass Co., Martins Ferry, OH.*
Named by: Boultinghouse
Y.O.P. Circa 1888
Other name: Expanded Diamond
Colors made: White, blue, and cranberry opalescent; sometimes the blue has a definite greenish caste.
Pieces made: Pitcher, tumbler, butter dish, covered sugar, creamer, spooner, berry set, cruet, sugar shaker

(two sizes), syrup, toothpick holder, salt shakers and celery vase.
Reintroduction or Repros: None known at this time.
Notes: *In *Harry Northwood, The Early Years, 1881–1900* James Measell states: "the precise origins of *Ribbed Opal Lattice* have not yet been ascertained." Northwood is definitely a possibility. Neila and Tom Bredehoft made no mention of *Ribbed Opal Lattice* in their book, *Hobbs, Brockunier & Co., Glass Identification and Value Guide,* so the attribution is doubtful. This is a highly collectible and beautiful pattern. The collector will find that putting together a complete table set is hard to do.

RIBBED OPAL RINGS

(See figs. 893, 899)

Ribbed Opal Rings tumbler. Note that the rings are horizontal; they do not connect or slant.

Maker: Probably Northwood Glass Co., Martins Ferry, OH.
Named by: Heacock
Y.O.P. Circa 1888
Other name: Ribbed Opal Spiral (too often confused with Ribbed Spiral, a popular pressed pattern)
Colors made: White, blue, and cranberry opalescent.
Pieces made: Pitcher, tumble, and sugar bowl.
Reintroduction or Repros: None known at this time.
Note: The name was changed since the opalescent rings do not connect or spiral. The tumbler shown above shows that each "ring" is unconnected. Since a covered sugar bowl is known, it is reasonably safe to assume that the rest of a table set was made (butter dish, creamer and spooner). The pitcher is an unusual, short tanker style. The covered sugar carries the same finial as the *Ribbed Coinspot* sugar.

RIBBED SPIRAL

(See figs. 80-82, 171-172, 205)
Maker: Model Flint Glass Co., Albany, IN.
Named by: Herrick
Y.O.P. Circa 1903
Other name: Ribbed Basket (Hartung, *Opalescent*) and pattern #911.
Colors made: White, blue, and canary opalescent. No green was made as previously reported.
Pieces made: Table set, water set, berry set, plates, (7", 9", 10") cups and saucers, toothpick, salt shaker, jelly compote, assorted ruffled bowls, lemonade tumbler and vases of all sizes (from 4" to 36" high). Also, toothpick in the *Ring Neck* mould.
Reintroduction or Repros: None known at this time.

RIB OPTIC/OPAL RIB

(See figs. 186, 618, 952, 1057, 1058, 1059, 1072–1074, 1101, 1105–1108, 1139, 1140, 1144, 1201, 1202, 1204, 1209–1211, 1216, 1220, 1221)

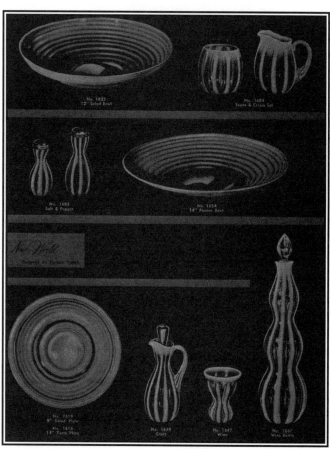

1953 catalog reprint of Fenton's *Rib Optic* showing the contemporary shapes of the cruet, wine glass, and decanter.

Maker: Fenton Art Glass Co., Williamstown, W.Va., for L.G. Wright Glass Co., New Martinsville, W.Va.
Named by: Fenton and L.G. Wright
Y.O.P. 1920s—present

Other name: Victorian name: Stripe. L.G. Wright's name: Opal Rib.
Colors made: Blue, topaz, cranberry, white, pale and dark green.
Pieces made: Barber bottle, cruet, rose bowl for L.G. Wright; Fenton's line: salt/pepper, wine bottle, wine glass, vase (several shapes), cream, sugar, ivy ball, plate, bowl, hat, (four sizes), cruet, pitchers (covered and uncovered), tumblers (with and without handles), and many different lamps. Most of these pieces are hard to find.
Reintroduction or Repros: Fenton may reintroduce a pattern or color at any time. If made after 1972, the piece should be signed with the Fenton logo.
Notes: Many of the shapes are very modern and should not be confused with the old. Figures 1209–1211 were made for the National Fenton Glass Society in 1998.

RICHELIEU

(See figs. 550, 551)
Maker: George Davidson & Co., Gateshead–on–Tyne, England.

Davidson trademark

Named by: Heacock
Y.O.P. See notes
Other name: No. 1889 Suite
Colors made: Blue and yellow opalescent
Pieces made: Bowls, three–part sweet dish, biscuit jar, basket and novelties.
Reintroduction or Repros: None known at this time.
Note: Some pieces are marked with the Rd #36945, which dates them circa 1885; others are marked #96945, which dates them circa 1888, and some are not marked at all.
See the following sketch.

1889.
TRIPLE SWEET,
Also made Crimped, 1889/8.

RIDGED

(See figs. 1205, 1206)
Maker: Fenton Art Glass Co., Williamstown, W.Va.
Named by: Elmore
Y.O.P. Circa 1926
Other name: Pattern #3
Colors made: Cameo, Florentine green, aquamarine, Celeste blue, Grecian gold, Persian pearl, Velva Rose and Jade. Others are probable.
Pieces made: Creamer and sugar
Reintroductions/Repros: Fenton may reintroduce a pattern or color at any time. If made after 1972, the piece should be marked.

RING

(See figs. 1046, 1047, 1053, 1136–1138, 1187)
Maker: Fenton Art Glass Co., Williamstown, W.Va.
Named by: Fenton
Y.O.P. Circa 1939, but possibly as early as 1933.
Other name: None
Colors made: White opalescent and cranberry in later years.
Pieces made: Pitcher, tumbler, bowl, candlestick, lamp and vases.
Reintroduction or Repros: Fenton may reintroduce a pattern or color at any time. If made after 1972, the piece should be signed with the Fenton logo.
Note: A 12" swung vase was produced in Cameo opalescent in the *Ring* pattern, circa 1927. See catalog reprint in the *Wide Rib* section.

RING–HANDLED BASKET

(See fig. 407)
Maker: H. Northwood Co., Wheeling, W.Va.
Named by: Heacock
Y.O.P. Circa 1903
Other name: None
Colors made: White, blue, and green opalescent
Pieces made: Basket
Reintroduction or Repros: None known at this time.

RING–HANDLED BASKET SALT SHAKER

(See fig. 565)
Maker: Uncertain
Named by: Peterson, *Glass Salt Shakers—1,000 Patterns*
Y.O.P. Circa 1903
Other name: None
Colors made: Opalescent blue and white, with a clambroth effect similar to the *Carnelian* (*Everglades*) salt shakers seen in figure 226. Also made in opaque colors.
Pieces made: Salt shakers
Reintroduction or Repros: None known at this time.

RIPPLED

(See fig. 1121)
Maker: Fenton Art Glass Co., Williamstown, W.Va.
Named by: Elmore
Y.O.P. Circa 1932
Other name: Pattern #100
Colors made: White, blue, green, and amethyst opalescent.
Pieces made: Bowls
Reintroductions/Repros: Fenton may reintroduce a pattern or color at any time. If made after 1972, the piece should be marked with the Fenton logo.

ROSE

Maker: U. S. Glass Co.
Named by: Original manufacturer's name
Y.O.P. Circa 1920s
Other name: Rose Wreath, Roses and Ruffles, and Pattern No. 15318.
Colors made: Blue and canary opalescent with a satin finish, sometimes decorated.
Pieces made: Trinket box, footed compote, cologne bottles, covered bonbon, vase, console bowl, candlesticks, handled cake plate, tray, and large dresser tray.
Reintroduction or Repros: Yes—by the Fenton Art Glass Co. They made *Rose* in: Colonial blue, pink, amber and green; milk glass (1964–1976, lamps were in the line until 1988).
Pieces made: Goblet, ring tree, footed candy box, compote (two styles), candy box, candlestick, oval vase, ashtray (two sizes, individual size with rack), creamer, covered sugar, salt shaker, lamp (four styles).

Blue Marble, 1970, pieces made: Basket, bowl, covered candy box, handkerchief vase, swung bud vase and compote. Carnival glass (1975)—only a compote is listed. Ebony (1979)—only a compote is listed. More colors and pieces are likely.

Note: Excerpt from a letter I received from Frank M. Fenton in September, 1999: "We did make the compote with a new mould made by Fenton...reproducing the U.S. Glass Co.'s compote almost exactly the same, except that our compote was not flared as much as the U.S. Glass flared theirs."

Rose trinket box.

ROSE SHOW

(See fig. 442)
Maker: H. Northwood Co., Wheeling, W.Va.
Named by: Hartung, *Carnival Glass 2*
Y.O.P. Circa 1907
Other name: La Belle Rose (Presznick)
Colors made: Blue and white opalescent; Carnival colors of marigold, green, blue, purple, pearl, ice blue, ice green and marigold on custard.
Pieces made: Bowls and plates.
Reintroduction or Repros: None known at this time.

ROULETTE

(See fig. 505)
Maker: H. Northwood Co., Wheeling W.Va.
Named by: Joe. B. Bell
Y.O.P. Circa 1906
Other name: None
Colors made: White, blue, and green opalescent.
Pieces made: Bowls
Reintroduction or Repros: None known at this time.

RUFFLES AND RINGS

(See fig. 506)
Maker: Jefferson Glass Co., Steubenville, OH., and H. Northwood Co., Wheeling, W.Va.
Named by: Hartung, *Opalescent*
Y.O.P. Circa 1905–1910
Other name: Carnations and Pleats (*Presznick 2*) and Jefferson Pattern #20
Colors made: White, blue, green opalescent and white opalescent with an iridescent marigold interior.
Pieces made: Bowls
Reintroduction or Repros: None know at this time.
Notes: This mould was somehow transferred from Jefferson to Northwood. See catalog reprint in the *Beaded Fan* pattern section.

SANIBEL

(See fig. 1252)
Maker: Duncan and Miller, Washington, PA.
Named by: Original manufacturer's name
Y.O.P. Circa 1941
Other name: Pattern No. 130
Colors made: Cranberry pink, Cape Cod blue, Jasmine yellow, white and crystal.
Pieces made: Vase (three shapes), bowl (many shapes that look like swirling shells), tray, ashtray (fish and life preserver), plates, relishes, candy jar, cigarette jar and decanter.
Reintroductions/Repros: None known at this time.
Note: Most of the items in the *Sanibel* line have a nautical theme ranging from fish to shells to life preservers. See the following advertisement.

Duncan and Miller ad that appeared in *China, Glass and Lamps*, June, 1941.

SCHEHEREZADE

(See fig. 458)
Maker: Unknown
Named by: Heacock
Y.O.P. Uncertain
Other name: None
Colors made: White, blue, and green opalescent.
Pieces made: Bowls
Reintroduction or Repros: None known at this time.

SCOTTISH MOOR

(See figs. 639, 915)
Maker: Unknown. West Virginia Glass Co., Martins Ferry, W.Va. is a possibility.
Named by: Uncertain
Y.O.P. Circa 1890
Other name: None
Colors made: White, blue, cranberry, amethyst opalescent and rubina.
Pieces made: Celery vase, pitcher, tumbler, cracker jar and cruet.
Reintroduction or Repros: None known at this time.

SCROLL WITH ACANTHUS

(See figs. 65-66, 197, 201, 232)
Maker: H. Northwood Co., Wheeling, W.Va.
Named by: Kamm 3
Y.O.P. Circa 1903
Other name: None, but this appeared in their "Mosaic" assortment.
Colors made: White, blue, and canary opalescent, novelties in green opalescent (see fig. 197); crystal, blue, apple green and purple slag.
Pieces made: Table set, water set, berry set, jelly compote, toothpick, salt shaker and cruet.
Reintroduction or Repros: None known at this time.
Note: Occasionally, some pieces are enamel decorated. Stopper is not original.

SCULPTURED ICE

(See fig. 986)
Maker: Fenton Art Glass Co., Williamstown, W.Va.
Named by: Fenton
Y.O.P. Circa 1982
Other name: None
Colors: Cranberry and non–opalescent colors.
Pieces made: Fairy light, and other pieces that were in the line in 1982.
Reintroduction or Repros: Fenton may reintroduce a pattern or color at any time. If made after 1972, pieces should be marked with the Fenton logo.
Note: See text for *Snow Capped Diamonds*.

SEA SPRAY

(See figs. 517, 1120)
Maker: Jefferson Glass Co., Steubenville, OH.
Named by: Hartung, *Opalescent*
Y.O.P. Circa 1906–1908
Other name: Jefferson pattern #192
Colors made: White, blue, and green opalescent.
Pieces made: Novelties
Reintroduction or Repros: None known at this time.

SEAWEED, OPALESCENT

(See figs. 215, 249–258, 383, 573, 643, 677, 678, 681–692, 838)
Maker: Originally by Hobbs, Brockunier & Co., Wheeling, W.Va. Moulds were acquired and reissued by Beaumont Glass Co., Martins Ferry, OH., circa 1899.
Named by: Heacock
Y.O.P. Circa 1890
Other name: Beaumont Beauty and Coral**
Colors made: White, blue, and cranberry opalescent; rare with a satin finish.
Pieces made: Pitcher (several shapes), tumbler, butter dish, covered sugar, creamer, spooner, berry set, cruet (several shapes), barber bottles (two shapes),salt shaker, syrup, sugar shaker, vase, toothpick, rose bowl, pickle caster, and miniature lamp.

Reintroduction or Repros: None known at this time.
Notes:**There has to be an exception to every rule and this is it. Throughout this book, names have been changed to honor what the manufacturer initially called the pattern. In this instance, it just does not make any sense to change the name back to the original—it will only cause more confusion. The name has been left as *Seaweed* even though the original name was stated as *Coral* in the Bredehoft's book, *Hobbs, Brockunier & Co., Glass Identification and Value Guide*. This is hard to believe as Hobbs, Brockunier already had an extensive plated amberina line called *Coral*, circa 1886. It has been noted that Bryce Brothers made a pattern called *Coral,* and a pressed opalescent pattern (see fig. 510) has also been dubbed *Coral*. As there are already at least three different patterns or types of glass using the name *Coral,* there is no need to add a fourth.

A *Seaweed* cruet made in the *Hobbs Swirl* mould has been reported. The toothpick holder and sugar shaker are difficult to find.

Cranberry *Seaweed* pickle caster on ornate frame. Hobbs supplied inserts for metal holders to a number of different silver plate firms, including Pairpoint, Meriden and Wilcox.

SHELL (SEE NEW YORK)

SHELL AND WILD ROSE

(See fig. 462)
Maker: H. Northwood Co., Wheeling, W.Va.
Named by: Presznick 1
Y.O.P. Circa 1906–1908
Other name: Called Wild Rose by Carnival collectors.
Colors made: White, blue, and green opalescent. Carnival colors of marigold, green, and amethyst.
Pieces made: Bowl and open–edge rose bowl.
Reintroduction or Repros: None known at this time.
Note: Occasionally signed with the "N" in a circle.

SHIELD BY JEFFERSON

Maker: Jefferson Glass Co., Follansbee, W.Va.
Named by: Hartung variation.
Y.O.P: Circa 1906
Other name: Pattern No. 262
Colors made: Blue opalescent, probably white and green.
Pieces made: Bowls and novelties
Reintroductions/Repros: None known at this time.
Note: Usually the shields are almost unrecognizable by the time the glass piece has been crimped and refired to obtain the opalescent effect.

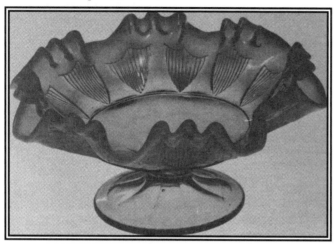

Blue opalescent *Shield by Jefferson* bowl.

SIMPLE SIMON

(See fig. 427)
Maker: Possibly Northwood
Named by: Heacock
Y.O.P. Circa early 1900s
Other name: Graceful
Reintroduction or Repros: None
Colors made: White and green opalescent, possibly others.
Pieces made: Vase
Reintroduction or Repros: None known at this time.
Note: This vase looks very similar to Northwood's *Graceful*, known in Carnival glass. The base on *Simple Simon* is rayed; the base on *Graceful* shown in *Harry Northwood, The Wheeling Years, 1901–1925* is opaque and it cannot be determined if it is also rayed. If *Graceful* is rayed then it is almost a certainty that *Simple Simon* is a Northwood piece.

SIR LANCELOT

(See fig. 399)
Maker: H. Northwood Co., Wheeling, W.Va.
Named by: Heacock
Y.O.P. Circa 1908
Other name: None
Colors made: White, blue, and green opalescent and possibly Carnival.
Pieces made: Novelties

Reintroduction or Repros: None known at this time.
Note: Occasionally signed with the "N" in a circle.

SNOW CAPPED DIAMONDS

(See fig. 990)
Maker: Fenton Art Glass Co., Williamstown, W.Va.
Named by: Elmore
Y.O.P. Circa 1983
Other name: None
Colors made: Cranberry
Pieces made: Fairy light
Reintroductions or Repros: Fenton may reintroduce a pattern or color at any time. If made after 1972, pieces should be marked with the Fenton logo.
Notes: I wrote to Frank M. Fenton on September 20, 1999, asking for information about this fairy light. Following is his reply: "I think the optic is the same as fig. 986. We used the same optic on 986 and 990 except that on 986 we struck the opalescent before it was blown in the mould, and on 990 we didn't strike it before it was blown in the mould, but instead struck just the edges. The process that we used in striking is for the piece to be chilled after it comes out of the optic mould, and before it goes back into the glory hole to be reheated before blowing into the regular mould. It's the same thing we do with *Diamond Optic,* when we make the *Diamond Optic* pieces without chilling them. They are then Ruby overlay *Diamond Optic.* If we chill and reheat them, they are Cranberry Opalescent *Diamond Optic.*" This fairy light was made for the attendees of the 1983 Fenton Convention.

SNOWFLAKE

(See figs. 830, 831, 836)
Maker: Hobbs Glass Co., Wheeling, W.Va., with continued production by U.S. Glass.
Named by: Uncertain
Y.O.P. Circa 1891
Other name: Daisy or Clover Leaf
Colors made: White, blue, and cranberry opalescent.
Pieces made: Oil lamp, hand lamp, and night lamp.
Reintroduction or Repros: Yes—by Fenton Art Glass Co., Williamstown, W.Va. See text for Daisy, Fenton.
Journal Quote: "The Hobbs Glass Co...they have made a great hit on a new line of lamps just ready for the trade. It is a square-shaped bowl made in crystal and three colors... blue opalescent, ruby opalescent and white opalescent. Its superior advantages promise a great sale for it. The bowl and foot of these lamps are screwed firmly together by a metal socket, which entirely obviates the excessive breakage attending all blown lamps. The socket is covered by a glass sleeve which conceals the metal, producing a brilliant effect and making practically an all glass lamp. The saving in breakage will make a handsome profit for the dealer. The lamps will be shown in the *Journal* next week." (*Crockery and Glass Journal*, May 14, 1891) See the following advertisement.

1892 Butler Brothers assortment of *Snowflake* hand, stand and table lamps, offered in "ruby opalescent, crystal opalescent, and turquoise opalescent." These were made by the U.S. Glass Co. at their factory H (formerly Hobbs Glass Co.) in Wheeling, W.Va.

SOMERSET

(See fig. 1281)
Maker: George Davidson & Co., Gateshead-on-Tyne, England.
Named by: Heacock
Y.O.P. Circa 1895. Rd #154027
Other name: None
Colors made: Blue and yellow opalescent, others are possible.
Pieces made: Bowls (round and square), pitcher and tumbler, juice set (5" pitcher, 3" tumbler), crimped oval plate (9"); other pieces are likely.
Reintroductions/Repros: None known at this time.
Note: The fanned ribs do not appear on the round pieces.

SPANISH LACE (SEE OPALINE BROCADE)

SPANISH LACE, FENTON

(See fig. 982)
Maker: Fenton Art Glass Co., Williamstown, W.Va.
Named by: Fenton
Y.O.P. Circa 1950 to present
Other name: Victorian original manufacturer's name was Opaline Brocade or Brocade.
Colors made: Milk glass, green pastel, pink pastel, blue pastel and turquoise (circa 1950s); silver crest (circa 1962 and for another 25 years, some pieces were decorated with violets); teal crest (made for Gracious Touch circa late 1980s); cranberry (circa 1993); and Lilacs, which is milk glass with a lilac crest.
Pieces made: Silver Crest: salt shaker, Gone with the Wind lamp, footed cake plate, footed bowl, bowl, basket (8" and 10"), vase (4" and 8"), bell, candleholder and footed candy box. Cranberry: 32 oz. pitcher and basket (experimental). Lilac: basket and vase.
Note: Following is a quote dated in April of 1999 from Frank M. Fenton explaining their production of *Spanish Lace*, which was inspired by the old *Opaline Brocade* design: "The original *Spanish Lace* pattern is a pattern produced in opalescent glass made by blowing the glass first in an optic mould and then in a final shape mould. The only piece among the early pieces that is pressed is a butter dish bottom which carries out the *Spanish Lace* design in a raised surface with the pattern showing on the surface of the piece. In the 1950s, the Fenton Art Glass Co. in Williamstown, W.Va., borrowed the patterns on the base to the butter dish and the name, *Spanish Lace*, and applied them to a series of pressed pieces beginning with a footed cakeplate and footed bowl in Milk Glass, Green Pastel, Rose Pastel, Blue Pastel and Turquoise. In 1962, they introduced the same surface treatment pattern in Silver Crest and called it *Spanish Lace*. They continued to make it for the next 25 years. Some pieces were decorated with violets. Pieces made in Silver Crest were the salt shaker, Gone with the Wind lamp, footed cake plate, footed bowl, bowl, basket 8" and 10", base 4" and 8", bell, candleholder, footed candy box. Fenton also produced its own version of the *Spanish Lace* pattern with a Teal Crest for the Gracious Touch line in the late 1980s. In 1993, they produced a 32 oz. pitcher in Cranberry Opalescent. This piece is the first authentic reintroduction of the original *Opaline Brocade* pattern. In 1994, they produced a basket and vase in Milk glass, not opalescent, with a Plum crest and a hand painted decoration called Lilacs. The surface treatment on the vase is similar to the earlier pressed *Spanish Lace* pieces made by Fenton in Milk glass." Also see text for *Opaline Brocade*.

SPIRAL

(See figs. 598, 599, 964–966, 969, 970, 973, 980, 1024, 1025, 1028, 1050, 1051, 1054, 1060, 1076, 1088, 1125, 1135, 1141, 1162–1164, 1188, 1203)
Maker: Fenton Art Glass Co., Williamstown, W.Va., and Fenton also made this pattern for L.G. Wright Glass Co. New Martinsville, W.Va.
Named by: Original name
Y.O.P. 1907–present
Other name: Victorian name Opal Swirl or Swirl, Spiral Optic.

Colors made: White, blue, green, topaz, and cranberry (not until 1939) opalescent; possibly others.

Pieces made: Pitcher (several sizes), tumbler, milk pitcher, barber bottle, syrup, creamer, cruet, sugar shaker, pickle caster, hats (at least four sizes), candlesticks, vases (many sizes and shapes), bowls, epergne, ginger jar, hurricane globe, candlestick, basket, lamps (many sizes and shapes); others are likely.

Reintroduction or Repros: Fenton may reintroduce a pattern or color at any time. If made after 1972, the pieces should be marked with the Fenton logo.

Note: See text for *Opal Swirl* and *Swirl*. Figures 1050/1190, 1162, 1164 are perfume bottles made for DeVilbiss in the 1940s. Frank M. Fenton states that Fenton actually has two different kinds of spiral. Sometimes they call it *Fine Rib Spiral* and sometimes *Wide Rib Spiral* using a different spot mould or different rib mould for the wide rib. Figure 1203 was made for QVC, a program on cable TV, in 1991. Figure 1088 was made for the "Cruet Lady" in 1992, and is so marked. See the catalog reprint on page 207.

SPOKES AND WHEELS

(See fig. 456)

Maker: H. Northwood Co., Wheeling, W.Va.
Named by: Heacock
Y.O.P. Circa 1906
Other name: None
Colors made: White, blue, and green opalescent.
Pieces made: Bowls
Reintroduction or Repros: None known at this time.
Note: Occasionally signed with "N" in a circle.

SPOOL

(See figs. 443, 466)

Maker: H. Northwood Co., Wheeling, W.Va.
Named by: Hartung, *Opalescent*
Y.O.P. Circa 1903
Other name: Spool of Threads
Colors made: White, blue, and green opalescent; purple slag and custard.
Pieces made: Novelties
Reintroduction or Repros: None known at this time.
Notes: The pattern that Hartung shows as *Spool*, Heacock renamed *Spool of Threads*, since it has the vertical ribs.

SPOOL OF THREADS

(See fig. 519)

Maker: H. Northwood Co., Wheeling W.Va.
Named by: Heacock
Y.O.P. Circa 1903
Other name: Spool, Hartung
Colors made: White, blue, and green opalescent and purple slag.
Pieces made: Novelties
Reintroduction or Repros: None known at this time.

SQUIRREL AND ACORN

Maker: Unknown
Named by: Heacock
Y.O.P. Circa early 1900s
Other name: None
Colors made: Green opalescent; others are likely.
Pieces made: Vase; others are probable.
Reintroductions/Repros: None known at this time.
Note: Unfortunately, Heacock knew nothing about this charming vase in 1981 when he first showed it in his book, *Old Pattern Glass According to Heacock,* and no information has surfaced since.

Green opalescent *Squirrel and Acorn* vase.

S–REPEAT (SEE NATIONAL)

STARS AND STRIPES FENTON/WRIGHT

(See figs. 617, 815, 886, 950, 957, 1063–1068)

Maker: Fenton Art Glass Co., Williamstown, W.Va., and also for L.G. Wright Glass Co., New Martinsville, W.Va.
Named by: Original name
Y.O.P. Circa 1940s—present
Other name: None
Colors made: Blue and cranberry.
Pieces made: Tumbler, creamer, barber bottle, cruet, basket, finger bowl, syrup, and many novelties or whimsies.
Reintroduction or Repros: Fenton may reintroduce a pattern or color at any time. If made after 1972, the pieces should be marked with the Fenton logo.
Notes: The new is almost as hard to find as the old. See catalog reprint on page 186.

Excerpt from a letter by Frank M. Fenton, September, 1999: "We made the barber bottle for a firm called Crow and Cuttle, which was a barber supply house. We made the spot mould for that pattern to work with their barber bottle. Later, with Crow and Cuttle's permission, we were able to use the same spot mould for items for L.G. Wright as long as we didn't make a barber bottle for Wright." See the catalog reprint on page 186.

STARS AND STRIPES, OPALESCENT

(See figs. 813, 814, 958)

Maker: Hobbs, Brockunier & Co., Wheeling, W.Va., and Beaumont Glass Co., Martins Ferry, OH.
Named by: Hartung, *Opalescent*
Y.O.P. Circa 1888 to 1896; Beaumont 1899
Other name: None
Colors made: White, blue, and cranberry opalescent.
Pieces made: Pitcher, tumbler, barber bottle, finger bowl and lamp shade.
Reintroduction or Repros: Yes—see Stars and Stripes, Fenton, above.
Note: See figure 617, which is a reproduction tumbler. It is very difficult to tell the old from the new. The new is usually much heavier and thicker. The old tumbler and finger bowl were polished at the top. As a result, they do not have a polished pontil in the base. The old pitcher and barber bottle should have a pontil mark. There is some controversy about the water pitcher. It was reportedly made by L.G. Wright to go with the many tumblers on the market, but no water pitcher appears in any of the catalogs from this firm. Pitchers with and without polished pontil scars are known, the latter assumed by many to be the Wright reproduction. But I (Heacock) have a theory that the version without the pontil scar is the later Beaumont production of the pattern. Both versions of this pitcher, shaped identically, are very rare.
Journal Quote: "Alex P. Menzies, the New York representative of the Beaumont Glass Co., has full lines of that company's ware and is showing their latest creation for the first time this week. It is a line of jugs in opalescent white, red, and blue, with a field of stars at the bottom and stripes running up the jug. The shapes are excellent..." (*Crockery and Glass Journal*, September 7, 1899)

STORK AND RUSHES

(See fig. 494)

IRIDESCENT TUMBLER

1C1132—9 oz., ht. 4 in., golden iridescent, embossed bird design, beaded bands. 1 doz. in box......Doz. 92c

Stork and Rushes tumbler. Butler Brothers catalog.

Maker: Dugan Glass Co., Indiana, PA.
Named by: Hartung, *Carnival*
Y.O.P. Circa 1910
Other name: None
Colors made: Blue and white opalescent, royal blue. Carnival colors of marigold, blue and purple.
Pieces made: Punch set, water set, berry set, mug and bowl.
Reintroduction or Repros: None known at this time. See catalog reprint in the *Lattice and Daisy* section.

STRAWBERRY

(See fig. 1245)

Maker: Fenton Art Glass Co., Williamstown, W.Va.
Named by: Uncertain
Y.O.P. Circa 1911
Other name: Pattern #74
Colors made: Lime green opalescent and Carnival colors of marigold, topaz, green, red, blue, purple, and amber. Also amberina, which is probably red that was not heated to a high enough temperature to be a true red.
Pieces made: Handled bonbon
Reintroductions/Repros: None known at this time, but Fenton may reintroduce a pattern/color at any time.
Note: Figure 1245 has a base color somewhere between canary opalescent and what Carnival collectors call lime green opalescent (not the be confused with the dark green opalescent Fenton made in the 1950s). This bonbon is considered rare.

STRAWBERRY AND DAHLIA TWIST

(See fig. 648)

Maker: Jefferson Glass Co., Steubenville, OH.
Named by: Uncertain
Y.O.P. Uncertain
Other name: None
Colors made: White and blue opalescent.
Pieces made: Epergne
Reintroduction or Repros: None known at this time.
Notes: This epergne is included in a Butler Brothers ad reprint illustrated in Freeman's book, *Iridescent Glass*. The base and trumpet vase are original.

STRIPE, OPALESCENT

(See figs. 187, 189, 263, 277, 350, 385, 725, 737–741, 837, 853, 862, 868, 1033, 1037, 1049, 1208)

Maker: Northwood Glass Co., Martins Ferry, OH.; The Northwood Glass Co., Ellwood City, PA.; The Northwood Co., Indiana, PA; Buckeye Glass Co., Martins Ferry, OH.; Beaumont Glass Co., Martins Ferry, OH.; Jefferson Glass Co., Steubenville, OH.; Nickel Plate Glass Co., Fostoria OH. (circa 1891); Model Flint Glass Co., Albany, IN. (circa 1900); possibly others.
Named by: Heacock
Y.O.P. Circa 1889; see other dates above.

Other name: Candy Stripe, Ribbon Strip, Venetian Thread, Venetian Rib and Opalescent Stripe.

Colors made: White, blue, cranberry, rubina, and rare in canary opalescent. Not all colors were made by all companies.

Pieces made: Pitcher (many shapes), tumblers (small size and shot glass), syrup jug (three shapes), sugar shaker (three styles), celery vase with ruffled top, cruet (many shapes), condiment set (two styles), toothpick holder, barber bottle, individual salt shaker (several shapes), finger bowl, rose bowl, bowls, oil lamps (many styles); lamp shades (many shapes), and wine decanter.

Reintroduction or Repros: Yes—by Fenton Art Glass Co., Williamstown, W.Va., which they called *Rib Optic*. See *Rib Optic* section.

Notes: About the only way you can determine who made which piece is to study the type of moulds each company used, such as Northwood's ring–neck and nine panel. It is also helpful to know which colors each company made. For instance, Model Flint Glass Co. made no cranberry, but they did make canary, white, and blue. The four–piece condiment set seen in fig. 189 was advertised in the 1889 Butler Brothers Catalog.

Journal Quote: "At the Buckeye Glass Works business is still good, with encouraging prospects for the future. The season has been a very prosperous one and the management is well pleased over it. Only one furnace, the large 15–pot one, has been in use but this has always worked to perfection and has turned out a large amount of ware, very little of which will be left unsold when the bars are drawn. There are now more fine fancy goods in the sample rooms than ever and a visit to it will pay any person. A line of goods is ready for the fall trade which ought to meet with a quick sale. The number of the new plain and opalescent dew drop table set is 527, and it is a pretty thing. The decorated vase lamps, six patterns with decorated shades to match, are very handsome. In Venetian thread ware, plain and decorated, they have a water set, new shapes in oil and vinegar bottles, new shapes in molasses jugs and lamp chimneys, salts, lamps in blue, white, and canary, and other articles. These Venetian goods are something the Buckeye has not been making and are very neat and decorations show to good advantage on them." (*Pottery and Glassware Reporter*, June 23, 1887)

See the following picture.

Yellow opalescent *Stripe* pitcher, tumblers, slop bowl and *Beatty Swirl* tray. The pitcher is similar in shape to *Ribbed Coinspot*, fig. 786 and *Stars and Stripes*, fig. 813.

STUMP MUG (SEE TREE STUMP MUG)

SURF SPRAY

Maker: Jefferson Glass Co., Follansbee, W.Va.
Named by: Heacock
Y.O.P. Circa 1906
Other name: Pattern No. 253
Colors made: White, blue, and green opalescent
Pieces made: Pickle dish
Reintroductions/Repros: None known at this time
Note: Heacock named this pattern *Surf Spray* because of the similarity to Jefferson's *Sea Spray*.

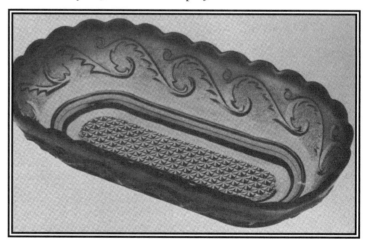

Green opalescent *Surf Spray* pickle dish.

SUNBURST-ON-SHIELD (SEE DIADEM)

SUNDERLAND

(See fig. 1286)
Maker: Henry Greener & Co., Millfield, Sunderland, England.
Named by: Heacock
Y.O.P. This pattern's Rd #138051 was assigned to Greener on November 14, 1889.
Other name: None
Colors made: Blue opalescent; others are likely.

Pieces made: Basket and tumbler; others are likely.
Reintroductions/Repros: None known at this time.

SUNSET
(See fig. 1129)
Maker: Co-Operative Flint Glass Co., Ltd., Beaver Falls, PA.
Named by: Uncertain
Other name: Sometimes mistakenly called "Cambridge Tomato"
Colors made: Heacock called this color Rubina Verde in one of his many articles.
Pieces made: Candlesticks, compotes, covered candy dishes, and bowls.
Note: The color was intended to shade from butterscotch to a deep red and then back to butterscotch. This does not always happen as this is a heat sensitive glass and difficult to control.

SWAG WITH BRACKETS
(See figs. 88, 89, 91-94, 135, 220, 221)
Maker: Jefferson Glass Co., Steubenville, OH.
Named by: Kamm 1
Y.O.P. Circa 1904
Other name: None
Colors made: White, blue, green and canary opalescent; crystal, amethyst, blue, and an odd yellow-green shade, all frequently gold decorated.
Pieces made: Table set, water set, berry set, toothpick, salt shaker, cruet, jelly compote and novelties.
Reintroduction or Repros: None in opalescent. The toothpick has been reproduced by the Crystal Art Glass Co. of Cambridge, OH., and later by Boyd's Crystal Art Glass Co. Crystal's colors: amber, amethyst, aqua, crystal, cobalt, Crown Tuscan, custard, custard light, forest green, milk blue, milk white, ruby, sapphire, sunset, taffeta and vaseline. Boyd's colors: candy swirl, chocolate, delphinium, deep purple, heather, ice green, impatient, lemon ice, Mardi Gras, persimmon, purple variant, rubina and tinkerbell. In 1978, they started marking with a "B" within a diamond. They called this pattern *Colonial Drape*.
Notes: See catalog reprint in the *Old Man Winter* pattern section.

SWAN, ENGLISH
Maker: Burtles, Tate and Co., Manchester, England
Named by: Heacock
Y.O.P. Circa 1885, marked with Rd 20086
Other name: None
Colors made: Yellow and pink opalescent
Pieces made: Swans in 3" and 4" sizes.
Reintroductions/Repros: None known at this time.
Note: The 4" swan could easily be confused with our own American swan by Northwood, Dugan, Fenton, and Imperial.
See the following picture.

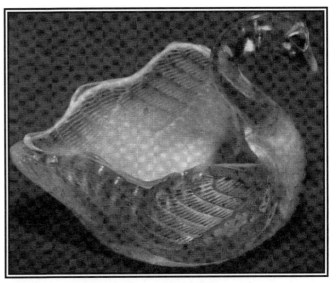
Yellow opalescent *English Swan*.

SWASTIKA*
(See figs. 304, 305, 353, 391, 648A, 848)
Maker: Dugan Glass Co., Indiana, PA.
Named by: Taylor
Y.O.P. Circa 1904
Other name: None
Colors made: White, blue, cranberry, and green opalescent.
Pieces made: Water set and syrup jug.
Reintroduction or Repros: None known at this time.
Notes: A very rare and exciting pattern. The water pitcher was made in two shapes—a tall tankard style is also known. The *Swastika* motif was produced using a spot mould to create the swastikas before blowing the item to its final shape. The *Swastika* motif is most easily identified when found on otherwise plain articles. For some reason, *Swastika* was incorporated into the *Diamonds and Clubs* pitcher and tumbler moulds which made for an interesting, but hard to distinguish, design.
* Swastika has not always had a derogatory connotation. The 1970 American Heritage Dictionary defines it as: "an ancient cosmic or religious symbol formed by a Greek cross with the ends of the arms bent at right angles in either a clockwise or counter clockwise direction."

SWIRLED FEATHER
(See figs. 597, 648K, 978, 995)
Maker: Fenton Art Glass Co., Williamstown, W.Va.
Named by: Fenton
Y.O.P. Circa 1953—present
Other name: Blown Twist
Colors made: Cranberry, blue, white, and green opalescent originally; new colors have been introduced.
Pieces made: Fairy lamps, vanity sets, candy jar, vase, hurricane lamp and cruet; others are likely.
Reintroduction or Repros: Fenton may reintroduce a pattern or color at any time. If made after 1972, the

pieces should be marked with the Fenton logo.

Notes: These pieces are often attributed to *Nailsea* but they are heavier than the old ones. Excerpt from a letter by Frank M. Fenton, dated in September, 1999: "We tried to get Mr. Wright to let us use the *Drapery Optic* mould for some other pieces in the early fifties, but he wouldn't do it. Finally he said 'if you twist it, you can use it, but don't use it straight.' "

In 1985 they made the 2007GO seven–piece water set in green opalescent, only this time they called it *Twisted Drapery Optic*. In 1986, they made an 8" *Peaches 'n Cream* cruet in limited production.

See the following catalog reprint.

Swirled Feather circa 1953. Fairy lamp and vanity set.

SWIRL OPAL JEWEL

Maker: Northwood Glass Co., Martins Ferry, W.Va.
Named by: Variation on Heacock's name
Y.O.P. Circa 1890
Other name: None
Colors made: Cranberry and blue opalescent.
Pieces made: Salt shaker; others are possible.
Reintroduction or Repros: None known at this time
Note: Limited, perhaps experimental production using the *Opal Swirl* spot mould in the *Jewel* pattern mould, which usually appears in rubina glass.

Blue opalescent salt shaker in the *Swirl Opal Jewel* pattern.

SWIRL OPAL ROYAL OAK

(See fig. 922)
Maker: Northwood Glass Co., Martins Ferry, OH.
Named by: Variation on Heacock's name
Y.O.P. Circa 1891
Other name: Opal Swirl in Royal Oak mould
Colors made: Cranberry opalescent; other colors are possible.
Pieces made: Creamer
Note: This must have been experimental. It is an important piece in that it helps confirm that Northwood had *Opal Swirl* spot moulds and may have made the straw holder in this pattern, a shape described in trade journals.

SWIRL, OPALESCENT

(See figs. 289, 296, 299, 300, 367, 374–376, 388, 574, 648J, 726–736, 839, 857, 866, 896, 922, 1006, 1008, 1017, 1032, *1055, *1056, 1085, 1115, 1118, 1124, 1257)

This blue opalescent *Swirl* lamp is one of many known; made in several sizes.

Maker: Hobbs, Brockunier & Co., Wheeling, W.Va., 1888; reissued by Beaumont Glass Co., Martins Ferry, OH., circa 1898; Nickel Plate Glass Co, Fostoria, OH., 1889; Jefferson Glass Co., Steubenville, OH., (#181 water set) circa 1905; a variant was also made by the Northwood Co., and Dugan Glass Co. (shards unearthed at factory site in Indiana, PA.); Fenton Art Glass Co., Williamstown, W.Va., circa 1907—present; and several English manufacturers.
Named by: Popular nomenclature
Y.O.P. Circa 1888—present. See above.
Other name: Hobbs pattern No. 326, Venetian Thread, Spiral Optic, Twist, Spiral (Fenton's name) and Opal Swirl (L.G. Wright's name).
Colors made: White, blue, cranberry, and green opalescent; canary is rare.
Pieces made: Pitcher (several styles), tumbler, butter dish, creamer, covered sugar, spooner, berry set, syrup, sugar shaker, cruets (at least four shapes), salt shaker, fin-

ger bowl, toothpick, mustard, rose bowl, celery, custard cup, bar bottle, bitters bottle, water bottle, lamp shades, cheese dish, straw holder, shot and juice glass, finger lamps and cruet set, English punch set, and vases.

Reintroduction or Repros: Yes, if you consider Fenton's intermittent production.

Notes: Fenton's name for this pattern is *Spiral*, circa 1907. They brought this pattern back into their line in 1939 and again in the 1950s and were still producing it in the 1990s. (See text for *Spiral*.) If the collector wants to acquire only old *Swirl* it would be a good idea to become familiar with the shape moulds used by Fenton. The only one which is difficult to discern is the water pitcher; Fenton usually uses the reeded or crimped handle, which helps to differentiate the new from the old.

Perhaps the different companies should be used in the pattern names for the many *Swirl* variants, but in some cases this may prove to be impossible. Hobbs and Beaumont used the same moulds and the same may be true of Northwood and Dugan. Thus, all variants are grouped under the generic name *Swirl*. The figure 896 straw jar matches the shape mould used by Beaumont in 1899–1900. However, it could have been made earlier by Hobbs or even Northwood (a straw jar was described in Northwood's displays in 1889). The finial on this jar was not broken off, it simply was never attached. The fig. 736 sugar shaker was made as late as 1909, appearing in Butler Brothers catalogs. Thus it was probably Dugan, the only factory making cranberry that year. The fig. 729 square–top pitcher matches shapes by Hobbs, Nickel Plate, and Beaumont. The Nickel Plate cranberry is usually more pink, with the opalescence less defined. The Hobbs cranberry is usually darker with the opalescent swirls more distinct, sometimes even raised. All pieces which have the raised opalescent swirls are old and were made by Hobbs. Hobbs also used this pattern with silver plated frames, primarily cruets and salt shakers to provide the Victorian table with a caster or seasoning set. Jefferson made this pattern in a water set, vases, rose bowls, crimped bowls, and possibly a sugar shaker.

Figure 1115 is not round as it appears, but oval. It measures 5½" by 3½". Figure 1118 has an unusual crimped top with six points. Figure 1124 tumble–up (guest set) is very rare.

See text for *Opal Swirl* and *Spiral*. See catalog reprint in *Coinspot* section. *The manufacturer is probably English.

SWIRLING MAZE
(See figs. 269, 811, 812, 894)
Maker: Jefferson Glass Co., Steubenville, OH.
Named by: Heacock
Y.O.P. Circa 1905
Other name: Maze
Colors made: White, blue, cranberry, and green opalescent.
Pieces made: Pitcher (three shapes), tumbler and ruffle–edged bowl.

Reintroduction or Repros: None known at this time.
Note: The crimped bowl is sometimes found with an edge treatment in speckled cranberry, which was previously thought to be a Northwood technique.

TARGET
(See fig. 1242)
Maker: Dugan/Diamond Glass, Indiana PA.
Named by: Uncertain
Y.O.P. Circa 1912
Other name: Pattern No. 1027
Colors made: Green opalescent; others are likely. Carnival colors of peach opalescent, white (Pearl Iris), marigold, and amethyst.
Pieces made: Vase
Reintroductions/Repros: None known at this time.

TARGET SWIRL
(See figs. 1009, 1258)
Maker: Probably English
Named by: Elmore
Y.O.P. Circa early 1900s
Other name: None
Colors made: Cranberry
Pieces made: Tumbler
Reintroduction or Repros: None known at this time.

THISTLE PATCH
(See fig. 490)
Maker: H. Northwood Co., Wheeling, W.Va.
Named by: Heacock
Y.O.P. Circa 1908
Other name: None
Colors made: White opalescent.
Pieces made: Novelties
Reintroduction or Repros: None known at this time.
Notes: This may be the same pattern which Hartung called *Thistle*. The piece Hartung illustrated is a pressed piece, not blown, so they probably are different patterns.

THOUSAND EYE
(See figs. 161-164)
Maker: Adams and Co., Pittsburgh, PA.; Richards & Hartley, Tarentum, PA., with production continued by U. S. Glass after the 1892 takeover.
Named by: Lee, *Early American Pattern Glass*
Y.O.P. Circa 1891
Other name: None
Colors made: Opalescent only in white; plain colors of crystal, apple green, canary, blue, and amber.
Pieces made: Table set, berry set, water set, plate, compotes, toothpick, hat, novelties, and rare twine holder—some are rare in opalescent.
Notes: Care should be taken not to confuse the *Thousand Eye* pattern for several other similarly designed *Raindrop* type lines. However, the other designs were not made in opalescent.

THREE FRUITS

(See figs. 414)
Maker: H. Northwood Co., Wheeling, W.Va.
Named by: Hartung, *Opalescent*
Y.O.P. Circa 1907
Other name: None
Colors made: White, green, and blue opalescent; ivory (custard) sometimes with nutmeg decoration; Carnival colors of blue, purple, green, marigold and aqua opalescent. Custard was sometimes iridized.
Pieces made: Bowls and plates in many sizes and shapes.
Reintroduction or Repros: None known at this time. See figure 415.

THREE FRUITS WITH MEANDER

(See fig. 415)
Maker: H. Northwood Co., Wheeling, W.Va.
Named by: Heacock
Y.O.P. Circa 1907
Other name: None
Colors made: White and blue opalescent; Carnival colors of blue, purple, green, marigold, and aqua opalescent.
Pieces made: Bowls
Reintroduction or Repros: None known at this time.
Notes: The *Meander* pattern is on the bottom side of the bowl and can be seen by turning the bowl over.

TOKYO

(See figs. 133, 150, 235, 507)
Maker: Jefferson Glass Co., Steubenville, OH., and Follansbee, W.Va.
Named by: Original manufacturer's name
Y.O.P. Circa 1905–1908
Other name: Pattern No. 212
Colors made: White, blue, and green opalescent; plain crystal, blue, and apple green. Colors were occasionally decorated with gold.
Pieces made: Table set, water set, berry set, salt shakers, cruet, jelly compote, toothpick holder, vase. Sometimes the vase was "pulled" so tall that the pattern became difficult to distinguish.
Reintroduction or Repros: The Fenton Art Glass Co. produced a compote in this pattern which they named *Scroll and Eye*, No. 8248, and categorized it as a nut dish. This nut dish was made in blue opalescent, lime sherbet (1977), cameo opalescent (1980), French cream (1981), amethyst, country peach and ruby (1982). The pieces were all marked. More pieces and colors are probable, Fenton may reintroduce a pattern or color at any time. If made after 1972, the pieces should be marked with the Fenton logo.
Notes: The stopper is not original. See catalog reprint in the *Astro* pattern section.

TRAILING VINE

(See fig. 625)
Maker: Coudersport Tile & Ornamental Glass Co., Coudersport, PA.
Named by: Gaddis, *Keys to Custard Glass*
Y.O.P. Circa 1903
Other name: Endless Vine*
Colors made: White, canary, and blue opalescent; decorated milk glass and custard glass, blue milk glass; rare in emerald green.
Pieces made: Table set, berry set, water set, and novelty bowls.
Reintroduction or Repros: None known at this time.
Notes: It is possible that only novelty bowls were made in opalescent. Any table set piece in opalescent would be rare.
Endless Vine named by Floyd W. Bliss. (*Spinning Wheel*, November 1972)

TREE OF LOVE

(See fig. 488)
Maker: Unknown. Possibly made by Sowerby and Co., Gateshead–on–Tyne.
Named by: Heacock
Y.O.P. Unknown—possibly late 1880s
Other name: None
Colors made: White opalescent.
Pieces made: Bowl and jelly compote
Reintroduction or Repros: None known at this time.
Notes: The name of this pattern is a variation of the *Tree of Life* name which graces far too many patterns. *Opalescent Tree of Life* was considered, but discarded; Portland Glass collectors might see it advertised and think it is a rare piece of Portland pattern glass, which it most decidedly is not.

TREE STUMP MUG

(See fig. 496)
Maker: Possibly Northwood Glass Co.*
Named by: Heacock
Y.O.P. Uncertain
Other name: Stump Mug
Colors made: White, blue, and green opalescent.
Pieces made: Mug
Reintroduction or Repros: None known at this time.
Notes: The size is small, possibly this was produced as a child's mug? *This wonderful mug does not appear in *Harry Northwood, The Early Years, 1881–1900* or *Harry Northwood, The Wheeling Years, 1901–1925* so the Northwood attribution is less likely.

TREE TRUNK

(See fig. 434)
Maker: H. Northwood Co., Wheeling, W.Va.

Named by: Hartung, *Opalescent*
Y.O.P. Circa 1908
Other name: None
Colors made: White, blue, and green opalescent; custard (sometimes with a pink stain); Carnival colors of marigold, blue, green, purple, white, ice blue, ice green and aqua opalescent.
Pieces made: Vases in many sizes and diameters ranging in height from 7" to 18".
Reintroduction or Repros: None known at this time.
Note: Usually signed with "N" in a circle. The design really does resemble tree bark as it shows irregular lines, bumps, knots etc. When the vase is swung to one of its taller heights the knots appear to resemble tadpoles. See *Feathers* text for catalog reprint.

TWIG (VASE)

(See fig. 646)
Maker: The Northwood Co., Dugan Glass Co., Indiana, PA.
Named by: Presznick 4
Y.O.P. Circa 1898; probably circa 1908 for Dugan
Other name: Paneled Twig, and Beauty in Carnival colors.
Colors made: White, blue, and canary opalescent; Carnival colors of marigold, purple and smoke.
Pieces made: Vases
Reintroduction or Repros: Yes, beware of pieces with solid glass branches at the base.
Notes: These vases were made in two sizes. See catalog reprint in the *Winterlily* pattern section.

A VASE BARGAIN.

Opalescent Vases—Large, handsome vases in assorted shapes and colors. Assorted flint, blue and yellow opalescent in each dozen. Boxed. Per dozen 88

Twig bud vase, as shown in a G. Sommers and Co. catalog.

TWIG, TINY

(See figs. 568, 1228)
Maker: The Northwood Co., and Dugan Glass Co., Indiana, PA.
Named by: Heacock
Y.O.P. Circa 1898; probably circa 1908 for Dugan.
Other name: Beauty
Colors made: White, blue, canary, and rare in green opalescent; Carnival colors of marigold, purple and smoke.
Pieces made: Vases
Reintroduction or Repros: None known at this time.

TWIST

(See fig. 556)
Maker: Model Flint Glass Co., Findlay OH., and Albany, IN. Model Flint joined the National Glass Co. in 1899–1900.
Named by: Kamm 4
Y.O.P. Circa 1901
Other name: Model Swirl, Ribbed Swirl, and Swirl
Colors made: White, blue, green, and canary opalescent; crystal, frosted crystal, amber, blue, and decorated crystal.
Pieces made: Pitcher, tumbler, vase (four sizes), butter dish, cake salver, celery vase and tray, comport, cracker jar, creamer, sugar, cruet (two sizes), cup and saucer, bowl (many sizes including berry set), syrup, mug, punch bowl (two sizes), rose bowl (four sizes), comport (two sizes), salt and pepper, miniature table set (creamer, sugar, spooner, butter dish). This pattern also had some square pieces—comports and nappies.
Notes: The miniature set has been incorrectly attributed to the Greentown glass firm. It most decidedly is not a Greentown product.

TWIST, BLOWN

(See figs. 259, 368, 394, 825, 826, 855, 1261)
Maker: Northwood* and West Virginia Glass, Martins Ferry (in their *Optic* mould). Both companies joined the National Glass Co. in 1899-1900.
Named by: Hartung, *Opalescent*
Y.O.P. Circa 1892 to 1905
Other name: Blown Twist
Colors made: White, blue, green, cranberry (rare) and canary opalescent.
Pieces made: Water set (twisted handle), sugar shaker, and celery vase.
Reintroduction or Repros: Yes, by Fenton Art Glass Co. Pieces made in 1953: fairy lamp, perfume, puff box, candy box, hurricane lamp, and cruet in white, blue, green, and cranberry opalescent. Fenton called this pattern *Swirled Feather*. See text for *Swirled Feather*.
Notes: *This pattern was made by Northwood while at Buckeye, and at his own companies in Martins Ferry, OH., Ellwood City, PA., and Indiana, PA. The pattern can also be found in the *Nine–Panel* mould.

TWISTED RIBS

(See fig. 522, 1232)
Maker: Dugan Glass Co., Indiana, PA.
Named by: Heacock
Y.O.P. Circa 1906 to 1908
Other name: None
Colors made: White, blue, and green opalescent, also crystal and Nile green; Carnival colors of golden and pearl luster. Golden probably refers to peach opalescent.
Pieces made: Vases
Reintroduction or Repros: None known at this time.
See the catalog reprint on the following page.

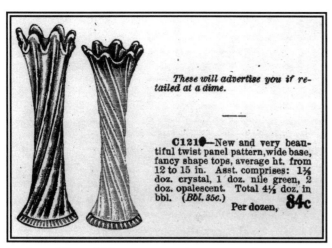

These will advertise you if retailed at a dime.

C121●—New and very beautiful twist panel pattern, wide base, fancy shape tops, average ht. from 12 to 15 in. Asst. comprises: 1½ doz. crystal, 1 doz. nile green, 2 doz. opalescent. Total 4½ doz. in bbl. (*Bbl. 35c.*) Per dozen, **84c**

Pair of *Twisted Ribs* vases, turned in opposite directions.

TWISTER

(See fig. 472)
Maker: Unknown
Named by: Joe B. Bell
Y.O.P. Uncertain
Other name: None
Colors made: White, blue, and green opalescent.
Pieces made: Bowls
Reintroduction or Repros: None known at this time.

VESTA (HOBNAIL IN SQUARE)

(See figs. 157, 489)
Maker: Aetna Glass & Mfg. Co., Bellaire, OH.
Named by: Original manufacturer's name.
Y.O.P. Circa 1887
Other name: Hobnail in Square
Colors made: Primarily crystal, white opalescent; rare in colored opalescent.
Pieces made: Water set, table set, berry set, celery vase, salt shaker, and assorted compotes.
Reintroduction or Repros: Yes—see figures 586, 587 and text for *Diamond Lace*.
Note: Heacock initially called this pattern *Hobnail in Square*. In his series *The Glass Collector, Collecting Glass,* he began advising the reader of the original manufacturer's names. Heacock believed original names should be used when known. Heacock advised us that the original name for this pattern was *Vesta* in his *Victorian Colored Pattern Glass Book 6, Oil Cruets From A to Z*. Thus the name change for this edition.

VICTOR (JEWELLED HEART)

(See figs. 146, 152, 198, 218)
Maker: Dugan Glass Co., Indiana, PA.
Named by: Original manufacturer's name
Y.O.P. Circa 1904
Other name: Jewelled Heart, Kamm 5
Colors made: White, blue, and green opalescent; crystal, blue, apple green and peach opal, purple and marigold Carnival (circa 1909).
Pieces made: Water set, table set, berry set (round or ruffle–edged), cruet, syrup, salt shaker, toothpick holder, novelties, chop plate, small size plates, and nappies. Also, a condiment set consisting of cruet, salt/pepper, and toothpick holder on a round, flat plate which functions as a tray.
Reintroduction or Repros: Yes, L.G. Wright has had various glass companies making this pattern for them for many years. In 1968, they began marketing this pattern under the name *Sweetheart*. Toothpick, creamer, covered sugar, goblet, wine, bowl, spooner, fairy lamp, and oil lamp are the pieces made in crystal, blue, amber, amethyst, pink, and ruby. Other pieces and colors are likely.

Over the last few years, Singleton Bailey of Loris, S.C., has been having the Fenton Art Glass Co. produce pieces for him in the *Farmyard* pattern with the *Victor (Jewelled Heart)* pattern on the exterior. These pieces were made in very limited quantities and colors as follows: Basket in black Carnival (60 pieces), Electric blue, Carnival (116 pieces) and red Carnival (66 pieces); Cuspidor in black Carnival (78 pieces); Chop plate in black Carnival (47 pieces), Electric blue (92 pieces), Sea green Carnival (150 pieces); Rose bowl in black Carnival (108 pieces), Electric blue (132 pieces); Whimsey bowl in black Carnival (72 pieces), Electric blue (138 pieces). These pieces are signed. More colors and pieces are probable, since Singleton Bailey has had Fenton make many items for him.

Excerpt from a letter by Frank M. Fenton dated in September, 1999: "Under the caption *Victor (Jeweled Heart)*, I have written a little note saying 'Don't forget MiMi.' Singleton Bailey of Loris, S.C., now owns that mould, but the mould originally was made by a fellow named Chuck Stone of Columbus, Ohio. Chuck's wife was named MiMi. He came to us to make glass out of the mould, and we insisted that the name MiMi be put on the bottom so that people would know it was not an old piece. When Singleton acquired the mould, he then put his own identification, the <DBs>, on it."
Notes: Heacock initially called this pattern *Jewelled Heart*. In his series *The Glass Collector, Collecting Glass,* he began advising the reader of the original factory names. Heacock believed original factory names should be used when known. The original factory name is used in *Dugan/Diamond, The Story of Indiana, Pennsylvania, Glass.*

(Continued on page 209)

Alaska

1

2

3

4

5

6

7

Tumbler

Water pitcher

8

9

10

11

Spooner

Butter

Sugar

Creamer

12

Celery Tray/Jewel Tray

13

Salt

14

Cruet
n.o.s.

15

Pepper

16

Sauce

17

Berry

18

Sauce

Carnelian

| **19** Spooner | **20** Butter | **21** Creamer | **22** Sugar | **23** Water pitcher | **24** Tumbler |

Encore

| **25** Water pitcher | **26** Spooner | **27** Butter | **28** Sugar | **29** Creamer |

Wild Bouquet

| **30** Sauce | **31** Berry | **32** Jelly | **33** Tumbler | **34** Water pitcher |

35 Spooner

36 Butter

37 Sugar

38 Creamer

114

Inverted Fan & Feather

39	40	41	42	43	44
Creamer	Butter	Sugar	Spooner	Water pitcher	Tumbler

Intaglio

45	46	47	48	49
Creamer	Butter	Spooner	Water pitcher	Tumbler

Beatty Swirl   Intaglio

50		51	52	115
Water tray		Sauce	Berry	

Circled Scroll

53
Sauce

54
Berry

Sauce

55
Water pitcher

56 Tumbler

57
Salt

58
Jelly

Pepper

59
Spooner

60
Butter

61
Creamer

62 Sugar

Beatty Swirl

Scroll with Acanthus

63
Water pitcher

64 Sugar

65 Water pitcher

66
Jelly

National

Paneled Holly

116

67 Berry

68
Spooner

69
Creamer

PRESSED OPALESCENT GLASS

Manila & Other
Albany Glass

70

Celery

71

Cracker jar

72

Tumbler–footed

73

Water pitcher

74

Tumbler–collared

75

Creamer

76

Sugar

77

Butter

78

Spooner

79

Toothpick

Ribbed Spiral

80

Jelly

81

Cup & saucer

82

Covered sugar

83

Lady's spittoon

84

Rose bowl

85

Sauce

86

Berry

Sauce

87

Bon–Bon

117

88 Tumbler **89** Pitcher Tumbler **90** Water pitcher

Swag with Brackets

Paneled Holly

91
Creamer

92 Sugar

93 Butter

94
Spooner

Swag with Brackets

95
Spooner

96
Butter

Frosted Leaf & Basketweave

97 Sugar

98
Creamer

99 Sauce

Hobnail & Paneled Thumbprint

100 Master berry

Carnelian

101 Sauce

Daisy & Greek Key

102 Water pitcher

103 Tumbler

104 Water pitcher

105 Powder or puff jar

Klondyke

Jackson

106 Butter

107 Rose bowl

108 Sugar

109 Creamer

110 Salt

Drapery, Northwood

111 Spooner

112 Butter

113 Sugar

114 Creamer

115 Water pitcher

116 Sauce

117 Berry

Sauce

118 Tumbler

119

PRESSED OPALESCENT GLASS

Palm Beach

119 Sugar

120 Creamer

121 Butter

122 Spooner

123 Tumbler

124 Water pitcher

125 Sauce

126 Finger bowl

Diamond Spearhead

Regal, Northwood

127 Butter

Fan

128 Sugar

129 Celery

130 Syrup

131 Spooner

Beatty Rib

132 Tumbler

National

133 Jelly

Tokyo

134 Jelly

Intaglio

135 Jelly

Swag with Brackets

136 Cruet: n.o.s.

Nautilus

An Assortment

137
Honeycomb and
Clover

138
Dolly Madison

139
Iris

140
Double Greek Key

141
Colonial

142
Frosted Leaf &
Basketweave

143
Regal, Northwood

144
Nautilus

145 New York

146
Victor

147
Waterlily with
Cattails

148
Regal, Northwood

149
Idyll

150
Tokyo

151 Tumbler
Waterlily with
Cattails

152
Victor
Sauce

153
Acorn Burrs
Sauce

154
Nautilus
Sauce

155
Iris

121

Hobnail & Thousand Eye

156	157	158	159	160
Hobnail, 4 Ft.	**Vesta**	**Hobnail**	**Hobnail**	**Over–All Hob**
Sugar, non–opalescent	Barber bottle	Hobbs	Hobbs Butter	Pitcher

Thousand Eye

161	162	Celery vase	163	164
Creamer	Spooner			Water pitcher

165 Creamer	166 Cruet, n.o.s.	167 Spooner	168 Water pitcher	169 Tumbler
122 Over–All Hob	**Adonis Hobnail**	**Hobnail, Northwood**		**Over–All Hob**

Ribbed Spiral

Water set

170   Caster set

171

172

Curtain Call

Adonis Swirl

173
Syrup

174
Spooner

175
Sugar

176
Pitcher

177   Tumbler

Adonis Swirl

Buttons & Braids

178   Gas shade

179

180

181
Pressed tumbler

182

Diamond Spearhead

Indiv. creamer

Finecut & Roses

Spooner

Bead and Panel

Cruet

183
Covered Sugar

Diadem

184
Breakfast sugar

185
Breakfast creamer

186   Butter

Beatty Swirl   123

An Assortment

187   Caster set
Stripe

188   Pitcher
Waterlily with Cattails

189   Caster set
Stripe

190   **Diadem**
Butter

191   **Wild Bouquet**
Cruet

192   **Diamond Spearhead**
Goblet

193   Butter
New York

Celery vases

194
Beatty Honeycomb

195   **Adonis Swirl**

196   Celery vase
Block

Rare green

197   **Scroll with Acanthus**

198   Tumbler
124   **Victor**

199   Spooner
Idyll

200   Gas shade
Duchess

201   Canary
Scroll with Acanthus

Ribbed Spiral

203

**Pump &
Trough**

204

205 Spooner

Banana Boat **202**

Alaska

208

Creamer

New York

209

Admiral

Butter

206

Butter

**Double Greek
Key**

207

Toothpick

Jelly

Maple Leaf **211**

212

213

Beatty Rib

210

Old Man Winter

Small basket

**Diamond
Spearhead**

Spooner

214

Peacocks on a Fence

Salad

125

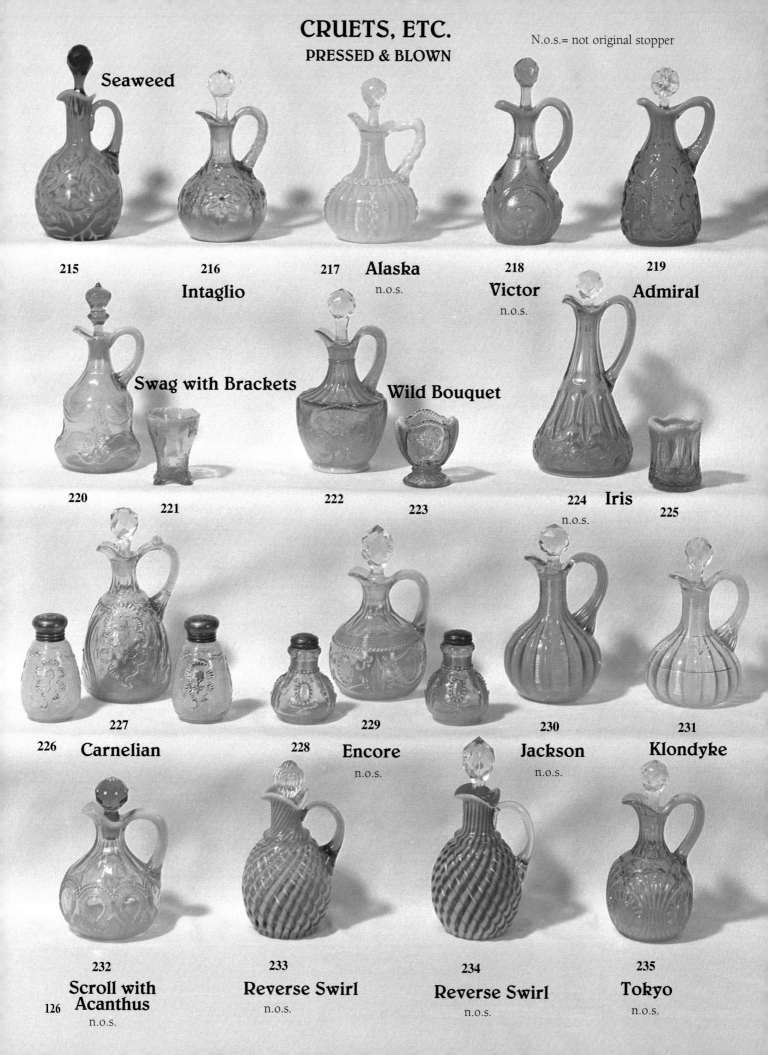

CRUETS, ETC.
PRESSED & BLOWN

N.o.s.= not original stopper

Seaweed

215

216 Intaglio

217 Alaska
n.o.s.

218 Victor
n.o.s.

219 Admiral

Swag with Brackets

Wild Bouquet

220

221

222

223

224 Iris
n.o.s.

225

226 **227** Carnelian

228 **229** Encore
n.o.s.

230 Jackson
n.o.s.

231 Klondyke

232 Scroll with
Acanthus
n.o.s.

126

233 Reverse Swirl
n.o.s.

234 Reverse Swirl
n.o.s.

235 Tokyo
n.o.s.

Ribbed Opal Lattice

Reverse Swirl

240

Sugar shaker

Salt shaker

238
Tumbler

239
Mustard

241   **242**
Toothpick

Chrysanthemum Swirl

236
Tumbler

237
Pitcher

Unfrosted

Salt & pepper

243

244
Toothpick

245
Cruet

246
Covered butter

247
Covered sugar

248
Celery vase

Seaweed, Opalescent

251
Celery vase

252
Pitcher

249
Sugar

250
Creamer

253
Toothpick

254
Spooner

255
Salt shaker

256
Oil cruet

257
Sugar shaker

258
Tumbler

Pitchers & Tumblers

259 **Twist**
Blown

260
Arabian Nights

261
Coinspot

262 Square–top
Coinspot

263
Stripe
Ring–neck

264 **Criss–Cross**
Consolidated

265
Daisy & Fern
Northwood

Poinsettia

Water set
squatty shape

266

128

267

Pitchers & Tumblers

269
Swirling Maze

Tankard shape

268
Honeycomb

270   **Opaline Brocade**   **271**

272
Poinsettia   **273**

274
Buttons & Braids

275

276
Buttons & Braids

BLOWN OPALESCENT GLASS

Unique opal handle

277
Stripe

278
Reverse Swirl

279
Daisy & Fern

Pitcher

280 **Daisy & Fern,**
Northwood

281 Tumbler

282   **283**
Coral Reef

284
Windows, Plain

285 Water carafe
Bullseye

286 Creamer
Reverse Swirl

287 Vase   **288** Spooner
Floradine

Fern, Ribbed

Toothpick

289
Swirl
Rubina

290
Herringbone

291
Toothpick

292
Daisy & Fern
Apple Blossom
mould Spooner

293
Lattice

294 Finger bowl
Windows, Plain

Fern, Opal

295 Pitcher

Swirl, Opal

296 Pitcher

Daisy & Fern

297 Pitcher

299 Swirl, Opal

Tankard, Beaumont

300

Rose bowl, Jefferson

301

Syrup

Coinspot & Swirl

302 Optic mould

Daisy & Fern

298

Lamp

Reverse Swirl

306

Baby Coinspot

Syrup

303

Butter

Opaline Brocade

304

305

Water set

Swastika, Opal

307
Pitcher
Herringbone

308
Cruet

309
Butter
Reverse Swirl

310
Pitcher
Christmas Snowflake

311
Spooner
Windows, Swirled

312
T.P.

313
Syrup
Criss–Cross

314
T.P.

315
Syrup

316
Tumbler
Daisy in Criss–Cross

317
Salt & pepper
Opaline Brocade

318
Finger bowl

319
Sugar shaker

132

Hobnail by Hobbs, Brockunier & Co.

Water pitcher
Old reeded handle

321

320
Lemonade pitcher

326
Creamer

327
Bride's basket

322
Syrup, Rubina

323 Milk pitcher

324
Celery

325
Tumbler

328
Syrup

329
Cruet

330
Barber bottle

333
Miniature water pitcher

334
Lemonade set on original tray

331
Berry bowl

332
Berry sauce

Daisy & Fern, Northwood

335

Cruet
Apple Blossom mould

336

Pickle caster
Apple Blossom mould

337

Toothpick

338

Cruet

Ribbed Opal Lattice

Lattice

Frosted

339

Cruet, frosted

340

Toothpick, unfrosted

341

Sugar shaker

342

Toothpick

Opaline Brocade

Fern Opalescent

343

Rose bowl

344

Syrup

345

Cruet

346

Salt & pepper

Blown Opalescent Syrups, etc.

347
Coinspot
9–panel

348
Coinspot
Ring–neck

349 Unfrosted
Lattice

350
Stripe

351 **Daisy & Fern**
Optic mould

352
Polka Dot

353
Swastika

354
Opaline Brocade
Old reeded handle

Windows, Swirled

355
Syrup, tall

356
Toothpick

357
Sugar shaker

358
Syrup, squatty

359
Salt shaker

135

BLOWN OPALESCENT GLASS

Sugar Shakers, etc.

360
Poinsettia

361
Daisy & Fern
Buckeye

362
Daisy & Fern
Northwood

363
Daisy & Fern
Apple Blossom mould

364
Daisy & Fern
Alternating panels

365
Lattice
Bulbous

366
Lattice
Tapered

367
Swirl
Tall

368
Twist, blown

369
Leaf Mold

370
Coinspot

371
Coinspot
Ring neck

372
Toothpick

373
Coinspot
9–panel

374
Toothpick

375
Swirl
Short

376
Toothpick

Assorted Tumblers
PRESSED & BLOWN

377
Encore

378
Idyll

379
Paneled Holly

380
Beatty Swirl

381
Lustre Flute

382
Lattice

383
Seaweed

384
Daisy & Fern

385
Stripe, Opalescent

Diamond quilted

386
Poinsettia

Pressed

387
Curtain Optic

Fenton

388
Swirl, Opalescent

389
Wide Stripe

Rare green

390
Daffodil

391
Swastika

392
Opaline Brocade

393
Poinsettia

394
Twist

395
Ocean Shell

396
Beaded Fleur–de–Lis

397
Leaf Chalice

398
Beaded Star & Medallion
Gas shade

399
Sir Lancelot

400
Winter Cabbage

401
Cabbage Leaf

402
Heart–Handled Open O's

403
Jefferson Wheel

404
Jackson

405
Reflecting Diamonds

406
Abalone

407
Ring–Handled Basket

408
Hearts & Clubs

Dolphin Compote

Dolphin Compote

409

410

411

409

411

Dolphin

Dolphin Petticoat

412

413

414 **Three Fruits**

Blossoms & Palms

Daisy & Plume

415

416

417

Three Fruits with Meander

Grape & Cherries

Greek Key & Scales

418

419

420

Beaded Stars and Swag

Netted Roses

Bushel Basket

OPALESCENT NOVELTIES

421
Heatherbloom

422
Little Nell

423
Zippers & Loops

424
Reverse Drapery

425 Palm & Scroll

426 Keyhole

427
Simple Simon

428
Carnelian

Rare green

429
Maple Leaf

430
Hilltop Vines

431
140 Jewel & Fan

432
Desert Garden

433
Daisy Dear

Cherry Panels

Pineapple & Fan

434

435

436

437   **Leaf Tiers**

Tree Trunk

438   **Reflections**

439   **Vintage**

440   **Piasa Bird**

441   **Palisades**

442

Rose Show

Carnival opalescent

443   **Spool**

444   **Jewels & Drapery**

445   **Fan**

446

Finecut & Roses

447   **Poinsettia Lattice**

448   **Berry Patch**

449   **Waterlily with Cattails**   141

Maple Leaf Chalice

Hearts & Flowers

Palisades

450

451

452

453

454

Pearl Flowers   **Fluted Bars & Beads**

455

456

457

458

Cashews   **Spokes & Wheels**   **Blocked Thumbprint & Beads**   **Scheherezade**

Shell & Wild Rose

459   **Buckeye**   460   **Basket, Fenton**   461   **Beaded Cable**   462

463

464

465

Diamond Point & Fleur-de-Lis   **Waterlily with Cattails**   **Lattice Medallions**

142

466
Spool

467
Aurora Borealis

468
Miniature Epergne

469   470
Beads & Bark

471
Wishbone & Drape

472
Twister

473
Reverse Drapery

474
Fancy Fantails

475
Blackberry

476
Button Panels

477
Pearls & Scales

143

OPALESCENT NOVELTIES

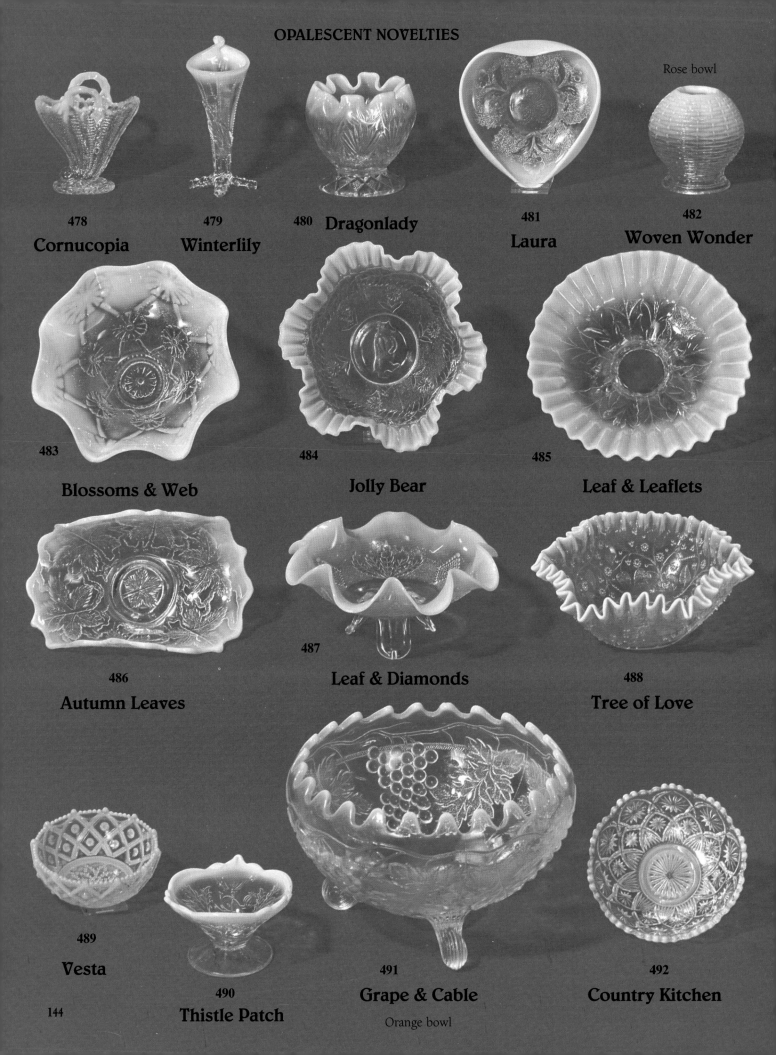

478
Cornucopia

479
Winterlily

480 **Dragonlady**

481
Laura

Rose bowl

482
Woven Wonder

483
Blossoms & Web

484
Jolly Bear

485
Leaf & Leaflets

486
Autumn Leaves

487
Leaf & Diamonds

488
Tree of Love

489
Vesta

490
Thistle Patch

491
Grape & Cable

Orange bowl

492
Country Kitchen

OPALESCENT NOVELTIES

Mug

Rose bowl

493
Corn Vase

494
Stork & Rushes

495
Opal Open

496
Tree Stump Mug

497
Grapevine Cluster

498 **Leaf & Beads**

499 **Wheel & Block**

500
Beads & Curly Cues

501
Meander

502
Beaded Drapes

503
Encore

504
Many Loops

505
Roulette

506
Ruffles & Rings

507
Tokyo

OPALESCENT NOVELTIES

Chop plate
508
Northern Star

Rose bowl
509 Beaded Fan

510 Coral

511
Barbells

512 Astro

513
Carousel

514
Woven Wonder

515
Windflower

516
Popsicle Sticks

517
Sea Spray
Olive

518
Open O's

519
Spool of Threads

520
Mikado
Olive

OPALESCENT NOVELTIES

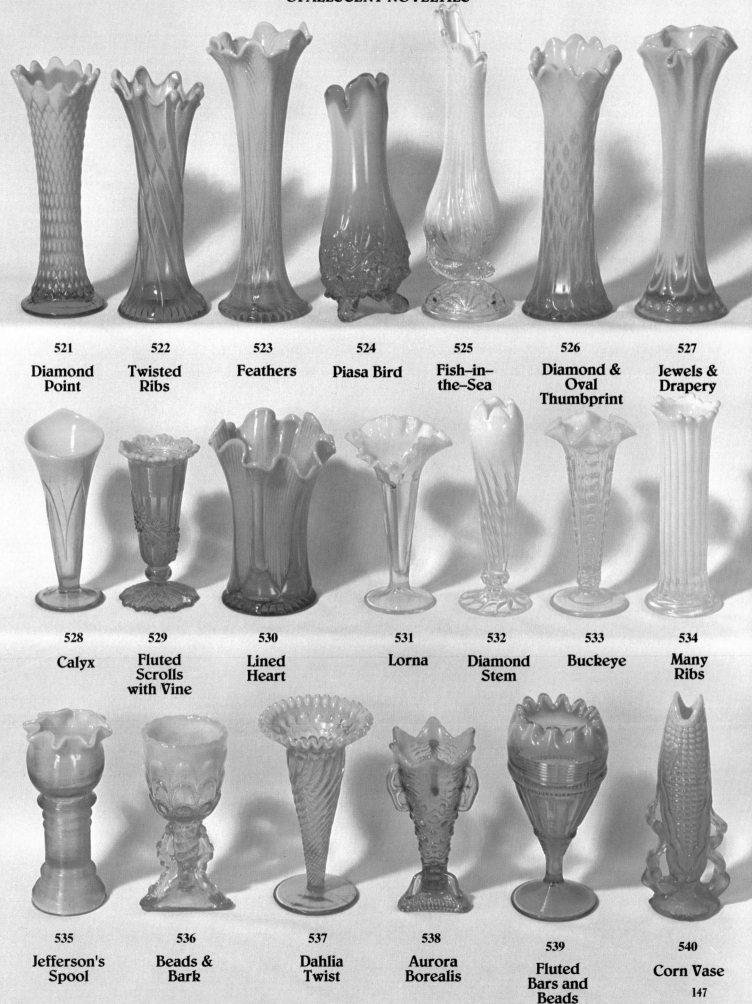

521
Diamond
Point

522
Twisted
Ribs

523
Feathers

524
Piasa Bird

525
Fish–in–
the–Sea

526
Diamond &
Oval
Thumbprint

527
Jewels &
Drapery

528
Calyx

529
Fluted
Scrolls
with Vine

530
Lined
Heart

531
Lorna

532
Diamond
Stem

533
Buckeye

534
Many
Ribs

535
Jefferson's
Spool

536
Beads &
Bark

537
Dahlia
Twist

538
Aurora
Borealis

539
Fluted
Bars and
Beads

540
Corn Vase

147

English Opalescent

541
Coronation

542
Piccadilly

543
Crown Jewels

544

545
Ascot

546
Contessa

547
William & Mary

548
War of Roses

549
Lady
Chippendale

550

Richelieu

551

Assorted Tiny Things

Toothpick holders, salt dips, etc...

Idyll

Twist

Manila

Beatty Rib

552

553 Salt dip

554
Beatty
Honeycomb

555

556 Mini spooner

557 Melon
with
Sprig

558
New York

559 William & Mary

560 Polka Dot

561 Over–All Hob

562 Adonis Swirl 563

564
Fern

565
Ring–Handle Basket

566

Reverse
Swirl

Ring neck

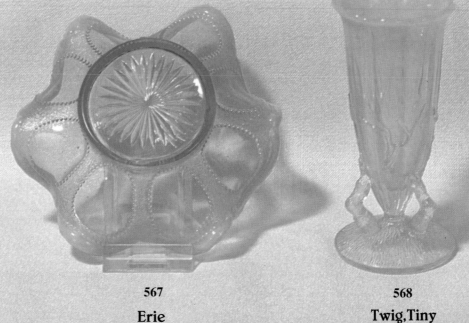

567

Erie

Nappy

568

Twig, Tiny

Vase

Assorted Tiny Things

Mini bride's bowl

Toothpick

569

Opaline Brocade

570

Colonial Stairsteps

571

Jackson

Mini epergne

572

Bullseye

Gas shade

573

Seaweed

574

Swirl, Opalescent

575

Circled Scroll

576   **577**

Beatty Honeycomb

578

Diamond Spearhead

579

Match

580

Toothpick

Beatty Rib

581

Mustard

582

Mug

583

Ind. Creamer

Beatty Honeycomb

Reintroduction/Reproduction Opalescent Glass

A representative example

Dolphin Candlesticks

584

Beatty Waffle

585

586   Diamond Lace

587

Moon & Star   588

589   Eyedot

Daisy & Button

590

591   Beatty Waffle

592

Dot Optic

593   Jersey swirl

594   Dolphin

595   Orange Tree

596   Cactus

597

Swirled Feather

598   Spiral   599

600   Daisy & Fern (Fern)

601   Coin Dot

602   151   Honeycomb

Reintroduction/Reproduction Opalescent Glass

A representative example

Not A Reproduction

603
Panel Grape

604

605
Daisy & Fern (Fern)

606
Inverted Fan & Feather

607
Corn Vase

608
Diamond Optic

609 Peacock

610

611
Moon & Star

612 Beatty Waffle

613
Coin Dot

614
Polka Dot

615 Hobnail

616

617
Stars & Stripes

618
Rib Optic

619
Argonaut

152

620
Hobnail

621
Hand Vase

622
Coin Dot

623

624
Fan & File

625

Trailing Vine

626

Wreathed Cherry

Creamer

Illustrations of

Pressed Opalescent Pattern Glass

627

Nautilus

Water pitcher

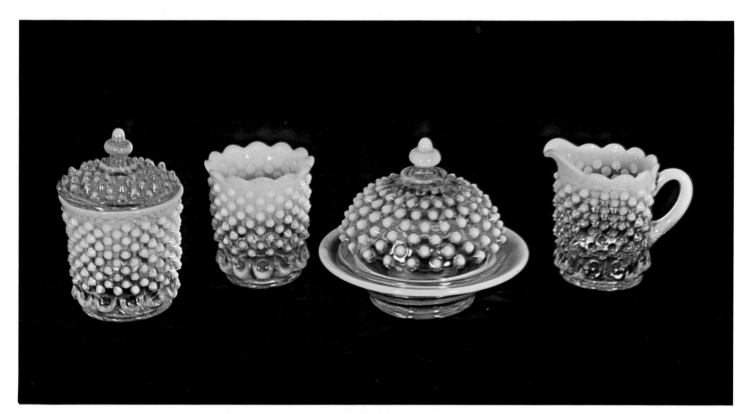

Table set

Butter   Creamer

Water pitchers

634
Diamonds, Opalescent

635
Honeycomb, Opalescent

636
Tankard shape
Reverse Swirl

Illustrations of

Blown Opalescent Pattern Glass

Celery

637
Coinspot
Jefferson

638
Daffodils
Oil lamp

639
Scottish Moor

640
Lattice
Spooner

641
Opaline Brocade
Spooner

642
Daisy & Fern
Cruet
n.o.s.

643
Seaweed
Butter

155

644
Daisy & Button
Bun tray

645
Maple Leaf
Dugan Glass

648
Strawberry and Dahlia Twist
Epergne

646
Twig (Vase)
Rare green, paneled

647
Fish–in–the–Sea
Vase

Encyclopedia of
Victorian Colored Pattern Glass

Book II
OPALESCENT GLASS from A to Z

648 A. Swastika
648 B. Opaline Brocade
648 C. Leaf Mold
648 D. Corn Vase
648 E. Manila
648 F. Chrysanthemum Swirl
648 G. Manila

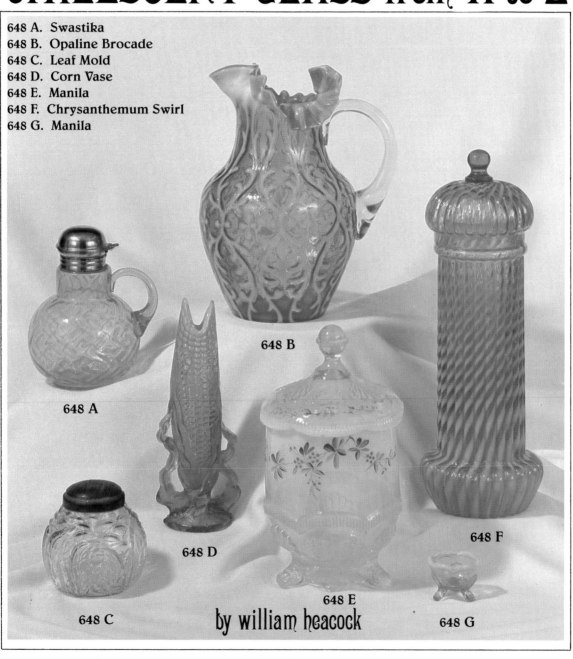

648 B

648 A

648 D

648 E

648 F

648 C

648 G

by william heacock

Encyclopedia of

Victorian Colored Pattern Glass

BOOK 9
Cranberry Opalescent from A to Z

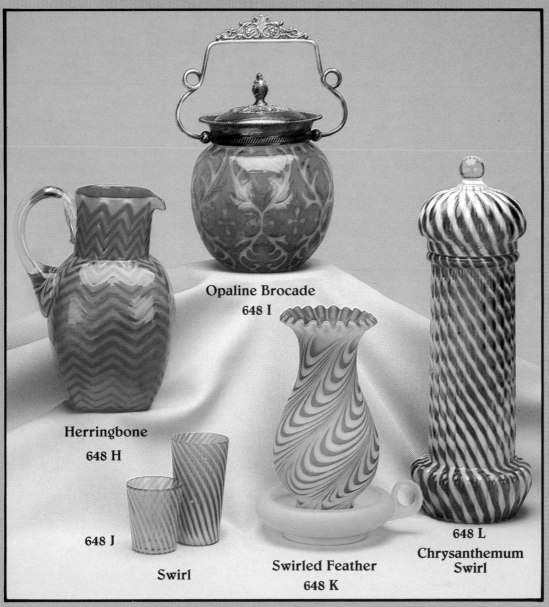

Opaline Brocade
648 I

Herringbone
648 H

648 J

Swirl

Swirled Feather
648 K

648 L
Chrysanthemum
Swirl

by william heacock & william gamble

649

Opaline Brocade

Wine Decanter

OPALINE BROCADE

Nine Panel Mould

654

650
Ribbon Tie Mould
Tankard

651
Tumbler

652
Squat Mould
Pitcher

653
Tumbler

Tankard

655
Butter

656
Spooner

657
Sugar

658
Creamer

659   Cracker jar

Wide Waist Mould

663
Cruet

Ribbon Tie Mould

160   **660**   Salt & pepper

661   Sugar shaker

662   Syrup
Ball–Shape Mould

Oval Indiana Mould

DAISY AND FERN (except fig. 669)

Pitcher **664**

Northwood Swirl

665

666

Ball Shape

Pitcher

667

Tumbler

668 Pitcher

Shoulder Mould

Northwood Swirl

669

Bulbous syrup

Daisy In Criss-Cross

670

Sauce

671

Berry bowl

672

Sugar shaker

673

Cruet

Sugar shaker

Spooner caster insert

674

Wide Waist

675

Rose bowl

676

Apple Blossom Mould

SEAWEED AND CORAL REEF

677
Triangular Crimp
Water pitcher

678
Celery vase

679
Square

Bitters bottles

680
Round
Coral Reef

681
Square Top
Water pitcher

682
Sugar

683
Butter

684
Spooner

685
Creamer

Toothpick

686
Bulbous Base

Coral Reef

687A & B
Salt & pepper

Cruet

162   **688**
Bulbous Base

Sugar shaker

689 Bulbous Base

690
Syrup

Tumbler

691

Satin Cruet

692
Bulbous Base

CRISS–CROSS, CONSOLIDATED

693
Frosted Satin
Pitcher

694
Salt shaker

695
Toothpick

696
Tumbler

697
Shiny
Pitcher

698
Sugar

699
Butter

700
Spooner

701
Creamer

702 Satin cruet

703 Shiny butter

704 Shiny cruet

REVERSE SWIRL & CHRYSANTHEMUM SWIRL

(R.S.)

(C.S.)

705
R.S. pitcher

706
R.S. tumbler

707
C.S. salt & pepper

708
C.S. pitcher

709
C.S. tumbler

710
Tankard

Chrysanthemum Swirl Variant

711
R.S. celery

712
R.S. spooner

713
R.S. sugar

714
R.S. salt & pepper

715
R.S. cruet

716
R.S. sugar shaker

717
R.S. syrup

718
C.S. cruet

164

719
C.S. toothpick

720
C.S. spooner

721 C.S. butter

722
C.S. creamer

723
Sugar shaker

724
C.S. syrup

OPALESCENT STRIPE & SWIRL

725 Pitcher
Ring Neck Stripe

726 Tumbler
Swirl

727 Pitcher
Swirl, Beaumont

728 Cruet
Swirl, Hobbs

729 Pitcher
Square–Top

730 **Swirl, Hobbs** **731**
Celery vase   Sugar shaker

732
Sugar shaker

733
Swirl, Nickel **734**
T.P.

735
Swirl, Hobbs
Syrup pitcher

736 Sugar shaker
Swirl

737
Stripe
Shank–shoulder cruet

738 Shank–waist cruet
Stripe

739 **Ring Neck Stripe**
Cruet

740
Toothpick

741
Stripe
Barber bottle

165

LATTICE & RIBBED OPAL LATTICE

742   Satin pitcher
Lattice (Buckeye)

743
Ribbed Lattice
Tankard

744
Lattice
Star crimp pitcher

Twist–handle pitcher
745
Lattice

Lattice

746   **747**
Ribbed Lattice   **Lattice (Buckeye)**

748
Sugar shaker
Ribbed Lattice

749
Butter

750
Lattice (Buckeye)
Sugar shaker

751
Ball–base cruet

Indiana Mould
752

T.P.

753
Lattice (Buckeye)

Ribbed Lattice

Spooner–caster insert

Tumbler

Salt & pepper

T.P.

754
Celery
166

755
Tumbler

756
Salt & pepper

757

758
Quilted Phlox Mould

759
Lattice

760
Ribbed Pillar Mould

WINDOWS

761
Square–Top
Pitcher

762
Tumbler

763
Windows Swirl
Pitcher

764
Tumbler

765
Tri–Corner crimp
Pitcher

766
Butter

767
Spooner

768
Sugar

769
Creamer

770
Celery

771
Barber Bottle

772
Cruet

773
Syrup

774
Toothpick

775
Salt & Pepper

776
Sugar shaker

COINSPOT

Northwood pitcher

Cruet

Beaumont pitcher

777
Star–Crimp

778
Indiana Mould

779
Three–Tier Tankard
Northwood pitcher

780
Tumbler

781 **Square Top**

Ribbed Coinspot

Northwood cruet

782
Ball Shape

783
Coinspot & Swirl

784
Barber Bottle

785
Syrup

786
Pitcher

787 **Ring Neck**
Cruet

788
Sugar shaker

789
Nine Panel

790
Wide Waist

791
Buckeye

792
Phoenix

168

FERN, POLKA DOT & BIG WINDOWS

793
Polka Dot
W.Va. pitcher

794
Fern
W.Va. pitcher

795 Beaumont pitcher
Fern, Square–Top

796
Big Windows
Buckeye pitcher

Fern

Décor. tumbler

Tumbler

797
Barber Bottle

Fern

798
Syrup

799
Sugar shaker

800
W.Va. Optic Mould

801
Cruet

802
Fern

803
Honeycomb

Polka Dot

Polka Dot

804
W.Va. Syrup

805 Indiana Mould cruet

806
Indiana Mould

MISCELLANEOUS OPALESCENT

Pitcher

Pitcher

807

Buttons & Braids

808

809

Arabian Nights

810

Tumbler

811

Shoulder–shape

Swirling Maze

812

Stars & Stripes

813

Pitcher

814

Barber Bottle

815

Indiana Mould

816

Barber Bottle

Hobnail

817

Pitcher

Hobnail

819

Sauce

821

Tumbler

170 **818**

Cruet

820 Berry Bowl

MISCELLANEOUS OPALESCENT

Poinsettia

822 **Drapery,**
Blown Opal

823 Tumbler

824 Pitcher

825
Twist, Blown

826

827
Poinsettia

828

Twist–handle
pitcher

Ribbed pitcher **Christmas**
Snowflake

829
Tumbler

830
Oil lamp

Snowflake

831
Oil lamp

832

Christmas
Snowflake

833

834

Curtain Optic

Indiana mould

835 **Poinsettia**

Night lamp

836
Snowflake

171

MISCELLANEOUS OPALESCENT

837 Caster set
Stripe

838 Pickle caster
Seaweed

839 Half shade
Swirl

840 Bar bottle
Chrysanthemum Swirl

841 Oil lamp
Reverse Swirl

Coinspot

842
Daisy & Fern
N. Swirl syrup

843
Indiana mould

844
Sugar shaker

845
Hobbs' syrup

846
Ribbed Coinspot
Sugar shaker

847
Lattice
Buckeye syrup

848
Swastika
Indiana mould

849
Diamonds, Opalescent
Coloratura mould

850
Criss-Cross, Consolidated

851
Polka Dot
Fancy Fans mould

852
Polka Dot
W.Va. mould

853
Stripe
Buckeye?

854
Daisy & Fern
N.Swirl mould

855
Twist, Blown
Nine panel mould

856
Wide Stripe
Nickel mould

857
Swirl
Hobbs mould

MISCELLANEOUS OPALESCENT

858 W.Va. mould
Coinspot

859
Windows
Tri–corner mouth

860 **Daisy & Fern**
Vase

861
Square barber
bottle

862
Stripe
Oil lamp

863
Hobnail
Vase

864 **Big Windows** **865**
Butter
Creamer

866
Swirl
Cruet

867
Lady
Toothpick

868
Stripe
Jack–in–the–pulpit

**Chrysanthemum
Swirl**

Tumbler

Fern

869

872

870
Sauce and berry bowl

871
Floral Eyelet

873
Sauce and berry bowl

173

MISCELLANEOUS OPALESCENT

Pitcher

Cruet

874 **Diamonds,**
Crackled tankard **Opalescent**

875
Crackled cruet

876 **Herringbone** **877**

878 Satin tankard
Lattice

879
Ellipse & Diamond
Squat ball pitcher

880
Wide Stripe
Pitcher

881
Honeycomb
Square top pitcher

Tumbler

Decanter

882
Herringbone

883
Grape

MISCELLANEOUS OPALESCENT

884

Diamonds, Opalescent

Dec. Tepee Cruet

885

Herringbone

Igloo mould cruet

886

Stars & Stripes

Indiana mould

887

Curtain Optic

Indiana mould

Daisy & Fern

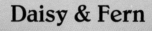

888

N. Swirl mould

889

Spooner

890

Creamer

Sugar lid

Tumbler

Sugar lid

891

Lattice

Ribbed Pillar mould

892

Honeycomb

Rainbow tumbler

893

Ribbed Rings

894

Swirling Maze

895

RIbbed Lattice   175

MISCELLANEOUS OPALESCENT

Swirl

Criss–Cross,
Consolidated

Coinspot

Ribbed Rings

896 Straw jar   **897** Ivy ball   **898**   **899** Tankard

Syrups

Mustard

900 Coinspot & Swirl   **901**   **902**   **903**   **905**

Ribbed Lattice   Big Windows   Hobnail   **904**
Criss–Cross, Consolidated

Fern

906   **907** Floradine **908**   **909**   **910**

Lattice   Sugar   Mustard   Celery   Butter

Buckeye sugar

MISCELLANEOUS OPALESCENT

Coinspot

Ribbed Coinspot

Windows

Coral Reef

Scottish Moor

911 Windows mould

912 Celery

913 Night lamp

914

915 Tankard

Coinspot

916 Ring Neck syrup

917 Nine Panel syrup

918 Indiana mould

Cruets

919 Coin Dot, Fenton

920 Diamonds, Opalescent

921 Wide Stripe

Sugar shaker

Sugar shaker

Tall salt

922 Swirl Opal Royal Oak

Royal Oak creamer

923 Ribbed Coinspot

Sugar lid

924 Honeycomb

925 Big Windows

926 Chrys. Swirl

927 Polka Dot

928 Coinspot

Water bottle

OPALESCENT BY L.G. WRIGHT

(Original Wright names used)

Daisy & Fern "Fern"

Diamond Optic

Eye Dot

929

930

931   Opal Swirl

932

933

934   Christmas Snowflake

935

936   Honeycomb   937

938   Opal Dot

178   939   Honeycomb   940

941   Eye Dot   942

943   Honeycomb

OPALESCENT BY L.G. WRIGHT

(Original Wright names used)

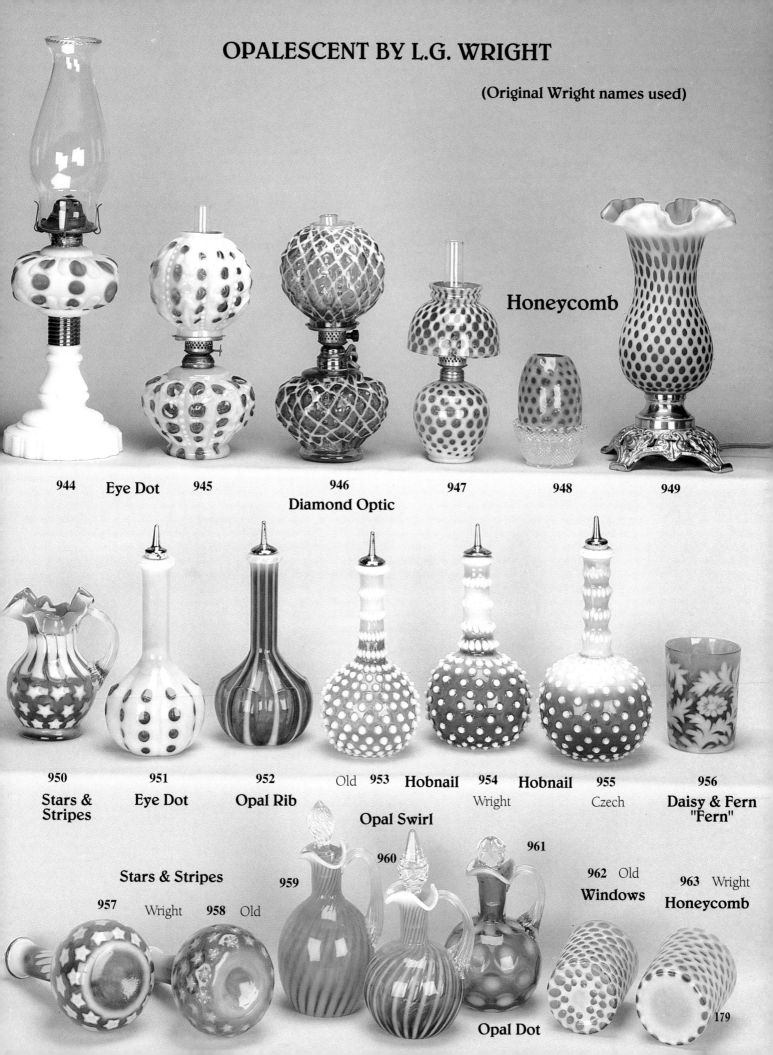

Honeycomb

944   Eye Dot   **945**   **946**   **947**   **948**   **949**

Diamond Optic

950   **951**   **952**   Old **953** Hobnail **954** Hobnail **955**   **956**

Stars &   Eye Dot   Opal Rib   Wright   Czech   Daisy & Fern
Stripes   Opal Swirl   "Fern"

Stars & Stripes   **959**   **960**   **961**   **962** Old   **963** Wright

957 Wright   **958** Old   Windows   Honeycomb

Opal Dot

179

FENTON OPALESCENT

964
Spiral Optic

965 Spiral Optic

Diamond Optic

966

967

968
Coin Dot

969
Barcelona mould

Spiral Optic

970

971

972

Polka Dot

973
Spiral Optic

974

Polka Dot

975

977

Swirled Feather

Perfume

180

976

978

979
Pearls
DeVilbiss

EXPERIMENTAL OPALESCENT BY FENTON

1978-1985

980	981	982	983	984	985
Spiral Optic	Heart Optic	Spanish Lace	Daisy	Diamond Optic	Wide Rib Spiral

986	987	988	989	990
Sculptured Ice	Feather Optic	Dot Optic	Coin Dot	Snowcapped Diamond

991	992	993	994	995
Coin Dot	Heart Optic	Honeycomb	Daisy	Swirled Feather

OPALESCENT LAMPS

Honeycomb

996
Opal Swirl

997
Coin Dot

998
Opal Swirl

999

1000   **Opal Swirl**

BY L.G. WRIGHT

OPALESCENT LAMPS
BY L.G. WRIGHT

1005
Daisy & Fern
"Fern"

1001
Honeycomb

1002
Opal Dot

1003
Daisy & Fern
"Fern"

1004
Christmas
Snowflake

183

EUROPEAN OPALESCENT

(Top Row)
&
Salt Shakers
(Bottom Row)

12" English vase

Gas shade

Vase

Iced Tea

1006
Swirl

1007
Opal Optic

1008
Swirl

1009
Target Swirl

1010
Hobnail

Hobnail

Hobnail

1011

8½" vase

1012

6" pitcher

1013

2½" tumbler

1014

8" pitcher

1015

5" tumbler

1016

4½" rose bowl

Salt & peppers

1017
Swirl, Nickel

1018
Wide Stripe

1019
Polka Dot

1020
Coinspot

1021
Ribbed Coinspot

1022
Lattice, Buckeye

Salt & pepper

Salt shaker

Salt shaker

Salt & pepper

MISCELLANEOUS OPALESCENT

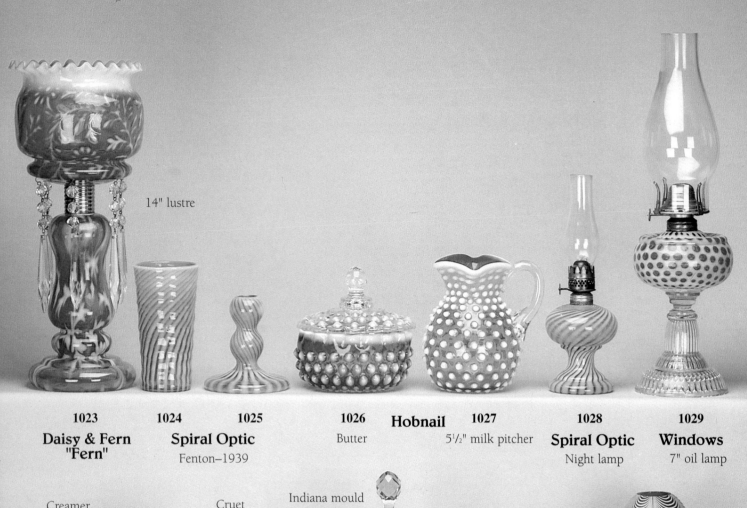

14" lustre

1023
Daisy & Fern
"Fern"

1024
Spiral Optic
Fenton–1939

1025

1026
Butter

Hobnail

1027
5½" milk pitcher

1028
Spiral Optic
Night lamp

1029
Windows
7" oil lamp

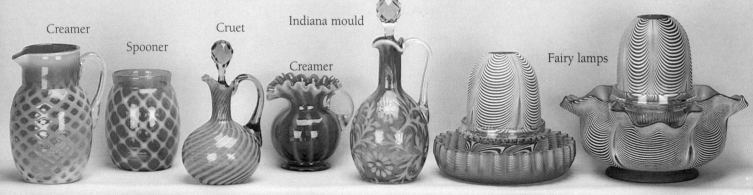

Creamer

Spooner

Cruet

Indiana mould

Creamer

Fairy lamps

1030
Lattice, Buckeye

1031

1032
Swirl

1033
Stripe

1034
Daisy & Fern

1035

Nailsea Type

1036

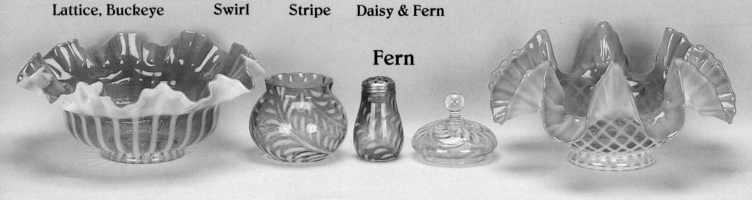

Fern

1037
Stripe
9½" bowl

1038
Spooner

1039
Salt

1040
Sugar lid

1041
Lattice
11" bowl

185

Two pages from a 1973 L.G. Wright catalog showing many items in cranberry opalescent. (Courtesy Steve Jennings)

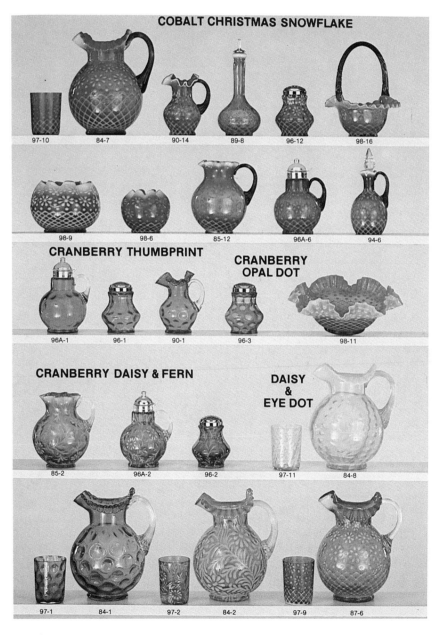

This page from a 1982 catalog shows the L. G. Wright shapes in *Christmas Snowflake* and the newly released *Eye Dot and Daisy* (Victorian name *Floral Eyelet*).

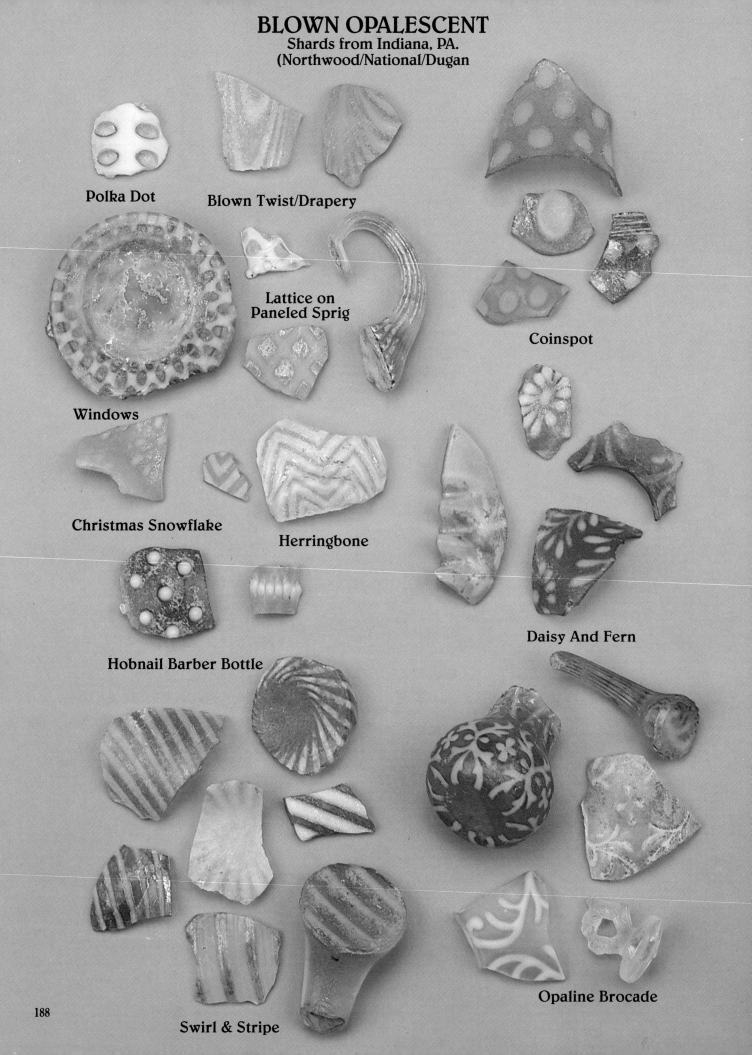

BLOWN OPALESCENT
Shards from Indiana, PA.
(Northwood/National/Dugan

Polka Dot

Blown Twist/Drapery

Coinspot

Lattice on Paneled Sprig

Windows

Christmas Snowflake

Herringbone

Daisy And Fern

Hobnail Barber Bottle

Opaline Brocade

Swirl & Stripe

BOOK 9 BACK COVER

Fenton

Fenton

1042
Dot Optic

1043
Coin Dot

1044
Diamond Optic

1045

1046

1047
Ring, Fenton

1048
Fern
Beaumont

1049
Stripe

1050

Spiral Optic

Fenton

Nickel

1051
Spiral Optic

1052
Wide Stripe

1053
Ring, Fenton

1055

1054
Spiral Optic
Fenton

1057
Rib Optic

1056
Swirl
Stourbridge

Captions for pages 190—198 are
listed on page 217.

1058   1059   1060   1061   1062

1063   1064   1065   1066   1067   1068

1069   1070   1071   1072   1073

1074   1075   1076   1077   1078

Captions for pages 190—198 are listed on page 217.

1079   1080   1081   1082   1083   1084

1085   1086   1087   1088   1089   1090   1091

1092   1093   1094   1095   1096   1097

1098   1099   1100   1101   1102   1103

Captions for pages 190—198 are listed on page 217.

1104 **1105** **1106** **1107** **1108** **1109**

1110 **1111** **1112** 1113

1114 1115 1116

1117 1118 1119 1120

1121

1122

1123

1124

1125

1126

1127

1128

1129

1130

1131

1132

1133

1134

1135

Captions for pages 190—198 are listed on page 217.

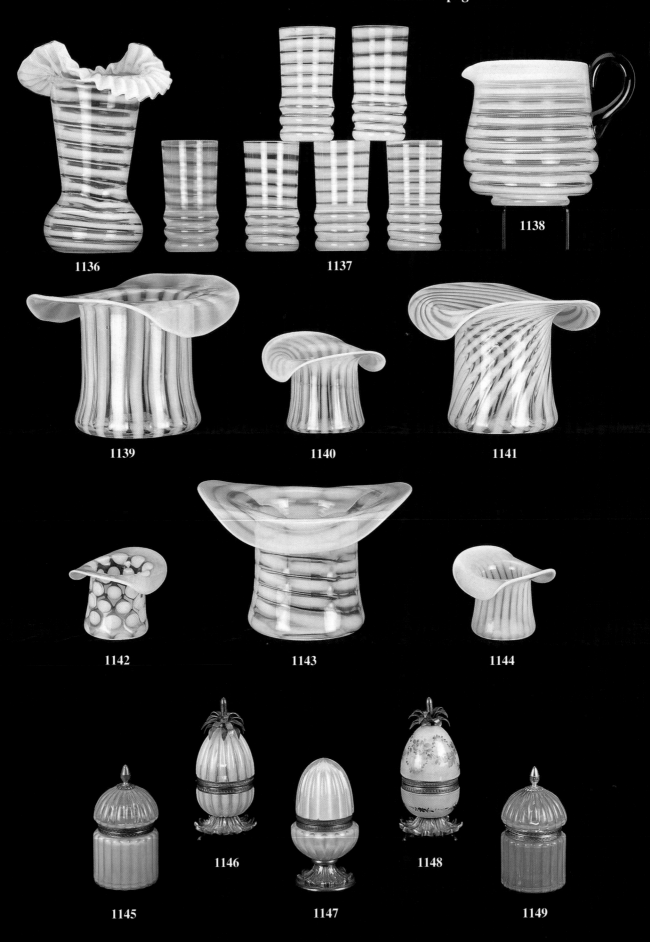

1136

1137

1138

1139

1140

1141

1142

1143

1144

1145

1146

1147

1148

1149

Captions for pages 190—198 are listed on page 217.

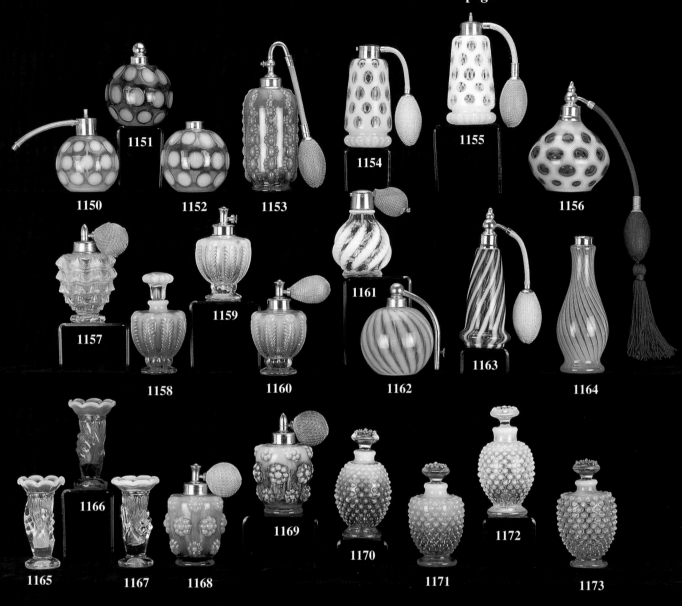

1150 1151 1152 1153 1154 1155 1156

1157 1158 1159 1160 1161 1162 1163 1164

1165 1166 1167 1168 1169 1170 1171 1172 1173

1174 1175 1176 1177 1178 1179

1180 1181 1182 1183 1184 1185

Captions for pages 190—198 are listed on page 217.

1186

1187

1188

1189

1190

1191

1192

1193

1194

1195

1196

1197

1198

Captions for pages 190—198 are listed on page 217.

1200

1201

1202

1203

1199

1204

1205

1206

1207

1208

1209

1210

1211

1212

1213

1214

1215

1216

1217

Captions for pages 190—198 are listed on page 217.

1218

1219

1220

1221

1222

1223

1224

1225

1226

1227

1228

1229

1230

1231

1232
Twisted Ribs

1233
Plain Panels

1234
Plain and Simple

1235
Unnamed
English vase
(1235 and 1238)

1236
National

1237
Unnamed
English tumbler

1238

1239
Quilted Pine Cone

Unnamed
English dish
1241

1240
Floating
Snowflake

Rare & Unlisted Opalescent Glass

1242

1243

1244

1245

1246

1247

1248

1249

1250

1251

1252

1253

1254

104

1242. Target
1243. Catalonian
1244. Diamond Stem
1245. Strawberry
1246. Grape and Cable
1247. Beaded Fantasy
1248. Panache

1249. Lincoln Inn
1250. Chanticleer
1251. Plume Twist
1252. Sanibel
1253. Inside Ribbing
1254. Miniatures

1255. Hobnail, Blown
1256. Melon with Sprig
1257. Swirl
1258. Target Swirl
1259. Over–All Hob
1260. Quadruple Diamonds
1261. Twist, Blown
1262. Coinspot
1263. Golfing

1257

1256

1258

1255

1260

1261

1262

1259

1263

Model Flint

Dolphin

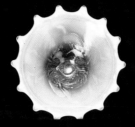

1264   1265   1266   1267

Kismet   Kismet

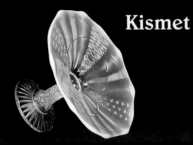
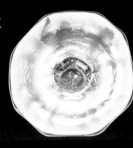

1268   1269   1270

1271   **Alhambra**   1272   1273

Ala–Bock

1274   **Kismet**   1275

1276. Princess Diana
1277. Driftwood and Shell
1278. Diamond Wave
1279. Grace Darling Rowboat
1280. Contessa
1281. Somerset

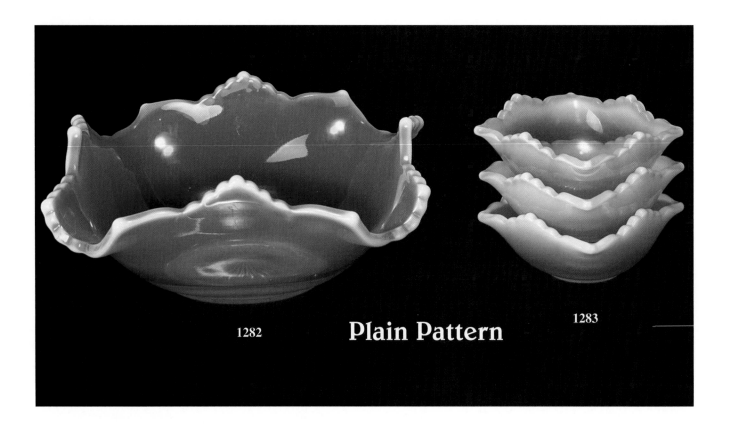

1282   **Plain Pattern**   1283

1285

1284   1286

Carriage   **Camelot**   **Sunderland**

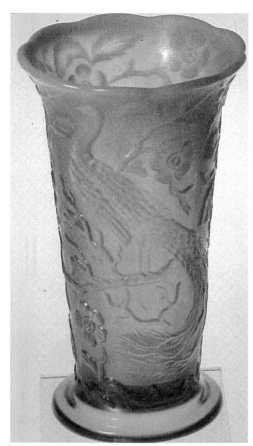

1287
Peacock

1288 **Cactus,** 1289
Northwood

1290
Intaglio

1291
Cleopatra's Fan

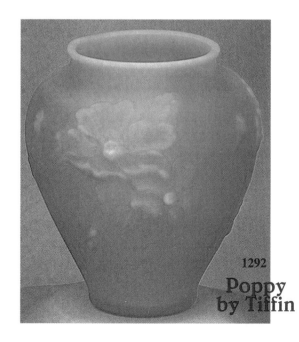

1292
**Poppy
by Tiffin**

1293
**Lady
Chippendale**

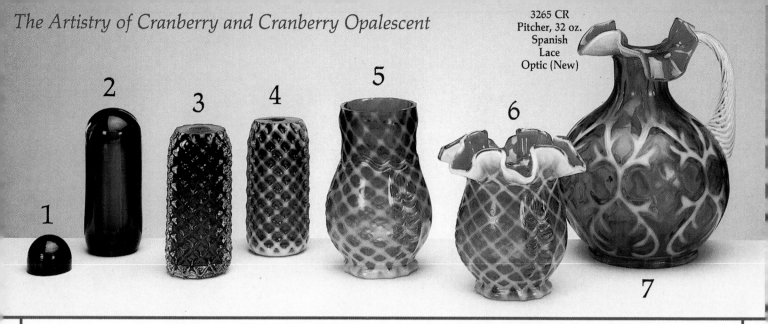

The Artistry of Cranberry and Cranberry Opalescent

3265 CR
Pitcher, 32 oz.
Spanish
Lace
Optic (New)

1 2 3 4 5 6 7

Truly the most unique of glassmaking accomplishments! Fenton Cranberry is achieved by a lengthy process requiring artistry, skill, technology and team work. Working together as a team, it takes up to 18 skilled craftsmen to make a basket or pitcher!

1

Cranberry glass begins with long Ruby Rolls containing gold which are made and heated in ovens for approximately 12 hours. A small bud is then snipped off of the roll and attached to the end of a hollow blow pipe. It is smoothed and shaped to give it a uniform shape for even color distribution.

2

The Ruby bud is then taken to a glass tank with crystal glass (or French opalescent glass for Cranberry opalescent) where a layer of crystal is gathered over top. The blocker then rolls the molten gob in hot soapy water to give it uniformity and lubrication. He then blows the first air bubble into the glass.

Courtesy of the Fenton Museum.

3-4

The gob is then reheated and blown into a spot mould to put the optic pattern on the piece. (4)-The opalescence comes out when the French opalescent is heated. So the protruding pattern receives more heat than the sunken areas causing the molecules to grow and turn white. This gives us the opalescent pattern.

5

After the optic pattern has been put on the piece, it is taken to the main blower. It is reheated and 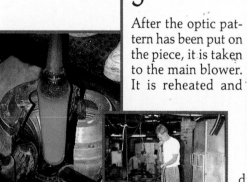  dropped into the final forming mould and blown out into the shape of the mould.

6-7

Once the piece has been blown into the forming mould, the bubble (called the overblow) is scraped off the top and reheated. It is given to the finisher who puts the ruffled crimp on the edge. It is then given to the handler to apply the handle if it is a basket or pitcher.

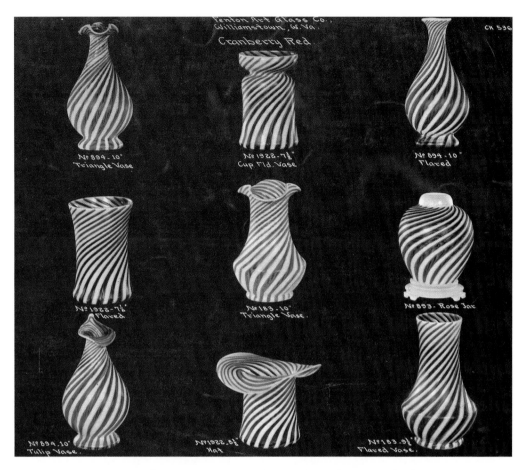

Assortment of Cranberry Spiral Optic by Fenton. Circa 1939

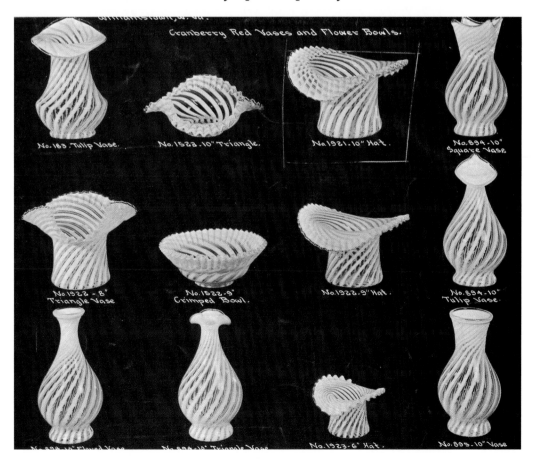

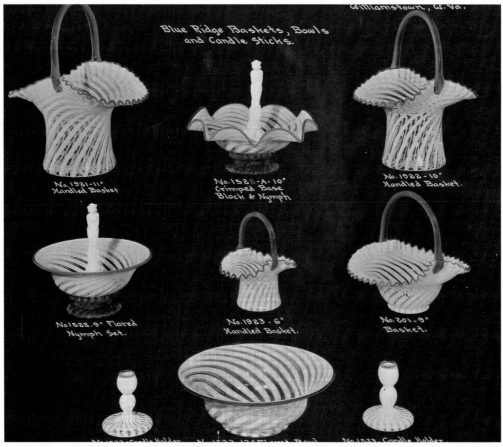

Assortment of Fenton's Blue Ridge using the Spiral Optic mould, circa 1939.

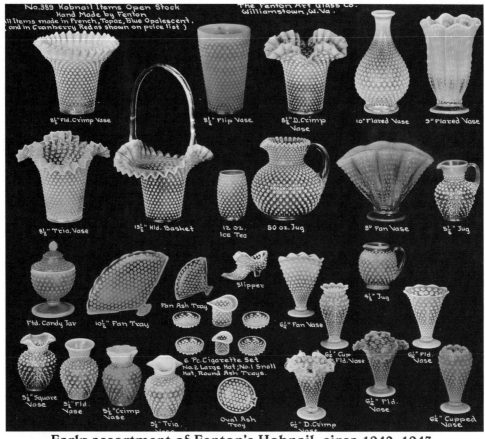

Early assortment of Fenton's Hobnail, circa 1940–1943.

Thus, the name change for this edition. In the *Glass Preview* (1980), Heacock reported a green opalescent *Victor* piece with the Diamond–D mark. This significant discovery was a milestone in attributing the *Victor* pattern to its rightful source—the Dugan Glass Co. The stopper is not original.

See the following catalog reprints.

See catalog reprint in the *Winterlily* pattern section.

OUR HEAVY OPALESCENT WATER SET ASSORTMENT.

Regular $1.00 sets to retail with a profit at 75c.

C1270—Comprising large heavy footed ½ gal. jug with pearl beaded edge and 6 fancy shape tumblers. 4 sets each of blue, green and flint opalescent, total 12 sets in bbl. (Bbl. 35c.) Per set. **42c**

Victor (Jewelled Heart) water set from a 1905 Butler Brothers catalog.

"OPALESCENT" BERRY SET ASST.

Big rich ones to retail at 50c.

C1009:. A new and beautiful pattern in the popular opalescent ware. Set comprises 9½ in. deep berry bowl and six 4½ in. nappies. 6 sets in round shape and 6 with fancy crimped edges, equally asstd. in blue, green and flint opalescent. 12 sets in bbl., wt. 85 lbs. Per set, **32c**

(NO PKG. CHARGE.)

Victor (Jewelled Heart) berry sets in opalescent hues from a Butler Brothers catalog (Mid–Spring, 1906).

VICTORIA AND ALBERT

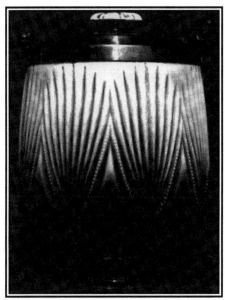

Victoria & Albert cracker jar.

Maker: George Davidson & Co., Gateshead-on-Tyne, England.
Named by: Heacock
Y.O.P. Circa 1897, sometimes marked with Rd #303519.
Other name: None
Colors made: Blue and yellow opalescent.
Pieces made: Cracker jar and small cream pitcher, quart-size pitcher, oval plate, and compote; other pieces are likely.
Reintroductions/Repros: None known at this time.

VINTAGE

(See fig. 439)
Maker: Jefferson Glass Co., Follansbee, W.Va., Dugan Glass Co., Indiana, PA., and Fenton Art Glass Co., Williamstown, W.Va.*
Named by: Hartung, *Opalescent*
Y.O.P.: Circa 1908
Other name: Jefferson pattern #245
Colors made: White, blue, and green opalescent and amethyst. Carnival colors made by Dugan: marigold, peach opalescent, ice blue, amethyst, and pearl (white). Colors made by Fenton: chocolate, and Carnival colors of marigold, blue, amethyst, green, red and aqua opalescent.
Pieces made: Bowl, powder jar, epergne, vase (two sizes), bowl (four sizes), plate (three sizes), card tray, punch bowl with base, cup, rose bowl, and compote. Not all pieces were made by all companies listed.
Reintroduction or Repros: None known at this time. Fenton may reintroduce a pattern at any time. If made after 1972, the pieces should be marked with the Fenton logo.
Notes: *This pattern was also produced by Northwood, but only on the exterior or backside of bowls.

WAR OF ROSES

(See fig. 548)

Maker: George Davidson & Co., Gateshead-on-Tyne, England.

Davidson trademark

Named by: Heacock
Y.O.P. Circa 1893; some pieces will be marked with the Rd #212684
Other name: None
Colors made: Blue and yellow opalescent.
Pieces made: Novelties
Reintroduction or Repros: None known at this time.

WATERLILY WITH CATTAILS

(See figs. 147, 151, 188, 449, 464, 1114)

Maker: Fenton Art Glass Co., Williamstown, W.Va., and H. Northwood Co., Wheeling W.Va.
Named by: Kamm 4
Y.O.P. Circa 1905
Other name: Cattails and Waterlily
Colors made: White, blue, green, amethyst opalescent; blue, chocolate; Carnival colors of marigold, blue, and amethyst.
Pieces made: Table set, water set, berry set, novelty bowls, tri–cornered bon–bon, handled relish, individual creamer and sugar, plates, assorted whimsies.
Reintroduction or Repros: None known at this time, but Fenton may reintroduce a pattern at any time.
Notes: This pattern was made in three different variants. Frank M. Fenton states his father made the version with the beads at the base of the pattern and he also confirms that the amethyst color was part of his company's early production. The Northwood version of the pattern is slightly different and is sometimes found signed with the "N" in a circle trademark. A Carnival version of the water set has a basketweave base on the pattern.

Excerpt from a letter by Frank M. Fenton dated in September, 1999: "The Northwood shape is quite different from the Fenton shape. We have now found a third *Waterlily and Cattail* tumbler which we have guessed might have been made by Dugan. We have never been able to locate a pitcher Dugan might have made. We have just acquired the mould for that tumbler at the L.G. Wright auction. It's an old Dugan mould. We haven't had time yet to check it out with the different pieces that we have here in the Museum. We'll let you know when that gets done."

WHEEL AND BLOCK

(See fig. 499)

Maker: Dugan Glass Co., Indiana, PA.

Named by: Hartung, *Opalescent*
Y.O.P. Circa 1905–1908
Other name: None
Colors made: White, blue, amethyst, and green opalescent; sometimes goofus decorated.
Pieces made: Bowls
Reintroduction or Repros: None known at this time.
Notes: This pattern was previously attributed to Jefferson. See catalog reprint in the *Corn Vase* section.

WIDE RIB

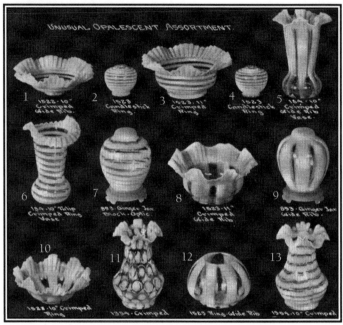

Unusual opalescent assortment. 1–4, 6. *Ring* 5, 8, 9, 10, 12. *Wide Rib* 7, 13. *Block Optic* 11. *Dot Optic*

Maker: Fenton Art Glass Co., Williamstown, W.Va.
Named by: Fenton
Y.O.P. Circa 1939, but possibly as early as 1933.
Other name: None
Colors made: White opalescent
Pieces made: Vase, bowl, rose bowl, and ginger jar on satin glass base.
Reintroduction or Repros: Fenton may reintroduce a pattern or color at any time. If made after 1972, the piece should be marked with the Fenton logo.

WIDE RIB SPIRAL

(See fig. 985)

Maker: Fenton Art Glass Co., Williamstown, W.Va.
See text for *Spiral* and *Wide Rib*.

WIDE STRIPE

(See figs. 389, 856, 880, 921, 1018, 1052, 1133–1134)

Maker: Early production in England, and Nickel Plate Glass Co., Fostoria, OH.; others are possible. Phoenix at Monaca, PA., is a suggestion.
Named by: Taylor

Y.O.P. Circa 1890

Other name: Nickel's pattern No. 84 and 94

Colors made: White, blue, cranberry (sometimes with a diamond quilt background) and scarce in green opalescent.

Pieces made: Pitcher, tumbler, syrup (two shapes), sugar shaker, cruet, toothpick holder, lamps (several styles), bowl and underplate, milk and juice pitcher.

Reintroduction or Repros: Yes, by the Fenton Art Glass Co. Fenton calls their reintroduction *Wide Rib*. See text for *Wide Rib*. Possibly a limited production by Imperial Glass Corp. during the 1930s.

Notes: This version of the *Stripe* motif has wider and fewer stripes running vertically. The difference between *Stripe* and *Wide Stripe* is sometimes minimal and a matter of opinion. Unfortunately, this was a very limited production pattern, as was the *Wide Stripe* produced in the diamond mould.

See the following photograph.

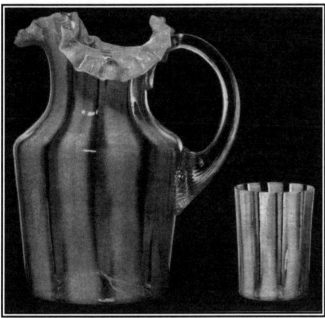

Blue opalescent *Wide Stripe* pattern, maker unknown. This could be Phoenix or La Belle.

WILD BOUQUET

(See figs. 30-38, 191, 222, 223)

Maker: The Northwood Co., and Dugan Glass Co., Indiana, PA.

Named by: Metz 1

Y.O.P. Circa 1898 for custard, and circa 1903 for opalescent.

Other name: Iris

Colors made: White, blue, and green opalescent; rare experimental pieces in canary opalescent and custard glass.

Pieces made: Table set, water set, berry set, cruet, toothpick, salt shakers, cruet set on tray (the tray is the same as *Chrysanthemum Sprig's*).

Reintroduction or Repros: None known at this time.

Notes: Many collectors prefer this pattern in opalescent without the goofus decoration which originally graced the pattern. However, removing the goofus decoration (unless it is badly worn) represents a sad misjudgment. Experienced collectors agree that the original decoration should not be removed. Do we change Mona Lisa's smile just because it isn't to our liking?

See the following catalog reprint.

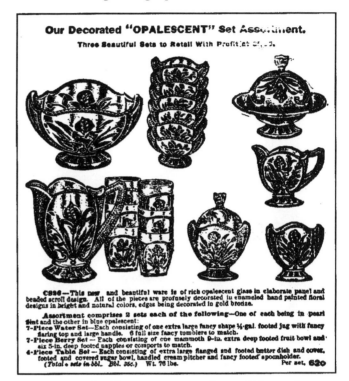

Assortment of *Wild Bouquet* items in white and blue opalescent from a May, 1903, Butler Brothers catalog.

WILLIAM AND MARY

(See figs. 547, 559)

Maker: George Davidson & Co., Gateshead-on-Tyne, England.

Davidson trademark

Named by: Heacock

Y.O.P. Registered July 14, 1903; sometimes marked with Rd 413701

Other name: None

Colors made: Crystal and yellow opalescent, others are possible.

Pieces made: Creamer, open sugar, compote, and novelties.

Reintroduction or Repros: None known at this time.

Note: In flattening the piece to make the compote, the

distinctive "hearts" and "diamonds" of this pattern became distorted.

WILTED FLOWERS

Maker: Dugan Glass Co., Indiana, PA.
Named by: Heacock
Y.O.P. Circa 1906
Other name: None
Colors made: White, blue, green opalescent and crystal. The crystal is often decorated with gold, red, and green.
Pieces made: Bowls and novelties
Reproductions: None known at this time.
Note: This pattern was part of their *Intaglio Ware* line and should not be confused with the pattern named *Intaglio*. Dugan's *Intaglio* is pressed glass with a pattern on the outside surface of the piece. The pattern is not raised as is typical in pattern glass; it is below the surface of the glass. See text for *Daisy May*.
See the following picture.

Green opalescent *Wilted Flowers* bowl.

WINDFLOWER, OPALESCENT

(See fig. 515)
Maker: Dugan/Diamond Glass Co., Indiana, PA.
Named by: Presznick 1
Y.O.P. Circa 1906–1916
Other name: None
Colors made: Primarily Carnival colors of marigold, blue, amethyst, ice blue and ice green. Rare in opalescent blue. White and green opalescent are possible.
Pieces made: Bowl, plate, and nappy.
Reintroduction or Repros: None known at this time.
Notes: The word opalescent must be included in the name of this pattern to differentiate between this and the much earlier pattern listed by Kamm.
See the following sketch, and catalog reprint in *Lattice and Daisy* section.

Design sketch for Dugan's *Windflower* pattern. Courtesy of Steve Jennings.

WINDOWS, (PLAIN)

(See figs. 284, 294, 761, 764, 765, 771, 859, 913, 962, 1029)
Maker: Hobbs, Brockunier & Co., Wheeling, W.Va., with later production by Beaumont Glass Co., Martins Ferry, OH.
Named by: Boul
Y.O.P. Circa 1889
Other name: Hobbs pattern #333
Colors made: White, blue, and cranberry opalescent.
Pieces made: Bowl (four sizes), caster set (two oils, salt/pepper in metal frame), celery (three styles), cheese and cover, syrup, pitcher, tumbler, plate (two sizes), sugar shaker, butter dish, creamer, sugar, spooner, toothpick, tray, bitters bottle, miniature lamp, lamps, and shades.
Reintroduction or Repros: Yes, by Fenton Art Glass Co. for L.G. Wright. The pattern was named Honeycomb. See text for Honeycomb.
Note: This is actually a tiny "honeycomb" design, but the six–sided holes are melted out and appear to be round. Percy Beaumont apparently acquired some of the original moulds from U.S. Glass (which owned the Hobbs factory) when he opened his own glassmaking factory in 1899. One catalog page is suspiciously similar to an earlier one found in a Hobbs catalog. The fig. 765 tri–corner, crimp–top pitcher was offered in an 1893 Butler Brothers catalog. Hobbs was closed by U. S. Glass later that year.

Do not confuse this with the *Windows Swirl* pattern, which is the same design, only blown into different shape moulds. The *Windows* water pitcher is known in two shapes—both are basically bulbous. One has a square top, the other has a ruffled tri–cornered top. Both have clear (not reeded) handles. Both have polished pontils. The water pitcher has been reproduced; the reproduction is also bulbous in shape. It has a plain handle and no pontil scar. The tumbler also has been highly reproduced. As with most reproduced opalescent tumblers, the weight is the key factor. Light weight glass is old—reproduction tumblers tend to have thicker walls and are heavier in weight. The finger bowl can be found in both the new and old form; unfortunately, like the tumblers, they are difficult to tell apart. The weight is the determining factor.

See the catalog reprint in *Coral Reef*.

See the following two catalog reprints.

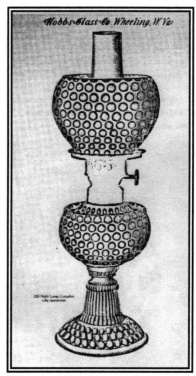

Opalescent *Windows* pattern night lamp by Hobbs Glass Co., from a 1891 catalog. This line was continued after the U.S. Glass merger.

The 1893 Butler Brothers catalog listed this *Windows* pattern water set in white, blue, and cranberry opalescent, with plain colors of crystal, blue, and amber ("Old Gold"). The finger bowl is called a slop bowl here.

WINDOWS, (SWIRLED)

(See figs. 311, 355–359, 762, 763, 766–770, 772–776)
Maker: Hobbs, Brockunier & Co., Wheeling, W.Va.
Named by: Heacock (variant)
Y.O.P. Circa 1888
Other name: Pattern No. 326
Colors made: White, blue, and cranberry opalescent.
Pieces made: Water set, berry set, table set, toothpick, mustard, cruet, salt shakers, sugar shaker, syrup (two shapes), cruet set, celery, and plates (two sizes).
Reintroduction or Repros: None known at this time.
Notes: This pattern was made from the same moulds used on the *Francis Ware Swirl* pattern. The pieces in this pattern are always oval, except the tumblers.
Journal Quote:
"Goods that will be hard to excel are the three new lines of the Hobbs Glass Co. They are just out and are 'rippers.' The numbers are 326 (FRANCES WARE SWIRL mould), 327 and 328. The former is made in ten effects, namely, crystal, crystal opalescent, sapphire, ruby, these four colors in satin finish decorated No. 7 and 'Frances.' In these they have a full line of tableware such as nappies, bowls, sugar sifters, molasses jugs, tumblers, pitchers, water bottles, finger bowls, celeries (boat and straight), salts, peppers, mustards, toothpicks, casters, also shades, oil bottles, etc. The shape is oval, entirely new, and all the articles named are made in this shape except tumblers."
(*Pottery and Glass Reporter*, January 17, 1889)

WINGED SCROLL

Maker: A. H. Heisey Glass Co., Newark, OH.
Named by: Popular nomenclature
Y.O.P. Circa early 1900s
Other name: Ivorina Verde, which referred to the "yellow-green ivory" color in which it was originally made. However, this pattern was also made in other colors, which probably explains why it is now called Winged Scroll. Pattern #1280.
Colors made: Crystal, emerald green, and custard. A few items have been found in milk glass and vaseline opalescent.
Pieces made: There are 50 different shapes known in this pattern, but only the tri-cornered nappy is known in opalescent.
Reproductions: Yes—a miniature butter dish was produced by Guernsey Glass Co., Cambridge, OH.
Notes: There are only a few other extremely-limited-production pieces of Heisey's early glass in opalescent, so anyone can consider himself fortunate to own even a single piece.
See the following picture.

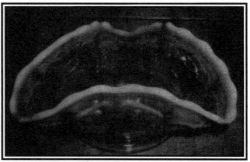

Heisey's *Winged Scroll* tri–cornered nappy in vaseline opalescent.

WINTER CABBAGE

(See fig. 400)
Maker: Dugan Glass Co., Indiana, PA.
Named by: Heacock
Y.O.P. Circa 1906
Other name: None
Colors made: White, blue, and green opalescent.
Pieces made: Novelties
Reintroduction or Repros: None
Notes: This is a variant of *Cabbage Leaf*, which has more leaves around the sides.

WINTERLILY

(See fig. 479)
Maker: Dugan Glass Co., Indiana, PA.
Named by: Heacock
Y.O.P. Circa 1906
Other name: None
Colors made: White and blue opalescent.
Pieces made: Novelties
Reintroduction or Repros: None known at this time.
Notes: Other colors are likely. See the following reprint.

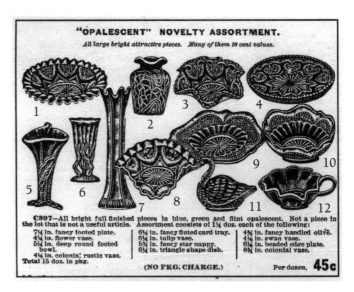

Opalescent assortment from Butler Brothers 1906 catalog.
1, 3, 4, 8. Victor (Jeweled Heart) 2. Venetian style
5. Winterlily 6. Twig 7. ? 9, 10. Blocked Thumbprint and Beads 11. Swan 12. Plain Nappy.

WISHBONE AND DRAPE

(See fig. 471)
Maker: Jefferson Glass Co., Steubenville, OH.
Named by: Heacock
Y.O.P. Circa 1904
Other name: None
Colors made: White, blue, and green opalescent.
Pieces made: Bowls
Reintroduction or Repros: None know at this time.

WOVEN WONDER

(See figs. 482, 514)
Maker: H. Northwood Co., Wheeling, W.Va.*
Named by: Heacock
Y.O.P. Circa 1908
Other name: None
Colors made: White and blue opalescent.
Pieces made: Bowls and novelties.
Reintroduction or Repros: None known at this time.
Note: *This attribution is somewhat questionable. In *Harry Northwood, The Wheeling Years, 1901–1925* the only mention of *Woven Wonder* is the statement that it may be part of the *Frosted Leaf and Basketweave* line.

WREATH AND SHELL (SEE MANILA)

WREATHED CHERRY

(See fig. 626)
Maker: Dugan Glass Co., Indiana, PA.
Named by: Kamm 7
Y.O.P. Circa 1908
Other name: None
Colors made: White and blue opalescent; Carnival colors of pearl (white), marigold and amethyst. Sometimes the cherries on the pearl Carnival will be decorated in red or gold.
Pieces made: Bowl, pitcher, tumbler, berry set, and table set.
Reintroduction or Repros: *The creamer shown is a repro. L.G. Wright acquired several of Dugan's original moulds in 1939 and began producing this pattern in 1940. They called this pattern *Cherry*. Wright had more moulds made and over the years increased the line to include 14 different pieces: bowl (three sizes), butter dish, compote, creamer, sugar, salt dip, salver, toothpick, tumbler, pitcher, goblet and ice tea. Colors: amber, blue, green, amethyst, amberina, vaseline, ruby.

Crystal with bright gold, red, and green decorations was made by Imperial Glass in the 1970s. Imperial also made purple, caramel, and red slag in the 1970s. The Wilkerson Glass Co. was making *Wreathed Cherry* in crystal in the 1990s.
Notes: Some of the original Dugan pieces were signed. See the following picture.

Wreathed Cherry tumbler.

ZIPPERS AND LOOPS

(See fig. 423)
Maker: Jefferson Glass Co., Steubenville, OH.
Named by: Heacock
Y.O.P. Circa 1903
Other name: None
Reintroduction or Repros: None known at this time.
Colors made: White, blue, and green opalescent.
Pieces made: Vase and novelties
Notes: Attribution is based on a Jefferson catalog.

1890 SUITE.

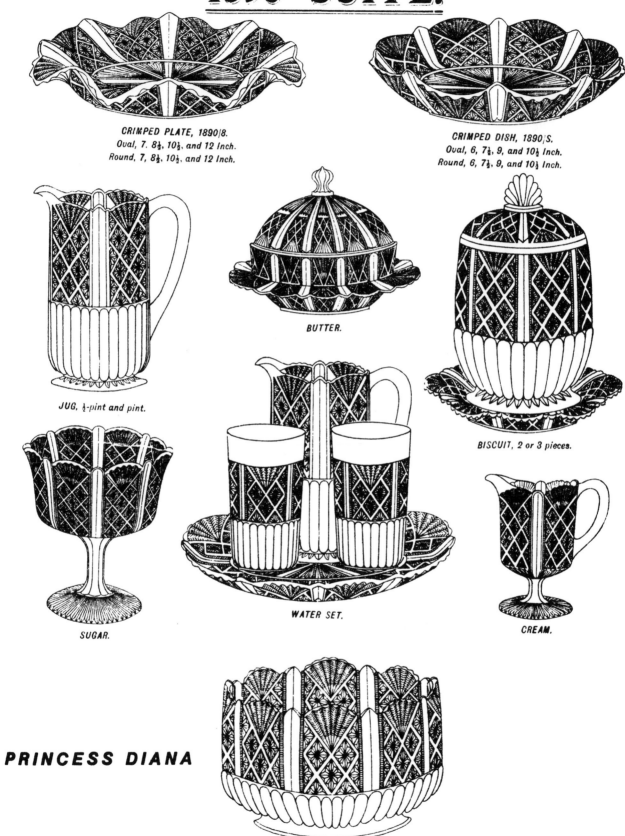

CRIMPED PLATE, 1890/8.
Oval, 7. 8½, 10½, and 12 Inch.
Round, 7, 8½, 10½, and 12 Inch.

CRIMPED DISH, 1890/S.
Oval, 6, 7½, 9, and 10½ Inch.
Round, 6, 7½, 9, and 10½ Inch.

BUTTER.

JUG, ½-pint and pint.

BISCUIT, 2 or 3 pieces.

SUGAR.

WATER SET.

CREAM.

PRINCESS DIANA

SALAD BOWL.

1058. Rib Optic wine

1059. Rib Optic wine bottle

1060. Spiral Optic No. 1921 basket

1061. Polka Dot footed ivy ball

1062. Dot Optic tankard

1063. Stars and Stripes creamer

1064, 1065, 1066. Stars and Stripes tumblers

1067. Stars and Stripes vase

1068. Stars and Stripes basket

1069. Jacqueline sugar

1070. Jacqueline creamer

1071. Jacqueline squat jug

1072. Rib Optic sugar

1073. Rib Optic creamer

1074. Rib Optic cruet

1075. Polka Dot sugar shaker

1076. Spiral Optic basket

1077, 1078. Hobnail Child's lemonade set.

1079. Eye Dot cruet

1080. Coin Dot large cruet

1081. Fern large cruet (satin)

1082. Opal Swirl barber bottle

1083. Honeycomb large cruet (pearl)

1084. Honeycomb large cruet (satin)

1085. Swirl cruet (old)

1086. Polka Dot cruet

1087. Honeycomb cruet

1088. Spiral cruet made for the "Cruet Lady" in 1992.

1089. Hobnail cruet

1090. Daisy and Fern "Fern" cruet (satin)

1091, 1092. Coin Dot cruet

1093. Honeycomb cruet (satin)

1094. Opal Swirl syrup

1095. Daisy and Fern "Fern" syrup

1096, 1097. Ribbed Opal Lattice sugar shaker (old)

1098. Daisy and Fern "Fern" barber bottle

1099. Coral Reef barber bottle

1100. Fern barber bottle (old)

1101. Opal Rib barber bottle

1102. Eye Dot barber bottle

1103. Coral Reef barber bottle

1104. Pulled Loop vase

1105. Rib Optic tumbler with cobalt handle

1106. Rib Optic covered pitcher with cobalt handle and coaster

1107. Rib Optic tumbler with cobalt handle

1108. Cobalt coaster

1109. Opal Dot "toy" lamp

1110. Nailsea–type flask

1111. Tangerine Diamond Optic candlestick

1112. Cornucopia candlestick

1113. Coin Dot vase

1114. Waterlily with Cattails bon–bon

1115. Swirl oval (5½" x 3½") decanter

1116. Dolphin fan vase, Cameo

1117. Nailsea–type plate

1118. Swirl vase

1119. Nailsea–type mini flask

1120. Sea Spray nappy

1121. Rippled bowl

1122. Dolphin fan vase

1123. Green satin Double Wedding Ring bowl

1124. Swirl Tumble–Up/guest set

1125. Spiral Optic vase

1126. Blue Amberina Honeycomb pitcher

1127. Cameo Dolphin cupped bowl

1128. Blackberry Spray vase

1129. Sunset bowl and base

1130. Mary Ann vase

1131. Hobnail mine vase

1132. Cameo Dolphin round comport

1133, 1134. Wide Stripe bowl and underplate

1135. Spiral Optic vase

1136. Ring vase

1137. Ring tumblers

1138. Ring pitcher

1139, 1140. Rib Optic hat

1141. Spiral Optic hat

1142. Dot Optic hat

1143. Block Optic hat

1144. Rib Optic hat

1145–1149. Opalescent lighters

1150–1152. Blue, amethyst, green Dot Optic perfume

1153. Pearls perfume

1154–1155. Blue and white Coin Dot perfumes

1156. Coin Dot perfume

1157. Flounces perfume

1158–1160. Blue and white Panache perfumes

1161. White Plume Twist perfume

1162, 1164. Blue Spiral Optic perfumes

1163. Cranberry Spiral Optic perfume

1165–1167. Topaz, blue, white mini hand vases

1168–1169. Blue, green Floating Snowflake perfumes

1170–1173. Cranberry, blue, white, green Hobnail perfumes

1174, 1177–1180, 1182, 1184, 1185 are all miniature vases by Fenton

1175. Miniature hat vase

1176, 1181. Miniature pitchers

1183. Miniature basket

1186. Hobnail lamp made up of two plates, mini vase, perfume, bowl and 14 prisms

1187. Ring lamp

1188. Spiral lamp

1189. Coin Dot boudoir lamp

1190. Opal Dot "toy" lamp

1191. Honeycomb "toy" lamp globe

1192. Coin Dot mini special order lamp

1193. Eye Dot "toy" lamp globe

1194. Curtain Optic fairy lamp

1195, 1198. Blue Eye Dot lamp with satin and glossy finish

1196. Honeycomb/Window Pane miniature lamp. Pearl finish.

1197. Daisy and Fern "Fern" lamp

1199. Buttons and Braids pitcher

1200. Buttons and Braids vase

1201–1202. Rib Optic tumbler and pitcher

1203. Spiral Optic epergne, made for QVC in 1991

1204. Rib Optic satin vase

1205–1206. Ridged Cameo sugar, creamer

1207. Green center–handled tray

1208. Stripe rose bowl

1209–1211. Topaz Rib Optic cruet, sugar, creamer.

1212. Beatty Swirl celery

1213–1214. Daisy and Fern heart–shaped tumbler & cruet

1215. Emerald green Diamond Optic ivy ball and base

1216. Cranberry Rib Optic ivy ball

1217. Cranberry Diamond Optic ivy ball on a satin crystal base

1218. Dot Optic "pancake" lamp

1219, 1223, 1225. Cornucopia console set

1220–1221. Rib Optic wine and flower stopper decanter

1222. Aquatic vase and under tray

1224. Blue Ridge Dot Optic vase–rare

1226. Ribbed Opal Lattice sugar shaker

1227. Center–handled tray–white

1228. Twig, Tiny vase

1229. Dot Optic perfume

1230. Heart Optic perfume

1231. Plumes and Spaces perfume

WORKS CONSULTED

Barrett, Richard. Popular American Ruby-Stained Pattern Glass. Manchester, VT: Forwards Color Productions, 1968.

Bond, Marcelle. The Beauty of Albany Glass. Berne, IN: Publishers Printing, 1972.

Bredehoft, Neila and Tom. Hobbs, Brockunier & Co., Glass Identification and Value Guide. Paducah, KY: Collector, 1997.

Freeman, Larry. Iridescent Glass. Watkins Glen, NY: Century House, 1964.

Godden, Geoffrey. Antique Glass and China. Cranbury, NJ: A. S. Barnes, n.d.

Hartung, Marion. Northwood Pattern Glass in Color. Emporia, KS: author, 1969.

– – – . Opalescent Pattern Glass. Des Moines: Wallace–Homestead, 1971.

– – – . Carnival Glass Series, Emporia, KS: author, 1960–1973.

Heacock, William. Collecting Glass. Vols. 1–3. Marietta, OH: Antique Publications, 1984–86.

– – – . The Glass Collector. Vols. 1–6. Marietta, OH: Antique Publications, 1982–83.

– – – . Fenton Glass, The First Twenty–Five Years. Marietta, OH:O-Val Advertising, 1978.

– – – . Fenton Glass, The Second Twenty-Five Years. Marietta, OH: O-Val Advertising, 1980.

– – – . Fenton Glass, The Third Twenty-Five Years. Marietta, OH: O-Val Advertising, 1989.

– – – . Old Pattern Glass. Marietta, OH: AP, 1981.

– – – . Pattern Glass Preview. Vols. 1–6. Columbus, OH: Peacock, early 1980s.

Heacock, William and William Gamble. Victorian Colored Pattern Glass, Cranberry Opalescent from A to Z. Marietta, OH: Antique Publications, 1987.

Heacock, William, James Measell, and Berry Wiggins. Dugan/Diamond, The Story of Indiana, Pennsylvania, Glass. Marietta, OH: AP, 1993.

– – – . Harry Northwood, The Early Years 1881–1900. Marietta, OH: AP, 1990.

– – – . Harry Northwood, The Wheeling Years 1901–1925. Marietta, OH: AP, 1991.

Herrick, Ruth. Greentown Glass. Grand Rapids, MI: author, 1958.

Jenks, Bill, Jerry Luna, and Daryl Reilly. Identifying Pattern Glass Reproductions. Radnor, PA: Wallace–Homestead, 1993.

Kamm, Minnie. Two Hundred Pattern Glass Pitchers. Grosse Point, MI: Kamm, 1937.

– – – . A Second Two Hundred Pattern Glass Pitchers. Grosse Point, MI: Kamm, 1940.

– – – . A Third Two Hundred Pattern Glass Pitchers. Grosse Point, MI: Kamm, 1943.

– – – . A Fourth Pitcher Book. Grosse Point, MI: Kamm, 1946.

– – – . A Fifth Pitcher Book. Grosse Point, MI: Kamm, 1948.

– – – . A Sixth Pitcher Book. Grosse Point, MI: Kamm, 1949.

– – – . A Seventh Pitcher Book. Grosse Point, MI: Kamm, 1953.

– – – . An Eighth Pitcher Book. Grosse Point, MI: Kamm, 1954.

Kovar, Lorraine. Westmoreland Glass 1950-1984. Marietta, OH: AP, 1991.

Lee, Ruth Webb. Early American Pressed Glass. Wellesley Hills, MA: author, 1931.

– – – . Victorian Glass. Wellesley Hills, MA: author, 1944.

Lechner, Mildred and Ralph. The World of Salt Shakers. Paducah, KY: Collector, 1992.

McGee, Marie. Millersburg Glass. Marietta, OH: AP, 1995.

Measell, James and Don Smith. Findlay Glass. Marietta, OH: AP, 1986.

Measell, James and W.C. Roetteis. L. G. Wright Glass Co. Marietta, OH: AP, 1997.

Metz, Alice. Early American Pattern Glass. Chicago: Metz, 1958

– – – . Much More Early American Pattern Glass. Beverton, OR: author, 1971.

Murray, Dean. More Cruets Only. Phoenix: Killgore Graphics, 1973.

Murray, Melvin. History of Fostoria, Ohio Glass. Fostoria, OH: Gray, 1972.

– – – . Fostoria, Ohio Glass II. Marietta, OH: AP, 1992.

Newman, Harold. An Illustrated Dictionary of Glass. London,Thames and Hudson, 1977.

Peterson, Arthur. Glass Salt Shakers 1,000 Patterns. Des Moines: Wallace–Homestead, 1970.

– – – . Glass Patents and Patterns. Sanford, FL: Celery City, 1973.

Presznick, Rose. Carnival & Iridescent Glass. Wadsworth, OH: Banner, 1964–67.

Smith, Don. Findlay Pattern Glass. Fostoria, OH: Gray, 1970.

Smith, Frank and Ruth. Miniature Lamps. New York: Thomas Nelson, 1968.

Taylor, Ardelle. Colored Glass Sugar Shakers & Syrup Pitchers. N.p: n.d.

Teal, Ron Sr. Albany Glass, Model Flint Glass Co. Marietta, OH: AP, 1997.

Unitt, Doris and Peter. American and Canadian Goblets. Petersborough, Ontario, Canada: Clock House, 1977.

Weatherman, Hazel Marie. Colored Glassware of the Depression, Era II. Ozark, MO: Weatherman Glassbooks, 1974.

Whitmyer, Margaret and Kenn. Fenton Art Glass 1907-1939. Paducah, KY: Collector, 1996.

Wright, L.G. L.G. Wright Catalog. N.d.

ON THE COVERS

Front cover, top row, l–r:
White Opalescent Country Kitchen Bowl
Blue Victor Pitcher and Tumbler
Front cover, bottom row, l–r:
Diamond Spearhead Cobalt Sugar
Vaseline Klondyke Pitcher
Cranberry Tumble–Up

Back cover, clockwise from upper left:
Cranberry Honeycomb Pitcher and Tumbler
Green Daffodil Pitcher
Cranberry Decanter
Green Rib Optic Pitcher and Tumbler
Vaseline Butter, Opaline Brocade

PATTERN INDEX